In Expectation o

Land's End to John C

March - June 2009

Ben Evens

In Expectation of a Kingfisher

Land's End to John O'Groats on foot
March - June 2009

Copyright © Ben Evens 2016

All rights reserved

No part of this book may be reproduced in any form by photocopying or any electronic or mechanical means, including information storage or retrieval systems, without permission in writing from the copyright owner of the book.

The right of Ben Evens to be identified as the author of this work has been asserted by him in accordance with the Copyright, Designs and Patents Act 1988 and any subsequent amendments thereto.

A catalogue record for this book is available from the British Library.

Front cover : Path to Maiden Castle, Cheshire
Back cover: On the West Highland Way, near Derrydaroch

ISBN: 978-1-5262-0126-3

First published 2016 by Ben Evens

Printed by The Print Room, Bolton
info@the-print-room.co.uk

The author may be contacted at: benjevens@outlook.com

Dedication

This book is dedicated to the memory of

Tim Stocks

sportsman, adventurer, wit, generally splendid chap

and a family friend

who died at the untimely age of 35.

Acknowledgements

I thank the following people for their help in the preparation of this book.

Firstly, Ann, my wife, for her unstinting help and advice in numerous ways before and during the walk. The proofreading of this book has been a labour of love and her eye for detail has been exemplary. To Nick, Juliet and Geoffrey, my siblings and to Bryony, our eldest daughter, who have had experience of producing books and who have offered me advice. To Andy, for letting me use some of his photos. To Peter Temple at The Print Room, for his friendly and helpful advice during the production phase.

To friends and relatives, who put me up for the night and who asked questions eagerly about my progress and listened patiently to my tales. Their enthusiasm for this undertaking and their encouragement and support have been invaluable.

To Susanna, who encouraged me by recounting her experiences of walking from John O'Groats to Land's End some years before I did my trek, and who gave me sensible and practical suggestions.

To Sally Thomas, for her book *A Walk for Jim,* which records her heroic journey from Land's End to John O'Groats. Reading this lovely book helped stir me into action.

Pre-amble

Ah! You noticed the hyphen.

Well it was an amble, a ramble, a stroll, a saunter ... with just an occasional bit of strenuous here and there.

But why did I think I wanted to do it? Well, you have to go back a long way. As far back as "I've always wanted to do it". I can't remember any specific date, but it probably goes back to my teenage years fifty years ago. Fifty years is a long time to harbour an ambition and then fulfil it. Sometimes one has ideas of things one would like to do but never really get round to them. I guess this was one of those. Rationality suggests all sorts of practical reasons why *not* to do it, mostly starting with 'lack of', like money, time, inclination, energy ..... so for years nothing happened.

As a walker I have achieved much with which to be satisfied. This includes various long-distance trails in England and Wales and the Long Distance Walkers Association annual Hundred-mile event; started 7, finished 3. Probably the best adventure was walking the Cambrian Way, on my own, in June 1997, taking three weeks in mostly beastly weather. I am gradually trying to conquer the 2000' summits of England and Wales so I've got plenty to aim at. I didn't feel a great need to do anything else particularly heroic; I didn't feel an urge to 'prove something to myself', but at the back of mind there was still that little niggle. No, not really a niggle because it didn't really keep niggling me, but a tiny dormant nugget of 'well, just suppose', very well concealed.

For quite a few years now my right knee has been playing up with arthritis. This has made walking less comfortable, partly because of pain and partly because I don't seem to be able to get along without limping. This has acted as a disincentive to tramping around the hills as I used to, although the desire to do so is still there. So whenever the 'dormant nugget' started one of its very occasional attention-seeking little forays, it received even more short shrift than in the past. The irony is that with retirement came the opportunity to find time. By about 2006 I had made a conscious decision that I would never walk from Land's End to John O'Groats. In my Presidential Address to the Sidcot School Old Scholars Association at Easter 2006 I said that I wanted to have a go at *cycling* from Land's End to John O'Groats.

By the winter of 2008 I had done up my old Viking Conquest, a present for my 21st birthday 46 years earlier, and pedalled it around the Peak District. I may not have given myself a fair enough test, I perhaps should have persisted with my training, but the upshot seemed to be that my knee liked it even less than walking. So that idea slid gently away. I had also been worried about various aspects of a cycling trip, not least it being all over far too quickly and with less time to enjoy the details of the journey. Even with a good knee it would have made me rather too anxious for comfort. So during the rest of 2008 I found myself gradually acclimatising to the fact that any End-to-End adventure was never going to happen.

Over the New Year holiday at the start of 2009 Ann, my wife, said to me, "If you really want to do it, do it!" My lifelong friend Alan was staying with us, as he always does over the New Year period, and I don't think we had been talking specifically about the possibility of Land's End etc, but something about the way the conversation was turning prompted Ann to say what she did. This rather stopped me in my tracks and the 'dormant nugget' emerged from its hiding place and started racing around shouting "Do it! Do it!"

I couldn't really believe that I was actually going to turn a dream into a reality. Not the reality of finishing a walk but the reality of starting it. I felt I needed three things: about three months of free time, money to pay for the venture and the goodwill of my wife to 'allow' me to go. She doesn't like the idea that she 'gave me permission', but this is how I sometimes referred to it as I went along.

Within hours I had done some very elementary thinking. Questions arose. The very first was - and this arose unbidden - how far will I expect to walk each day? The answer arrived without conscious thought - about 10 or 11 miles a day. I knew the distance was likely to be about 1100 miles so I reckoned I would need about 100 days. After this all the other practicalities came flooding in. Not least was when? I knew the answer to this straightaway. I wanted to start in the winter and arrive by about midsummer. This had been part of the long-held dream. I felt I wanted to attune myself to seasons and weather and place my feet upon the earth and be at one with natural things. I wanted to 'carry the spring to the north', a phrase I repeated many times to folk along the way. I wanted to 'savour' every aspect of the adventure.

A major task was clearing the decks of duties and responsibilities. I am a Quaker and fairly heavily involved with churchly business, but just at this time in 2009 I was 'between' various tasks and I felt I could escape without letting down too many people, but undoing and handing over took a while.

I have never done the lightweight camping thing and didn't intend to start at the age of 68. Offa's Dyke and the Pennine Way are old friends and I didn't feel a need to revisit them. I wrote letters to friends and relations who lived at places along possible routes, asking if they could put me up, in principle, at some future near-enoughish date. I had a good response and the route gradually sorted itself, doing some gentle zigzagging here and there. I then set about finding Bed and Breakfast stops to infill between my friends and relations. This was a massive task. Working on the 11 miles a day principle meant looking for overnight stop places. In the end some days were only about 8 or others were 14, 15 or even 16 miles. The whole busine out accommodation was extremely time-consuming, even with the internet pulling its weight.

By the time I left home I had booked every night as far as Frodsham in Cheshire. Other 'staging posts' further on had been booked, and I had to proceed in faith that places to stay would be found as I went along. I had some addresses and phone numbers and Ann did sterling research work on my behalf. I did not want ever to arrive at a destination without knowing where I was going to rest my head for the night; and in fact this never happened. However, the time scale came down from being booked at least two weeks in advance from Cheshire northwards to about a day in advance by the time I reached the north of Scotland.

Basically my route was to take me up the middle of Cornwall, north of Dartmoor, a flirt with the Quantocks, across the Somerset levels, over a corner of the Mendips and across the Avon at Keynsham, between Bristol and Bath. I trod a little of the Cotswold Way, down to Gloucester and then along the west side of the Malverns. I followed the Worcestershire Way, the Severn Way from Bewdley to Bridgnorth, across the flattish parts of Shropshire and Cheshire and then through industrial Lancashire.

I kept west of the Forest of Bowland, up the Lune to Sedbergh, then Appleby and down the Eden. Then Brampton and into Scotland at Kershope Bridge. The route continued through Newcastleton, Hawick, Selkirk, Peebles and out onto flatter country via Dolphinton, Carnwath, Carluke and on to Airdrie. Round the east side of Glasgow onto Milngavie from whence I followed the West Highland Way to Fort William. The Great Glen Way took me to Drumnadrochit. Then I continued to Beauly, Dingwall, Alness, Tain, Dornoch and Golspie. I followed the coast the rest of the way. And of course, on to Duncansby Head, the proper finishing point.
There was no temptation to visit Buxton, where I live, even though it could have been included in a possible route.

This book is not meant to be a guide for others, but just an account of my experiences. However, I think there are enough geographical indicators in the text to give anyone keen enough to be bothered, a reasonable idea of my route.

This route seems pretty tame in terms of strenuosity and considering my fondness for 'hills' I did not really go over very many. The main idea was not to be heroic, but to get from one end to the other as easily as possible.

Another worry in the planning phase was "Will I actually be able to walk as far as Cheshire, let alone Scotland?" I didn't really know how my body would hold *up* and I didn't really know whether my knee would let me *down*. Ah! the *ups* and *downs* of planning! There was no point in booking up places far ahead if I was never going to get there.

I needed to prepare myself mentally and physically for what I reckoned was going to be the biggest adventure of my life. Most of the mentally bit didn't really happen. I was too involved with the enormousness of the preparation to give much thought to how I was going to feel about it all once I'd started. Physically I was very out of condition. I'd done a 20 mile walk in the Mendips over the 2008 Easter weekend and a toughish 16 mile walk in the northern Berwyns in August 2008. And hardly any walks of 10 miles plus since. My instinct had been, right from the start, to walk a modest distance each day and 'recover' each evening in the hope that I would not suffer from accumulated tiredness. In the event this worked out very well indeed. However, I felt I needed to undertake some sort of 'training' to get myself at least minimally prepared. I had thought that my first week of walking would be of very modest distances each day and that this would be part of my acclimatisation process. Anyway, during February and March I undertook an absurdly feeble training regime. I went out twice a week with walks gradually increasing in length. The first week was a walk of one mile and another of two miles. The next week was two miles and three miles and the next a three-miler and a four-miler. You get the idea. Up to about 10 miles. Then I ran out of time and just hoped I would be ready.

There was not a lot of time to *savour* the *expectancy* before setting off. There wasn't really time to have doubts, because of being too busy. Preparations for things I had to take involved weighing everything, often to the nearest ounce. The departure time came all too soon and I felt I was only just ready. Subsequently I sometimes felt that if I had had another week or even a fortnight before departure I might have felt easier about, for instance, ongoing accommodation arrangements. But then I didn't want to book too far ahead in case I didn't make it that far. In the end I think my hasty arrangements were, in fact, thorough enough and I wasn't really complaining.

As for the mental preparation, this didn't really turn out to be necessary. Once I'd started walking I fell naturally into the routines that I had used on previous very much shorter long distance walks, albeit quite some years previously, and I had no problem with that aspect of the expedition at all.

There is a great deal of emotional anticipation before a big adventure like this. I can remember on quite a few occasions at work when it had been a lovely day and I had longed to be 'out there doing it'. During the first few days I was able to look back on such occasions and say to myself, "Yes, I really am out here doing it".

There is an inconsistent use of tenses all the way through this book. Sometimes I write in the present tense and sometimes, as if I was looking back, the past tense. This is just the way it is, so I hope you can cope.

The maps are not all to the same scale. Due to the varying lengths of the stages the maps have been made to 'fit the page' at the expense of consistency of scale. The little circles on the maps indicate overnight stops.

"The tourist who dashes from Land's End to John O'Groats during
the brief span of one summer
will find little to interest him in my pages,
because I detest excess speed."

From *This was England* by Horace Annesley Vachell - 1933.

I hope readers of this tale will find plenty of interest herein,
be they dashers or dawdlers.

Travelling to the South West

Thursday 19ᵗʰ March 2009
Buxton to Sennen Cove

My journey from Buxton in the Peak District to Cornwall was by public transport. The 0640 Transpeak bus took me to Whatstandwell where I made an easy connection to the train to Derby. Here I changed onto a Plymouth train and was whisked eagerly southwards. There was a ground frost early on and it was foggy until the Cotswolds gradually emerged south of Gloucester. It was sunny thereafter and the journey was very pleasant. There was blackthorn on display in Derby, then here and there pussy willow and forsythia. Gorse appeared in Devon. There was not a great deal of obvious 'leafing' on the trees and bushes but it was all looking very expectant. It had become a beautiful sunny day, but there was a cold easterly wind brisking through Plymouth station. Once over the Tamar and into Kernow there was plenty of trackside gorse and primroses, a far cry from 1000' feet up in Buxton! It was good to see good old-fashioned GWR lower semaphore signals. I spotted a golf-course just after Par. You can invent your own quips at this point.

I realised that my nerves were jangling for most of the journey. This was partly due to the enforced idleness and the thought of a momentous venture. I wanted my walk to be 'just ordinary' but nobody told my nerves that. All this was the tension of anticipation. This glorious long train journey from the Midlands to Penzance made me realise that the walk hasn't started yet. I pondered on the eleven weeks of planning after decades of believing it would never happen. Now - the reality is happening. But it tingles and fidgets with each passing mile.

I was interested to see a field of daffodils between Camborne and Hayle. I've never been in Cornwall before Easter and I came to realise that, of course, this was being grown as a crop and I met many more such fields over the next few days.

At Penzance I changed onto a rattly bus which eventually took me to Sennen Cove, where I was booked into a B and B.

My log records that evening, "The whole venture is based on a lot of assumptions: that my knee will not conk out; that my bodily strength will be enough; that there will be overnight accommodation; that my determination will be enough ...."

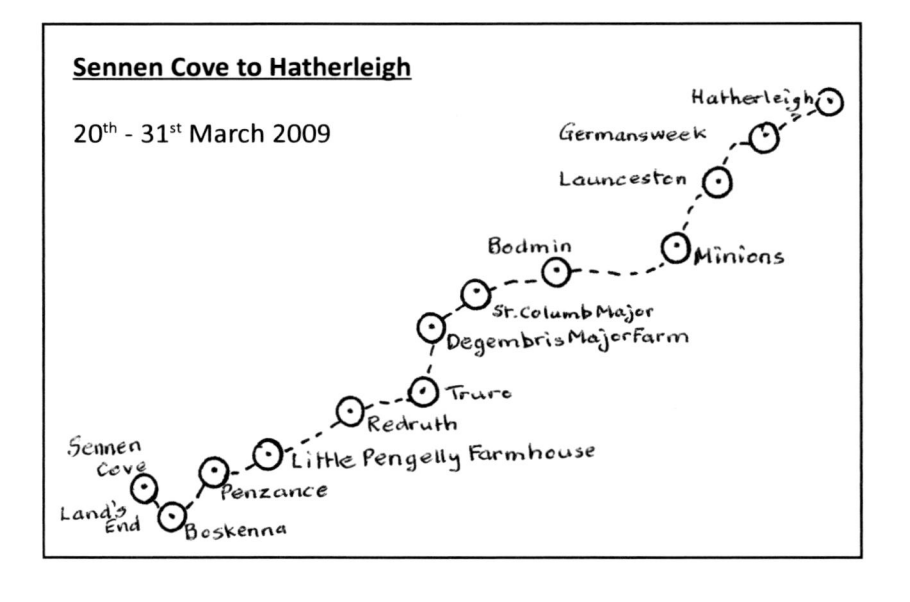

Sennen Cove to Hatherleigh

20th - 31st March 2009

> "To me the meanest flower that blows can give
> thoughts that do often lie too deep for tears."
>
> From "Intimations of Immortality" from
> *Recollections of Early Childhood* by William Wordsworth.

Sennen Cove to Sidcot

Friday 20th March
Sennen Cove to Boskenna - 10.5 miles

I left the B and B at Sennen Cove at 0850 and took my time along the cliff path, that is to say, anti-clockwise round the coast. It was only a mile or so to Land's End and I arrived when there didn't seem to be much happening. I fiddled around seeing if I could perch my camera somewhere and put the self-timer on, but a kind lady arrived and took a picture of me. The Longships lighthouse is lurking mistily somewhere behind me. I thought I ought to have a morning coffee, but the café wasn't open. Eventually the hotel opened at 1030 and I had a drink there. I received a lovely text message from Ann, which I found most encouraging. It said, "Congratulations! To have even started to realise a dream is special. Happy walking!"

So, at 1103, with nobody to see me off, I started properly. After the first few moments the nerves settled down and I concentrated on watching where I put my feet and gradually the buildings at Land's End disappeared behind me. The going at first was dry and gritty with grass and rock underfoot. It was a dry day. The coastal scenery is pretty good round here and I took several pictures. I was following the South West Coast Path and all I had to do was keep the sea on my right. Once or twice the path takes a 'short cut' and doesn't follow the cliff edge religiously. After a couple of miles I was presented with an option to go up onto a headland, but lazily thought it was just a side path, so I continued on the nice strong track which led me astray more than I wanted it to. I tried to correct this by cutting into a field but was defeated by hedge banks and barbed wire. I returned to the track and eventually got onto the coast path again at Carn Trevean. I reckon I am a quite good map reader, but one actually has to remember to look at the map once in a while for this skill to take effect. Throughout the walk, with the exception of a few miles in southern Scotland, I used the OS Explorer maps, mostly the most recent editions. I vastly prefer these maps at 2½" to the mile as they show lots of detail. I find knowing where the field boundaries are particularly useful.

Half a mile west of Porthgwarra I deliberately and knowingly abandoned the coast path and zigzagged inland, probably saving no distance at all. I continued along to the Minack Theatre at Porthcurno where I had a substantial lunch. This was to be my main meal of the day as I knew I wasn't easily going to find evening food near the B and B. I continued round the bay and carried on eastwards. The path is delightful, twisting and turning with plenty of ups and downs. I recorded twenty different wild flowers and also noticed, so far is the spring advanced, a dandelion clock. I had previously decided that I would record the flowers I saw every day. I jotted them down in my notebook as I saw them and each evening I entered them into a rather elaborate grid in my 'Log Book'. I carried an A6 size notebook in my trouser leg pocket for daily jottings; and kept an A5 hardback Log Book where I stored essential advance information. My B and B was about half a mile inland at Boskenna. I ate a snack in my room as an evening meal. I had to go quite a way up the lane in the dusk to find a signal on my mobile so that I could ring Ann.

Well, I am on my way!

Saturday 21st March
Boskenna to Penzance - 9.4 miles

Starting off I noticed I was experiencing what my log tells me was 'very slight upper body strain'. This was just getting used to my rucksack after the first day's walk and the feeling soon disappeared. I retraced my steps to the coast path and continued in decent weather. The wind was easterly, and remained so for several more days, so the air was pleasantly fresh. Of the three times I fell over on my way north, two were in the first two days. The circumstances were virtually identical. At times along the coast the path goes into a bushy tunnel where small trees and shrubs lean inland across the path, often with very limited headroom. Generally the ground had been dry but in the little tunnels the surface had not dried out and tree roots were there in abundance for the unwary. Stooping to avoid the 'roof' I managed to slip or trip, falling inelegantly, but not causing any damage to my person, beyond a muddy trouser knee. After a while I found myself at Lamorna Cove where a sign in the car park warned people to beware of uneven ground!

I was unexpectedly delighted to find a café there and enjoyed a coffee. Somewhere between Lamorna and Mousehole I met a couple and the young lady informed me, "If you can't see Lizard Point, it is set fair". Lizard Point was only just hazily visible. One of the things about walking along the coast, I mused to myself, is that one has a sense of *coast.* That thought seemed important enough to jot down in my notebook. Walking along on one's own, there is certainly plenty of time for thinking, or even not thinking. Some thoughts seem to make sense at the time. One thought that did seem important, and with which I was occasionally confronting myself, was the problem of how I was going to manage to motivate myself. The start, at Land's End, was one thing, but every day, day after day? I will have to wait and see.

Mousehole was very warm in the sheltered harbour area at noon. Children were playing on the strip of sand, clad only in bathers. I was asked by a man how far I was going, and when I said John O'Groats he said, "Oh, well done!" I felt like saying, and maybe even did say, "Tell me that when I'm two days from the end, not two days from the start!"

Somewhere along the way today, someone asked me if I was bound for Poole. This is the south and eastern end of the South West Peninsula Coast Path and local folk are probably well used to seeing walkers part way through the 600 odd miles. As I write this it occurs to me that that path, if undertaken in one go, is a darn sight hillier and harder than my route at half the distance again. However, I didn't know that at the time. What I did find intriguing with the folk I met was having the power of whether to tell them where I was going or not. Sometimes I would be asked outright, "Are you going far?" This was a splendid opening for me to admit that I was trying to reach John O'Groats. But if I wasn't asked - should I announce it? Sometimes as I drew near someone I would say to myself, "I won't tell them". Modesty did occasionally prevail. But today, "Poole?" was the question and I said I was only following the coast path as far as Marazion. No mention of John O'Groats!

I stopped to read the stone erected in memory of the eight Penlee Lifeboatmen who lost their lives in atrocious conditions in 1981. I called in at a nice little café in Newlyn to have lunch. I continued to Penzance, arriving at about half-past two.

Just before leaving Buxton I had bought myself my first, and so far only, digital camera. This is a Canon 'Power Shot' SX110. I wanted a decent number of megapixels, a good zoom, 10x optical, and a 2½" by 2" screen. The facilities available on this large-ish compact are vastly underused so far. It is quite heavy for its size, I think. I had planned, in my innocence, to rely on throwaway AA batteries, which I felt pretty sure would be widely available. By the time I had

used it for two days the two batteries were crying for mercy and the two spares I was carrying had been pressed into service. I was somewhat disconcerted by this situation. I walked up the main street in Penzance and went into Jessops and explained my predicament. I had expected the batteries to last much longer than appeared to be the case. I was told that my camera was quite 'powerful' and used up a lot of juice. I was advised that what I really needed to use were rechargeable batteries. I had already decided against this in the planning phase, as I did not want to carry the
extra weight of the charger. However, I did not relish the idea of discarding batteries every two days for three months so I reluctantly, but of necessity, purchased a pack with four rechargeable batteries and a charger for £19.99. I presented my debit card for payment. After some fiddling about, the lassie said my card wasn't working. I suspected it was really her machine that was faulty. Somewhat annoyed and worried I paid cash and then asked where the nearest ATM was.

I made my way further up the street to the NatWest Bank (which was my bank). I had only intended to try my 'not working' card in the ATM and, if possible, take out some money as well. It being Saturday afternoon, and remembering that some NatWest Banks had been experimenting with Saturday *morning* opening, it was with gratitude and delight that I found not only the ATM, but that the Bank was actually open. So at 1458 approximately, I went in and told my tale. The young girl tried my card and pronounced it perfectly healthy. I withdrew as much cash as I needed over the counter. Meanwhile, the manageress had shut the front door at 1500. It was one thing for the girl behind the counter to make my card work, but would it work in the ATM outside? So it was arranged that I would go out and try my card in the ATM. I did this and withdrew £10 without any fuss. The manageress obligingly stood in the window until I gave her the 'thumbs-up'. What lovely people! On my way back through the town I popped into Jessops again and told them, "It's your machine that's wonky"! I also found an Orange shop and went in to get my mobile topped up. I haven't had a mobile very long and hardly ever use it under normal circumstances, but it proved to be extremely useful all along my walk. I'm unavoidably carrying the charger for that as well!

The Cornish coast path was excellent even though it involved a lot of ups and downs, but, perhaps, because of that.

I went to the bus station and caught a bus to Carbis Bay where I spent the night with my friends Bill and Marion. Bill was senior to me at Sidcot School, a Quaker Boarding School in Somerset, which I attended in the fifties. Bill and Marion were the first of several Sidcot Old Scholars that I stayed with along the way.

I was able to break off from yarning to watch Ireland just beat Wales to win the Grand Slam for the first time in 61 years.

Sunday 22nd March
Penzance to Little Pengelly Farmhouse - 12.1 miles

I took the bus back into Penzance and started walking at about 1015. In the first two minutes I contrived to get on the wrong side of the sea wall, despite it being a 'good' path. I scrambled over huge boulders to regain the correct route. Whilst walking along beside the railway I was intrigued to find a short stretch of single track railway at Long Rock. I asked myself, "Are there any other mainline single track sections on the old Great Western"? It was cooler today with a fresh breeze, but fine and sunny and dry underfoot. I called in at a café on the shore between Penzance and Marazion. The views back got better the further round Mount's Bay I went. St. Michael's Mount stood out splendidly. On a small lake at Marazion I was surprised to see, but perhaps shouldn't have been, a little egret.

I knew that it would be difficult to find an evening meal handy for the B and B I was to stay in, so I thought it would be best to have my main meal at lunchtime. Just in case, I popped into a little shop in Marazion and bought an apple and a bar of something. I pressed on and eventually left the coast at Trenow Cove. Due to careless map-reading I did an unnecessary detour on my way to Perrannuthnoe. Discovering the Victoria Inn I entered with the intention of seeking lunch, only to be told, "We're not doing any more 'walk-ins' or we'll run out of food". I could see the place *was* pretty full. I had not heard the expression 'walk-ins' before. It gradually dawned on me that there had been a lot of pre-booking because it was Mother's Day! I carried on by field paths to Chiverton and then down to the main Helston road at Rosudgeon. I knew there was a pub along that stretch of road somewhere. I had deliberately strayed off my intended route in order to find a meal, but it meant the best part of two miles along a busy-ish main road. I did indeed find a pub, 'The Falmouth Packet'. At 1340 they had no food left! I wandered on and found a garage with a bit of a shop and satisfied myself with a cold lunch from whatever was available.

I managed to leave the main road soon afterwards and strolled along pretty little lanes to the village of Germoe. I found a seat in a delectable spot just outside the church with green sward and a delightful murmuring stream in front of me. The mid-afternoon sun was warm and I sat there doing nothing much except 'enjoying'.
I felt at peace with the world. Lovely.

Reluctantly moving on I continued along a dinky little lane. After a short distance I thought, "This feels like a wild strawberry sort of lane", and blow me, a few yards further on round the bend I found my first wild strawberry flowers. It was to be many weeks before I found my first wild strawberry *fruit*, high above Loch Ness.

When holidaying in the area some years ago I had wanted to climb and explore Tregonning Hill. The hill lay slap bang in the middle of the line I wanted to take, but I tamely stuck to the lanes to the north, leaving the hill for another day with more time to do it justice. I passed an area called 'Great Work' which I guessed is a reference to the days when mining was at its height. For the next day or two the map indicated many 'Shafts (dis)'. I finally reached my B and B at Little Pengelly Farmhouse at five o'clock, where I received a warm welcome from Maxine. She told me that the spring is about a month behind and that the trees daren't put their leaves out for fear of being blown over.

At one point during the day I came across a field almost covered in plastic mini-poly-tunnels. The map indicated a beeline across the middle of the field and I wondered whether there had been an official diversion around the edge. There was nobody to ask so I managed to 'stride' over the plastic strips without too much difficulty. When walking I normally have no hesitation in walking a beeline across a ploughed field, if that seems to be the right of way and also the easiest option. In so doing, if one dislodges a few clods or disturbs a few seedlings, then that is the way life is. Many farmers, of course, leave an unploughed or unseeded strip and the intention is clear. But dare one walk on top of the poly-tunnels and risk ripping the plastic? Later in my walk I came across strips of plastic which were 14 feet wide, but luckily the path ran parallel and I was not presented with a moral dilemma.

Monday 23rd March
Little Pengelly Farmhouse to Redruth - 12.4 miles

Monday dawned cold and sunny with a little light cloud at times. My route was by quiet lanes and fields. During the first mile I met my first 'fierce dog' which wasn't actually fierce at all. I had been wondering what I might do about dogs and had decided that I would speak to them, whatever the circumstances. Not knowing whether any such dog might be male or female, or young or old, I had decided I would say, "Hello, old thing!" in a friendly, cheerful voice. By and large this seemed to work pretty well. As additional 'protection' I was carrying my faithful 'cherry-slasher'. This is a piece of cherry tree pruning which I had found by a plantation of cherry trees near Stoke by Nayland when I was prowling around Suffolk a few years earlier. It is not the most wonderful of walking sticks but it is good for beating down nettles and brambles and the like. My Suffolk trip was just after the foot and mouth epidemic and there seemed to be miles of un-walked paths, which had become overgrown with nettles. Thousands of them felt the sting of my trusty blade! So, in case a particularly fierce dog came at me I had my stick in hand. Never needed it.

Many times I came across a field of daffodils being grown as a crop. One field, which I photographed, had the flowers pretty well in full bloom. I was later told that these might just catch the local market, but might well have to be ploughed back in. A year or two back the season was very 'telescoped', with everything coming into bloom within the space of a fortnight and much was wasted. Ideally the season needs to be much more spread out over many weeks so that the processing and distribution can be more easily dealt with.

I went into the Post Office in Praze-an-Beeble to post home a map or two and then thought it must be nearly coffee time. Lo and behold across the road was a café. I went in and had two coffees. The enterprising young man running the café asked me, "Are you going far?" When I replied that I was on my fourth day out from Land's End and bound for John O'Groats he said, "Ah! you're the first through this year!" I think he gets a lot of cyclists, presumably on their first day out.

The walking was very pleasant. At times I heard a sort of muted gunfire, but decided it was probably bird-scarers. I saw the occasional old chimney, a further reminder that I was in a mining area. 'Chy' is a Cornish word that crops up in place names and a search of a map of the area will throw up quite a few. However

'Chy' is also a map abbreviation for chimney! The street leading into the village of Troon had a stream running down beside the road edge, giving the place a bit of character and interest. Leaving the village I entered an area thick with old mines and workings; one can follow an industrial archaeological trail around the very extensive site. I had my lunch sitting on a bit of wall by an old shaft. Coming into Carnkie, with plenty of time in hand, I decided to make a deliberate detour onto the top of Carn Brea. Having seen this hill with its landmark tower on the summit quite a few times in the past, but never having got there, I thought now would be a good time.

For some years as a child I had an interest in trains and would often be found at the station in Keynsham, between Bristol and Bath. This is the town where I was born. I particularly liked the King and Castle Class locomotives and one of them was Carn Brea Castle. I had long wondered where this was. There is a castley sort of building at one end of the hill which is now a restaurant. The original building was a twin-towered fortress, built in the 14th century, but remodelled later, I guess. Can't remember the number of the engine either. Probably 70 something something.

Having enjoyed the view I poddled on down into Redruth, arriving in the town centre at 1545. My overnight stay was in a Guest House on the convenient side of town.

Tuesday 24th March
Redruth to Truro - 10.0 miles

I was soon away from Redruth and along some quiet paths over a gentle hill. This gave me a view ahead which I hadn't really had since the start of the walk. This was nothing amazing, but just a sense of middle distance and the enormity of the undertaking. The weather was cool and overcast, but there was the occasional sunny interval. I passed through the village of Carharrack and then through a rather muddly bit with a waste disposal site or a new industrial complex or something. There was new fencing and a path diversion, but it soon sorted itself. Lanes and field paths took me down into a deep valley to the village of Twelveheads and then there was a long climb up again. After passing Wheal Jane I found a pleasant bridleway which I followed for a mile or more before joining quiet roads that took me to the A390, at this point being the Truro bypass. From here it was only a short walk to the home of Patrick and Marion who were to put me up for the night.

This had been a short day's walk of only ten miles and I hadn't really stopped anywhere, it being rather uninvitingly cool, so I arrived in time for lunch and a very warm welcome. I had known Patrick since I was a child, and we share Bristol memories. Marion was at Sidcot, although some years my senior. She is also a distant relation, a fourth or fifth cousin, I think. I enjoyed a relaxing afternoon and evening doing nothing very much. Patrick reminded me of an old Bristol story I had rather forgotten.

If you are not familiar with the way Bristolians speak you need to know that it is quite usual for them to put an 'l' (ell) on to the ends of words, so that 'idea' becomes 'ideal', 'area' becomes 'areal'. I have heard city councillors, nay aldermen, in the Council Chamber refer to agendal and propagandal. You may sometimes hear an ell in the middle of a word, quite spontaneoulsly. I am reminded of the young soldier, who, upon being asked about being recruited for a spell in the tropics, responded with, "Africal's a malarial areal innit?" What Patrick reminded me of was the story of the father, introducing his three daughters to an acquaintance which went like this - "This one's Idal, and the second one is Eval and the third one is Normal".

Wednesday 25th March
Truro to Degembris Major Farm - 12.3 miles

I walked down into Truro town centre and did a bit of shopping, not least to buy a non-leaking replacement water bottle. I also visited the Post Office. Maps were posted home at regular intervals, usually two or three at a time.

I found my way through a few streets and under the railway to find the start of a pleasant path that Patrick had suggested I follow. This joined a quiet lane after a while and I continued to Idless, where flowering camellias made a lovely show. Soon I turned off the road to enter St. Clement Woods. There were loads of paths in the woodland, obviously much used by locals for a stroll or dog-walking. The trees were still pretty bare, although if I tried hard I could just about imagine leaves in bud, poised to break free. The exception was the larches which were just starting to come out, albeit in sheltered spots. The ground was starting to fill out with bluebell leaves.

I kept in the trees for nearly a couple of miles before descending to Treworgan. A mile or so of fields and track took me to the village of Trispen. I arrived here rather sooner than expected, but nonetheless entered the Clock and Key pub and made a substantial meal of soup and ham salad and chips etc, knowing there would not be an evening meal option at the B and B. On slightly higher ground now I found the north-westerly wind to be rather strong, hitting me on my port quarter as I moved basically northwards. In fact this was probably the windiest day so far. It was therefore rather cool, despite it being a bright and sunny day. I kept telling myself, "It's still only March"!

I found myself proceeding rather sluggishly after the heavy meal. It was a rather more iffy day with my silly knee and I found the wind slightly disorientating.

Lanes and fields took me to the busy and noisy A39, of which I was obliged to be within earshot for a mile or so. Leaving the A39 I followed a track and met several guys who were inspecting an existing, or surveying for a new, power line. There were certainly plenty of pylons about. A little further on the landowner came careering across the field in his pick-up and stopped to speak to me, initially thinking I was something to do with the national grid people. He soon realised I couldn't be, with my rucksack and all, and drove off again at high speed. I didn't know quite what was going on, but the landowner seemed rather anxious about something.

I crossed some more fields and came down into Mitchell. Still feeling rather in need of sustenance I went into the Plume of Feathers and sat quietly with a latte. I still had a couple of miles to go, so I toddled off through the village and under the busy A30 and along quiet lanes to Degembris Major Farm. There seemed to be several Degembrises in the vicinity. Opposite the farm was Degembris Minor and I'd already passed a house with the same name a mile back. I guess the postman understands it.

I spent a quiet evening having a snack and working out a route for the next day. Because of my advance planning, before I left home, I knew where I was to lay my head each night. However the detailed planning of a day's actual route was normally done the evening before. This meant trying to find as many field paths as possible, then bridleways and tracks and then quiet lanes and so on. Fields are OK except for when the path peters out or is blocked or diverted. A country lane is more reliable in terms of getting you somewhere, but is harder on the feet and traffic can be a problem. In a field one has to contend with stock and barbed wire and electric fences and progress can be slow. Little lanes often have banks, hedges and verges which can have a good variety of wild flowers.

It was quite interesting trying to judge what the terrain would be like from just looking at the map. I sometimes found myself saying as I went along, "Oh, so this is what it's like". One can have a preconceived idea of what it will be like, and when the actuality differs one can subsequently remember the preconceived picture, which then has to be cancelled out in one's mind. The reasoning behind the intricate route planning was to get from A to B as simply and straightforwardly as possible. I wanted to get to John O'Groats, and in these early days I didn't want to stray far from a direct-ish line; mainly because I wasn't sure whether my bodily strength - and especially my knee - might conk out. People I met, friends, folk at the B and B, or whatever, would occasionally tell me of 'a very nice garden' or 'an old church' that I really ought to visit. I explained that that was very kind of them to suggest it, but I didn't really want to walk an extra couple of miles in order to make these visits. I am sure they are very nice places and I am sure they will still be there if I was to make a return visit at a later date. This may sound a bit ungrateful, but I felt I had to be rather single-minded in my determination to stick to the planned route. I didn't feel I was depriving myself of pleasurable experiences as I seemed to be getting plenty already, with Spring starting to burst at the seams.

Thursday 26th March
Degembris Major Farm to St.Columb Major - 8.4 miles

The day started rather damp with some rain. Although it was still cool the air felt softer. I made good time along several miles of road to Luke's Shop, then down to Retyn Farm before taking a line across some fields. Here I had my first awkward adventure. Following a right of way I came to a point where the route was blocked by an electric fence. There were cattle nearby so I guessed the power was on. I am told you can test it by touching it with a blade of grass to see if it tingles, but I have never really tried that. I took my pack off and then wriggled under the wire on rather muddy grass and pulled my pack through. I then went a little way to the hedge-cum-bank to find no evidence of a stile or gate, present or past. On the other side of the bank was a stream and then another hedgebank. I didn't want to retreat to the lane a couple of fields back, when the way ahead would, hopefully, be satisfactory, provided I could get over this obstacle. I reckon I am prudent enough to turn back if I am up in the hills in bad weather, but here I think it was just plain stubbornness that took over. Acting prudently didn't seem to be an option. In the end, and with the help of my faithful cherry-slasher, I climbed over a barbed wire fence into a very restricted and brambly spot, climbed up a stony bank, climbed down to the stream bed, went over/through the stream, which was luckily not too deep, climbed up the stony bank the other side, down again with more brambles, nettles and barbed wire, before getting eventually into a field which was pretty boggy. Having survived this I came to a farm yard where the mud and muck was disgustingly yucky, but I managed to squelch my way through. All part of life's rich tapestry! Actually, looking back, this mini-adventure was really rather enjoyable in that it gave me something to deal with, something to make me swear a bit, something to make me break out into a sweat; an adrenalin surge - a change from placid plodding.

From then on the way was pleasant enough with the sun trying to make itself felt a bit. I got back onto lanes and kept on into St. Columb Major. My destination was the home of my second cousin, Janet, and her husband Chris. They lived right outside the village, conveniently on the east side, thus making my onward progress the next day easier.

I hadn't seen Janet for years and years and I had never met Chris. I arrived, after my shortest day so far, just in time for lunch. In the afternoon, Janet drove me to Mawgan Porth and we walked on the beach and then drove a little further to have a look at Bedruthan Steps, with its sticky up rocks. In the evening we spent a lot of time chatting and catching up with family news.

As my walk progressed, I developed a definite-ish routine for doing evening jobs. This included the aforementioned route planning, but also keeping my wild flower log up to date, and also looking at my digital photos and writing in my log book where the pictures were taken. There might also have been tasks with washing underwear etc. However, I found it rather disconcerting when staying with friends or relations, because the evening would be frittered away in conversation, albeit much enjoyed, and I would retire to bed with many of the tasks still to be done.

Chris and Janet are very involved with folk music. They belong to the Bodmin Folk Club and Chris writes the periodic folk newsletter for that part of Cornwall. The Bodmin Club meets on a Friday evening and I discovered that I was indeed going to be staying in Bodmin the very next day - a Friday. It was arranged that I would attend their Folk Evening as their guest. I asked whether I would be allowed to take part, not being at all familiar with Folk Clubs and how they operate. Chris and Janet thought it might be possible for me to have a slot, should I wish to take part. Read tomorrow's exciting instalment! (Don't hold your breath!)

Friday 27th March
St.Columb Major to Bodmin - 12.0 miles

I left at nine o'clock and enjoyed quiet lanes and fields through Tregonetha and St. Wenn. Down, down into a deep valley and up, up the other side. The field edges and lane banks were full of flowers, as they had been every day. By now I had seen 46 different kinds of wild flower since leaving Land's End. I had seen the three-cornered leek, a Cornish speciality, every day so far. I didn't see one today and on only three days after that - the next two days and then, most surprisingly in the Tweed valley in Scotland two months later. It was a great joy to me to be on the lookout all the time I was walking. My eyes were often on the verges and banks looking out for something new. The ever-present delight was primroses.

Whenever there was a clump, which was frequently, it wasn't just a clump, it was a big clump. I also found pink primroses, but these seemed to be never further than about a quarter of a mile away from a house or settlement. So long straight bits of road were never boring as there were always flowers.

I had decided that I would very much like to attend the Bodmin Folk Club in the evening and thought that I could offer a couple of unaccompanied English Folk Songs. I chose 'Searching for Lambs' and 'The Turtle Dove'. I felt pretty secure on all six verses of Searching for Lambs but needed to remind myself of the order of the two middle verses of the four-verse Turtle Dove. The lanes were pretty empty but I suspect I startled a few cows in the nearby fields as I got into the swing of my rehearsals, not overly loud, you understand, but pleasantly full. I probably sang some bits of other songs as well, just to keep myself company, and to see whether I wanted to alter my choices.

Leaving an elevated stretch I descended to the appealingly named Withielgoose and down into the valley by Withielgoose Mills. Here I stupidly misread the map - no, more like misread the terrain. I eschewed what turned out to be the correct path, that I thought was just leading to somebody's house, and climbed steadily through woodland. By now I realised I had gone wrong, but it didn't matter as I was able to get back on course within a mile or so.

As I descended gradually into the wide valley in which Bodmin sits, I found my rucksack talking to me. At home I have a large, old, rather heavy rucksack. This was too big for my needs. I also have a much smaller rucksack which is a good-sized day sack. I had dearly hoped that I would have been able to use that, but the trial packing a few days before departure proved that it was just annoyingly too small. So, I borrowed Ann's rucksack which was mid-way between my two. This served me very well for all of my journey, but it has a voice of its own. The leather straps rub against other bits and produce little noises. They don't seem to do it all the time, but certain kinds of terrain or gradient, and no doubt the way the load is distributed inside, brings on little voice-like squeaks. On this occasion I was walking down a gentle gradient and up speaks the little voice. It was quite regular and rhythmic and was in 4/4 time with a stress on the first beat. The sounds produced were not all of the same 'pitch', as it were, and seemed to be saying, "Much too hea-vy; much too hea-vy". I didn't really agree with this sentiment, as presented to me, because although it would have been nice to have had a lighter pack, I wasn't ever really discomfited by its weight, which was about 24 pounds. The rhythm also seemed to fit the name of the landlady of the B and B I was going to that night, a one syllable first name and a three syllable surname, again with a smaller stress on the third beat.

I arrived in Nanstallon and found a seat in a bus shelter opposite the primary school. The children were having their dinner-time playtime. This was a pleasant reminder of my years as a primary school teacher. I had expected it to rain during the day when I left in the morning, but so far it had held off, although it got colder in the afternoon. I joined the Camel Trail and followed it into Bodmin, arriving at the Shire Hall by about half-past two. This gave me plenty of time to reconnoitre and do a little shopping. After checking in at the B and B, I found my way to a Chinese Restaurant before moving on to the Barley Sheaf where the Folk Club meet.

I easily met Chris and Janet outside and they took me in. I've never really been in a proper folk club, although I am very fond of folk songs and the like. In the busyness of my life, going to a folk club has never quite reached the top of my leisure priorities, so this was to be a new experience. I was introduced to the evening's compere/host and it was arranged that I could have a slot. The main event of the evening was a visit from the two Askew Sisters and they were excellent. Local members in ones or twos, including Janet and Chris, performed their items. The usual thing seemed to be to do two items and then let someone else have a go. Various instruments were used as well as voices. Well, my turn came, and the full room was told of my reason for being in Bodmin, on the long journey north. Everybody else's contributions had been impeccable and I was rather nervous that I would let the standard falter. I gave them 'Searching for Lambs' and this went off fairly well. I got going on the 'Turtle Dove' and then what I feared would happen, did happen. At the start of the second verse I fluffed it and had to start again. I thought I had been starting verse three instead of verse two (not that it would have mattered), but thinking I had done it wrong I stopped. In fact I had been right all along and I should have stuck to my guns. Anyway, I got through the rest without further ado and was applauded warmly. What a nice bunch of forgiving people! The joyful thing was being amongst all these experienced singers. I was aware that they were joining in with my unaccompanied singing with quiet, gentle, humming harmonies, beautifully subdued so as not to drown me out. That was just lovely. For days after I had that hearteningly warm feeling, knowing that I had 'Sung at the Bodmin Folk Club'! I guess I just love enjoying simple pleasures.

Saturday 28th March
Bodmin to Minions - 16.5 miles

The rain that had threatened yesterday came on in real earnest within a few minutes of setting off. I paused under the shelter of a supermarket entrance to put my over-trousers on. However, this was a short-lived heavy shower which turned out to be the only significant rain of the day. A cold wind remained and I was glad of my gloves and hat. I have some rather superior fleece lined waterproof gloves at home, but I thought these were too unnecessarily heavy to cart about, so I brought a very small lightweight pair of fleece gloves, which served me very well. As I progressed through the spring and into summer, the need for gloves, I guessed, would be rather less. I have, very occasionally, in the past, when gloves were not being carried, used a spare pair of socks as a substitute.

I passed over the A30 and after a very short distance along the A 38 I turned north-east along a good track climbing over Long Downs then on lanes to Little Downs. Soon after that I saw a fox, sauntering nonchalantly, but a car came by and it disappeared. A little further on at Mount Pleasant I met a lady who was busy canvassing. I stopped and we chatted. She was, as I remember, the Lib Dem candidate for the Bodmin Moor ward of Cornwall County Council. Having established that there wasn't going to be a café in the village we parted and I pressed on. This was indeed Bodmin Moor. The agricultural feel to the countryside was gradually mingling with stretches of open moorland and old industrial mining. Soon after that I came to St Neot and luckily the Post Office was still open and I was able to post home the CD of the Askew Sisters I had bought the evening before. One of the good things about Post Offices, if they are open, is that they do tend to sell padded envelopes. I also bought a little food in case I needed it for my lunch. But lo and behold, round the corner was the London Inn, so I went in and had some tomato and basil soup with a baguette.

I pressed on, fortified and warmed, and kept to the road, dropping down to Treverbyn Bridge over the River Fowey and up again. Walking through central Cornwall often means crossing the grain of the land and there are numerous deep little valleys to cross. I was glad of these valleys, as going *down* and going *up* made a change from just going *along*. Somewhere along the way today I saw a sign outside a cottage which said, 'Cluck eggs and Duck eggs'.

Later, on a little narrow lane, I hutched up into the hedge to let a rare vehicle go by, but the car stopped and the two farmer occupants, father and son??, asked me if I wanted a lift. They were very friendly and sincere. I explained that I was walking 'all the way' and it wasn't in my plan to have lifts anywhere. They then offered me a coffee, which would have meant going to their (I guessed) nearby farm. I declined this also with many thank-yous. If I had had a lift to the farm for a coffee, would I have been brought back to the same spot before I could continue? It seemed easier not to get into that sort of a conversation. They said, "God Bless You" and drove on. Another couple of miles brought me to the village of St. Cleer. I went in to the Market Inn and drank an indifferent mug of coffee.

Down the lane from the pub was a lovely old well. This is the most elaborate well I have ever seen, almost like a little house, with arches and pillars and a steeply pitched roof and with a grating inside covering the well itself. It was mostly made of granite - not sure about the roof, but that was stone as well. If you've got granite, use granite. I then scooted in and out of little bits of housing estates, then onto field paths before climbing from a little settlement called Crow's Nest for nearly two miles up to Minions. My day had been dry underfoot until the last half mile or so when I got into a very boggy lane which I managed carefully to endure. The transmission masts on nearby Caradon Hill were very prominent.

I was staying at the 'Minions Village Shop cum Tea Rooms cum B and B'. The sign outside proclaimed it to be the 'Highest Post Office in Cornwall' and 'Open Most Hours For Most Things'. A display in the Tea Rooms warned visitors of the Big Cats that might still be found in the area. Minions has plenty of interest for visitors, with the prehistoric stone circles, The Hurlers, the Cheesewring, old tin mines and moorland to walk on. I would like to come back here sometime and do it more justice. I went to the Cheesewring pub for an evening meal, 995 feet above sea level and the sign said 'The Highest Pub in Cornwall'. It also said 'Good Food'. Aye, and it were, too. This had been my highest point and my longest day's walk so far.

Sunday 29th March
Minions to Launceston - 13.2 miles

I set off the next morning in bright sunshine with clear skies and just the gentling of a breeze. I was immediately onto moorland and climbed to over 1100 feet, the second highest point in England along my route. This was excellent walking underfoot for a couple of miles. There was ice on pools and puddles, but the feeling of height and space and clean, keen air was glorious. Views presented themselves to the east with the long edge of Dartmoor showing up well. If ever there was a time for enjoying every moment of every step, then this was it. Enjoying is too slight a word, perhaps. This was a deep sense of at-one-ness with everything around me; a sublime feeling of wholeness, tinged with a tingling of excitement. The view ahead did not make me feel daunted, in fact the opposite - this was the excitement, knowing I would be somewhere that way in a day or two. It was a special moment, one of many to be experienced in the coming weeks. The words I have just used seem inadequate to convey what I really felt. Heck! That's what beautiful sunny mornings do to you.

Without actually going right up to it, I paused to look up at the Cheesewring, a weathered stone 'sculpture' that is perched on the rim of a quarry face. Almost immediately afterwards I met a couple who were poking about looking for little carved emblems of Fleur de Lys which were put on stones in the 19th century by the Duchy of Cornwall to mark the outer limits of allowed quarrying.

Coming off the moorland I descended by a winding lane to the little village of Henwood where I sat for a few minutes on a seat on the village green. This was simply made with two granite uprights and a solid granite crosspiece - a bit cold on the bum. Another feature of the area I had noticed for a day or two was the vertical slate hanging as a wall covering. I wondered if the slates had come from Delabole near the north coast of Cornwall. Leaving the village I saw the most tremendous rhododendron I have ever seen, towering about twenty feet above the lane, dwarfing the nearby five-barred gate, and in full bloom. The walking was pleasant along the lanes and I passed by Kingbeare and down into the valley of the River Lynher. At Berrowbridge I paused on the bridge, as I always did when crossing streams and rivers, and gazed into the clear, gently flowing water, with its olive browns and greens and splashes of orange and lazy fish.

This pausing and gazing and dreaming was symptomatic of my whole approach to the walk. Even on my 16 miler the day before there was no great sense of urgency; and today, as on nearly every other day, there was time to stop and chat with folk, and just let everything happen around me. I wanted to achieve the goal of walking all the way to the far north if I possibly could, but much more I wanted to *enjoy* the adventure. I wanted to savour the intimacy of every flower, of every slip of birdsong, every wisp of scented wood-smoke. Everything and anything - whatever there was. I didn't seek to make things happen, I wanted to let them happen to me.

Climbing up from the valley I was struck by the unusual construction of several retaining walls. These were made of rather thin layered stones arranged in sections alternating between vertical and horizontal. There would be a sort of pier or pillar about five feet high and two feet wide with the stones laid horizontally, and these would repeat about every eight or ten feet; and the 'infill' was with perhaps thinner stones laid vertically in four or five rows. I made my way to the village of North Hill hoping to find some late elevenses. The Racehorse Inn seemed the only likely option, but it didn't open until 1200. I waited outside for a few minutes, enjoying the sunshine, before going in for a coffee.

Moving on I wandered through fields before lazing on a grassy bank to eat my lunch, somewhere between the delightfully named places of Lemalla and Coquarnel. My note book records, "This is much more of a day for saying, 'Ah! This is the life'"! I kept on through Lewannick and down a shady track to Treguddick Mill and up the lane to Treguddick. (Gothic writing on the map).

Back in the nineteen-thirties when my parents were newly married they bought a picture which hung on the wall all through my childhood and is in my possession even now. This picture was painted by the Cornish artist Harold Harvey in 1935 and is titled 'A Cornish Homestead'. The internet tells me, describing the picture, that 'Several farm buildings occupy the middle ground; in the foreground a man sits on a white horse which drinks from a pond, a brown horse alongside; beyond are green fields and hills'. My dad told me that he thought the hills in the background were Bodmin Moor, but that he had often wondered what the location was of this picture. Some years ago I took a photograph of the picture. Ann I took the photo with us when we had a summer holiday in Cornwall. During our stay we visited Bill and Marion, whom I'd stayed with on my second day out. I showed Bill the photograph on the off-chance that he might be able to recognise the background hills. After a very short look and think he told me he was pretty sure that the hill in the background was Bray Down, on the edge of Bodmin Moor, and that the farm was Treguddick Manor. He then astounded me by saying that the farmer there was a nice chap and a very obliging fellow. The reason that Bill is so knowledgeable is because he is a retired mining engineer cum mineralogist cum geologist and archaeologist. He enjoys tramping around the moors and fields of Cornwall looking for whatever might be of interest to him. Fossicking he calls it. He goes and has a word with a farmer or landowner and seeks permission to wander about. He had at some time in the past been to Treguddick and done his fossicking there. Ann and I subsequently visited Treguddick in our quest to discover if Bill could have been right, but our time was limited and our explorations, such as they were, were inconclusive. Now I went through the farm and up a way Ann and I hadn't explored previously and took various photos in attempt to find the spot from which the picture was painted. A lot can happen in 74 years! The pond may have been filled in, new buildings put up, trees chopped down and so on. The artist may have used considerable artistic licence in his composition. However, I did find a pond, perhaps not quite where I thought it ought to be, the trees behind the farm and the buildings looked very reminiscent of those in the picture, but not exactly true in every detail. The overall 'feel' of the place makes me believe that Bill was right.

Feeling very satisfied with this outcome I soon found myself on the brink of the A30. Not wanting to walk for nearly a mile along the gutter of the fast-moving dual carriageway I walked in the field alongside. After some minutes I noticed three large bulls in the same field - no cows present - so I decided the least worst thing to do was to remove myself fairly quickly. This meant climbing the stony hedge-bank and then clambering through a brambly bit of ditch before finding myself in the aforesaid gutter. I tramped on as far as Kennards House and escaped onto a quieter road leading into Tregadillet and on into Launceston.

I had by now learnt that one is to say Laan-son. I was entering the town and wondering how I was going to find the road where the B and B was when I met a couple out for an early evening stroll. They were friendly, and perhaps because I was poised, map in hand, they asked if they could help me. I explained what I was doing and where I was headed and they told me the way I needed to go. Before moving on they said, "Tell Gillian that you met Les and Ernestine". Gillian ran the B and B! I had been expecting a warm welcome from Gillian as I had heard of her from my friend Susanna, another Sidcot scholar, a couple of years younger than me. Some years before my venture she had walked from John O'Groats to Land's End and had fallen ill at Launceston and stayed at Gillian's B and B and had been looked after tenderly.

I was, indeed, warmly welcomed and settled in. I went out for a meal in a wine bar in the town, which was very noisy, being largely occupied by young men who were down for a golfing weekend. Thus ended a truly delightful day. I little knew then that there were many more to come ......

Monday 30th March
Launceston to Germansweek - 11.3 miles

After some pootling about in 'Laanson' doing bits of shopping I got going at about ten to ten and followed the Two Castles Trail for a few hundred yards and then climbed up through fields and shortly found myself coming the back way into a Garden Centre. This was an unexpected and fortuitous discovery. I guiltily crept round three sides of a many-windowed restauranty bit to find the loo. I had, unusually, been wondering how I was going to find a 'comfort stop' this morning, following some earlier mismanagement. This was a great relief. On just about every other day along the whole walk I wasn't troubled by this kind of situation, generally due to careful management before leaving my overnight stop. Pick your way as you will through the euphemisms.

I followed a main-ish road for less than a mile then escaped along a back road to Crossgate. I then turned east momentarily and crossed the River Tamar by an old bridge. I was now leaving my first county behind and joyfully entered Devon at 1205. This was a significant marker for me in that it meant I had finished with Cornwall and I felt I was actually making some progress. For the rest of my journey northwards I did occasionally note when I entered a new county. It wasn't always particularly obvious when that happened.

I trundled on and soon found myself with Council workmen patching the road surface. They seemed to be working, as far as I was able to establish, a circuit of roads and there seemed to be two teams of men. The first lot were spraying a black oily liquid on to the relevant bits that needed patching, then a few minutes later the second team came along with the tarmac. Then the first team, who had, no doubt, whizzed along the main road and come back round, followed the second team, this time spreading grit. I was able to pass by without undue inconvenience. I arrived at St. Giles on the Heath village in time for a hopeful lunch, but pub and Post Office and everywhere I could see seemed to be closed. Undismayed, well nearly, I kept on and towards the end of the village I passed a house called Keynsham. Now Keynsham is the town in north Somerset where I was born and lived as a child and I don't ever remember seeing a house named after it. Perhaps the owners used to live there. Any tenuous connection between myself, my journey and the occupants of the house, assuming they were at home, seemed too remote to even contemplate the idea of calling in and begging a lunch on the strength of it. So I didn't. A little while later I sat on the grass verge and ate my grub. I nearly always had some food with me, but I didn't always use it if a pub or a caff presented itself. I generally relied, quite enjoyably, on oaty biscuits, cheese or ham or a pasty, and fruit.

The weather was overcast all day and rather cool but it didn't rain. My notebook records that I was glad of my silk long johns today. I had never worn silk before this year and I had heard people say how warm they kept with silk underwear. I borrowed a friend's catalogue and ordered some long johns. They were reasonably comfy, but a bit on the baggy side. They did seem to make a difference, warmth-wise though. I used them on and off during the first three weeks, but Ann took them home after Easter.

The lane I was following was fairly level and I glimpsed Dartmoor away to the right and Bodmin Moor was receding behind me. I followed this lane for several miles to Ivyhouse Cross. I paused at the crossroads, which was very near to Broadwoodwidger Primary School. The village of Broadwoodwidger is about three miles away, but I guessed the school served a wide rural area. A male teacher came out of the school - it was after 'home time' - and I had a chat with him. He told me there were 25 children on the roll and hardly any children coming into the area. He wondered how long it would be likely to stay open. Just then a school bus arrived with older pupils on board, I guessed from a comprehensive in Launceston. A boy and a girl got off and as the bus started to move on a girl sitting in the bus waved to me. Then lots more of them started waving and I waved back. I could imagine that hard-bitten teenagers might 'wave' at a stranger, in a mocking kind of way, just 'having a laugh'. Such a thought flashed through my mind but was instantly banished as I felt that this was a genuine, friendly wave; a sincere gesture of greeting from sweet, unsophisticated rural children. OK - that was what I imagined, but it seemed better to give these youngsters the benefit of the doubt, rather than casting them in a cynical role.

I carried on, warmed by this tiny episode, following a grassy lane and then into fields. The last half mile or so was rather boggy underfoot, the first un-dry bit of the day. I easily found my B and B in the village of Germansweek and was given a warm welcome by Roger and Nicky. They gave me a substantial evening meal and the accommodation was very comfortable. Roger was a willing talker and listener and we yarned for quite a while.

Tuesday 31st March
Germansweek to Hatherleigh - 11.0 miles

I was away before nine o'clock on a day much as the day before, overcast but dry. Lanes took me through Eworthy and on to Northcombe. The next mile or so was over a stretch of land known as Broadbury. I had been half expecting a reasonably substantial hill, but the lack of contour lines on the map belied this. It is perhaps the near enough highest bit of land thereabouts but the gradients are so gradual that it does not stand up prominently. There was a bit of scrubby moorland which half put it right with my preconception. There were good wide views to the north and north-west. I thought, "Is that cloud or Exmoor in the far distance?" Yes, I think it was Exmoor. An interesting find was discovering a thrush's anvil with lots of beautifully coloured snail shells scattered nearby.

I sat on an old milk churn stand for a few minutes in the hamlet of Patchacott and then carried on along delightful lanes to the village of Northlew. I thought it was high time for elevenses, but the pub in the village square seemed to be closed - perhaps a bit too early. Looking around this charming little village I spotted the church hall where some activity seemed to be taking place. I went over and entered. Inside was a most splendid example of a community holding itself together by its own efforts. In the one room there was a temporary Post Office: Tuesdays 0930 until 1230. This was indeed a Tuesday. The young lady comes out from the Hatherleigh Post Office in a little van and sets up her office in one corner. In another corner a woman was selling pasties and other home-baked goodies. A man was taking orders for bread. There was a table with tinned food and domestic cleaning materials and such. And ... in one corner ... a lady was serving coffees and teas and biscuits. What more could I have wanted! One is aware of Post Offices closing all over the place, but this seemed to me to be a very good initiative.

Dragging myself away, I wandered along, passing an old collapsing barn or cottage that revealed broken walls. I said to myself, "That is crumbling cob". I vaguely remembered that cob was a mixture of clay and straw, and used as an old-fashioned building material. I couldn't be sure that this really was cob, but I like to think so. I hoped that someone would take this ruin in hand, rather than letting it be a sign of a gradually disintegrating village, which from my coffee-time experience it probably isn't.

At the bottom of the hill was the most immaculate fairy-tale thatched cottage. New looking roof, smoke curling out of the stone chimney, three thatched porches and a roof over the well in the

Thatched cottage at Northlew

Devon primroses

Thrush's anvil

garden. Cream coloured walls, looking very bright and clean. So, I thought, someone *is* taking trouble to make the village look good. I walked on feeling very optimistic.

My line was more northerly now, via Lambert Cross and on to Gribbleford Bridge, where I sat under a hedge and ate my lunch. It was less than three miles now into Hatherleigh and I arrived at my hosts' house, on the east side of town at about three o'clock. George was in my elder brother's form at Sidcot, and is an old friend. He and his wife Margaret have been regular and faithful attenders at our Old Scholars' reunions at the school every Easter. I was made extremely welcome and the talking began!

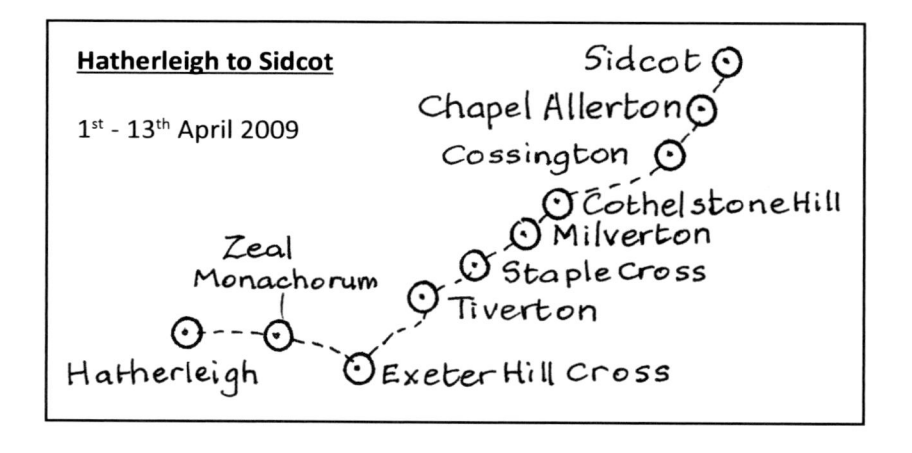

Hatherleigh to Sidcot

1st - 13th April 2009

- Sidcot
- Chapel Allerton
- Cossington
- Cothelstone Hill
- Milverton
- Staple Cross
- Tiverton
- Zeal Monachorum
- Hatherleigh
- Exeter Hill Cross

Hatherleigh to Sidcot

Wednesday 1st April
Hatherleigh to Zeal Monachorum - 11.5 miles

I left at 0845 and arrived at 1545 which means I had a pretty sauntering kind of day. The route was all along tarmac and was virtually due east in an easy line. I actually ended up a tiny bit further south than when I started. It was almost cold enough for gloves early on but it became sunny and warm later, with altocumulus clouds and some fractus. The Dartmoor high tops were hazily present away to my right. Leaves seemed to be making their presence felt on bushes and trees here and there. I had plenty of time to peer lazily over bridges and pause in woods to listen to the birds. I heard a woodpecker drumming and guessed it was a great spotted.

I came through Monk Okehampton, and passed Splatt Cross and Cadditon Cross. At one point during the morning I was passing an isolated house and four chocolate Labradors came charging out of the yard and ran into the road, barking madly. I felt a bit intimidated. Over-friendly dogs can be a bit daunting, especially at high speed, and I wasn't sure how friendly these were. A lady came to the door of the house, having heard the noise and called them off, apologising the while. A little later I descended to the valley of the River Taw to Bondleigh Bridge, where I ate my lunch perched on a stile just where the Tarka Trail crossed my path. I was intrigued by a nearby notice which announced: 'ALL DOGS MUST BE KEPT STRICTLY ON THE FOOTPATH AND ON A LEAD. IF THIS NOTICE IS NOT ADHERED TO PROSECUTION WILL FOLLOW'. It wasn't clear to me where one obtained the glue so that one could adhere oneself to the notice.

After my picnic I walked up the hill with an old workman who was going back to the farm at the top. He was anxious that I should never leave gates open and that I should keep to the footpath. He told me, in a lovely Devon dialect, of the ninety-six young cows that escaped some while back, because of a gate left carelessly open. "They found their way two mile and ended up in North Toddon (North Tawton). All over the place, they were. Up the 'igh Street and into people's gardens. It were the devil of a job rounding them up". He also told me of a similar occasion when forty heifers were found following the combine harvester along the lane. We talked about rights of way and he told me another story.

"My boss, he'd put 'is slurry pit where the footpath were and he wanted to get it diverted. Waal, this little bloke come out from the Council and 'e ad 'is little notebook and a fussy look about 'im. My boss, 'e said, 'I think the path should go round this side of the 'edge', and the little bloke said, 'Oh, no, I think it should go round this way'. My boss 'e come a bit stronger and said it really should come where 'e'd said, like. Waal, the little man, 'e thought 'e knew better and said, 'No it must go round *this* side of the 'edge, and I'm goin' round to 'ave a good look'. My boss, 'e said, 'You go round there if you wants to, but I'll go and fetch the tractor and back-loader and pull you out of the bog!'" By this time we had reached the farm and we parted.

I gentled on and passed Newton Cross and Great Wooden. I felt like asking, "The Great Wooden what?" Zeal Monachorum seemed a neat little village, partly on top of a hill and some of it down in the valley, all sitting prettily in the early spring sunshine. I sat out of the wind on a seat just outside the church for a while, just doing nothing except enjoy the warmth. The Waie Inn is a large building at the bottom of the hill, which seemed to serve as a community and sports centre as well as being a friendly pub with very decent en-suite accommodation and good food, all at a very reasonable price.

Thursday 2nd April
Zeal Monachorum to Exeter Hill Cross - 12.3 miles

I left at nine o'clock and although I had thought to go through fields to start with, I changed my mind and kept to the lanes, because there was a very heavy dew. My route was taking me even further south today, one of the longer 'necessary diversions' that I had to make occasionally. This was because I was to stay with old friends, Ann and Christopher, who lived just outside Crediton. I had meant to go via the village of Bow, but less than a mile after leaving the Inn I found the road was closed due to resurfacing. I turned left and after a while was obliged to join a main road for a couple of miles. However, before getting that far I met a man out walking his dog. The dog was called Milo. We exchanged 'good mornings' and he turned Milo and himself around and we walked along together. He thought I must be doing 'a cracking pace' to do 12 miles a day. I don't think he knew much about walking. He was amazed to discover that I was walking from Land's End to John O'Groats. I don't think he had ever realised that people did such a thing, let alone come along his bit of lane and past his house. After a few minutes he said, "Do you mind if I ask how old you are?" I turned it round and said, "Well, how old do you think I am?" He thought for a bit and then said, "Fifty-eight?" I replied, "Try sixty-eight." He was even more amazed than he was before and we walked on, passing his house, so that he could find out a bit more about what I was up to. After a while he turned back and I carried on. I don't know what Milo thought about it all.

As I progressed up the country I occasionally heard references to an 80 year old man who was walking northwards as well. I never came across him personally.

A little further on a man driving a car stopped and offered me a lift. He soon twigged though, and said, "I guess you are walking deliberately and won't want a lift", as though, in his experience

End-to-End walkers were two a penny. I did my usual explaining and he wished me the best of luck and drove on. Once I was on the main road there was a point where I walked for a hundred yards or so along the Two Moors Way. My daughter Beth and her partner Andy had walked the Way a year or so before, so I had a tiny taste of their adventure and devoted a few minutes to thinking about them.

I arrived in the village of Copplestone, hoping I might find a café. I didn't find a café as such, but the Convenience Store came up trumps with a coffee. I sat outside the shop and took my time. I got into conversation with a gentleman, who was less interested in my exploits than telling me about himself. That was fine by me. He said he was a Cornishman and was happier underground. He said he owned a pair of walking boots that cost £299 and were not being used. "I can't walk much now", he explained. He was familiar with the Bodmin Folk Club and admitted he was a singer/songwriter. He eventually drifted away and I drifted on.

I kept for a mile along the A377 and the pavement petered out after a while. The traffic was a bit busy and for a short way I felt rather exposed to danger with some blind bends. Before too long I turned off down a lane to Knowle and kept to some tracks for a while which were very pleasant. I crossed back over the main road at Barnstaple Cross and kept along a quieter back road which led me down into Crediton. Coming down a hill into the town, I passed a comprehensive school at lunch time. There were five teenage boys standing on the pavement smoking. As I approached them one of them perkily asked, "What's with the pink bag, man?" He meant my rucksack, which does have some pink material on it, and presumably implying that this was a somewhat ladylike colour to be carting about. I hardly broke my stride, but before I had left them, with grins and smiles all round, I think we agreed between us that 'pink was a man-thing'.

I was in need of a haircut and very soon came across 'Sarah's Barber Shop. Haircuts for Men and Boys. No appointment required'. I went in and had the full works - a hair trim, a beard trim and a hair wash, all done by Julie. Then I went in search of lunch which I enjoyed in a café on the main street. I was in plenty of time and could have gone straight to Ann and Christopher's, but decided to borrow a mile or two off tomorrow. I trundled across Lord's Meadow, which looked quite lovely in the by now very warm afternoon sunshine. I continued up a lane and through fields, bypassing Shobrooke village and eventually came out at Exeter Hill Cross. I rang Ann and she came and fetched me and took me back to their house. It was lovely seeing Ann and Christopher again after a good many years. My Ann and Ann had shared a house years ago before we were married. Good food, lovely garden to stroll in, plenty of catching up with old times, comfy bed - just the job.

Friday 3rd April
Exeter Hill Cross to Tiverton - 11.7 miles

Christopher drove me back to Exeter Hill Cross and I gentled along peaceably and after a few miles I reached the village of Thorverton. As always, I was on the lookout for a mid-morning coffee break and was not sure that I was going to just here. What I did find was a village car park in which were two vehicle-cum-buildings. One was a sort of hybrid static caravan-cum-whatever and the other was a converted library van. The first was the village Post Office and the other was proudly labelled 'Not the Village Shop'. There was a steady coming and going into and out of the car park as folk visited the Post Office and the shop. I spoke to a gentleman who I guess probably ran the 'Not the Village Shop'. He pressed me to view the inside where cunning use had been made of the old library shelves. He said that this shop and Post Office were both rather experimental. He called his shop by the name he did because he didn't want people to take it too much for granted and to realise the fragility of its existence. They were community initiatives that seemed to me to be flourishing, but I may have hit a busy moment. A kind lady called Jane, who I think worked in the shop, was busy around the back of her car across the car park. She was feeding twigs into a Kelly-kettle and boiling up water. I had never properly seen one in action. Jane kindly brewed me a coffee and I sat outside the Post Office on a bench revelling in the morning sunshine and the sense of good fellowship that the place seemed to generate. To say the least, I was very impressed with a community pulling itself up by its own boot straps. I remembered the similar situation at Northlew a few days previously.

Tearing myself away from this companionable place I walked down the pretty street to the bottom of the village where I stopped to take photos of the stream, burbling happily in the sunlight, with a hawthorn tree in fine leaf, hanging beautifully over the stream-bank at the side of a diminutive village green bedecked with daffodils. I guess idyllic really would sum it up.

I now turned sharply northwards, climbing out of the village. The dominant feature was good red Devon earth. Several newly sown fields, red-brown under a clear sky, stretched away before me as I climbed to Bidwell Cross. I followed the lane for a few miles over a shoulder of hill and down to Bickleigh in the Exe valley, where the green sheen on the trees was really starting to develop. I could have entered an eatery at Bickleigh Mill but chose to sit just outside by the stream and eat my own bits and pieces. I then kept to the Exe Valley Way for about another four miles into Tiverton, arriving just before four o'clock. The Exe Valley Way signs looked a bit sad and in need of sprucing up a bit. A lot of the way was in woodland beside the river and was cool after the heat of the middle of the day.

I spent the night at the Angel Guest House which was quite friendly. I think they are used to End-to-Enders on bicycles. The 'Golden

Panda' fed me a quite good sweet and sour chicken and an orange sorbet.

As I progressed up country I was crossing watersheds which were not always particularly obvious on the ground. Before reaching Tiverton I had already crossed streams or rivers that flowed in to either the English Channel or the Bristol Channel/Irish Sea. West Cornwall - English Channel; Redruth - Bristol Channel; Truro - back to the south again; St. Columb - back to the north; the Tamar at Launceston - quite clearly southbound; Hatherleigh area - northbound; then the Exe down south again. Looking ahead, once I was into Somerset and beyond, the water I crossed was always flowing into the Bristol Channel or the River Severn until I reached Whitchurch in Shropshire, where streams ran northwards, but still flowing into the Irish Sea. At Ravenstonedale in Cumbria I switched from the Lune catchment into the Eden. These still run westwards. After Newcastleton the westward flow changed to the Tweed catchment running into the North Sea. After that the Clyde went west, then at Crianlarich the River Dochart is eastbound via Loch Tay. At Glencoe and Fort William the water flows west, but somewhere near Loch Oich in the Great Glen the flow was into the North Sea. Any water in the last mile or so into John O' Groats arguably flows into the Atlantic.

Saturday 4th April
Tiverton to Staple Cross - 11.8 miles

I enjoy Saturday mornings and this was no exception. I pottered about the town, which seemed to have a decent shape to it and a history and old buildings. I felt I could easily go back there at some time in the future, as long as it was a sunny Saturday morning! I decided that I did not need to stock up on food as the man in the Tourist Information Centre told me there was a Spar shop in Sampford Peverell.

I was wearing trainers and carrying another pair of trainers for 'clean'. I visited several shoe shops in the hope that I might find some alternative footwear for evening use that would also be lighter to carry. I didn't want to wear flip-flops, even though these would have been very light. I never have worn them and as I prefer to wear socks, I wasn't sure how the front strap thing would fit between my toes. So that was a no-no. I did look at some "Crocs" which seemed to be made of plastic and were quite light, but I thought they were very ugly and not really me. I don't mind not 'being me' on occasions but this seemed like a footstep too far! I came away empty-handed, or should that be empty-footed? In a chemist's I bought an elasticated knee support. I thought this might help my 'silly knee', but I didn't really feel comfortable with it and abandoned its use after a day or so. I enjoyed visiting the Pannier Market, where at one stall there were four or five live chickens outside the door to help advertise the sale of 'local farm fresh free range eggs'. I bought a padded envelope to post a map home later on and also a Guardian. I visited a café and had a coffee and a Belgian bun and read as much of the paper as I wanted. I didn't want to carry it any further so gave it to another chap who looked slightly startled, but was happy to receive it after an explanation. However, I tore out and kept the Araucaria Prize Crossword to have a go at later.

I eventually started properly at about 1115 and worked my way out of town and took to the towpath of the Grand Western Canal. This made excellent walking and I met quite a few people over the next few miles. My route from Crediton was dictated by an overnight stop, a few days ahead, with my cousin at West Bagborough, which shelters under the Quantock Hills. My target for today was to reach Staple Cross, a tiny hamlet not far from Hockworthy. I left the towpath after a bit and made my way into Halberton. To my mild dismay I could not find a pub or café. I carried on and found myself back on the towpath which led me into Sampford Peverell. I did not find the promised Spar shop but instead found the Post Office at

Friendly welcome at Thorverton

Devon red

False oxlip

quarter to two. I wanted to post my map home but the PO had closed at one o'clock. The obliging postmaster allowed me to leave it for the Monday post. I paid slightly more for this privilege as the postal rates were going up on the Monday. I bought some cheese and two bananas and sat down near where the lane goes in a tunnel under the main road just out of the village and tucked in.

The day was cloudy with some sunshine and the next few miles were very quiet and pretty. After an easterly-bound morning I now struck northwards, skirting the fringes of the Culm Valley and climbed up to a broad ridge with views widening out. There was the beginning of a Brendonish hint about the banks and lane edges. The characteristic feature of the Brendons, I always think, is the beech 'hedges', and here they were. The Blackdown Hills were clearly in view. Just to the left of the Wellington Monument I could see, and had to ask myself, "Is that the Poldens? It surely can't be the Mendips???" And through a gateway I glimpsed the 'not so distant' Quantocks. I thought, "Ah Somerset, there you are!" I was born and bred in Somerset and I started feeling much more at home. I arrived at my B and B at Staple Cross Cottage, situated very conveniently next door to the pub. After a meal at the Staple Cross Inn (very nice food), I went to the car park across the road and managed to get a signal on my mobile. I spoke to Ann, as I did every evening and also spoke to my old friend Alan, who had been rather poorly.

There had been plenty of cumulus humilis around during the day and later on even some congestus, but at dusk the sky cleared to a splendid cool sunset.

Sunday 5th April
Staple Cross to Milverton - 9.3 miles

This was a beautiful morning and I felt pleased to be on my way. It felt very adventuresome, as did every morning, really. After less than a mile of lane I turned down a track to Hole Farm and I was surprised to find, halfway down, a narrow-gauge railway running round the hillside. I couldn't work out where it started and finished. It almost felt like a rich man's plaything, but I guess it must have had some industrial use. One of life's intriguing little mysteries. Just after the farm I crossed a stream on some dinky little stepping stones and passed from Devon into Somerset. Several fields later found me in the quiet little village of Ashbrittle. The last time I had been here had been in the middle of the night on the 100 kilometre Long Distance Walkers Association (LDWA) 'Wellington Boot' challenge walk some years before. Everything was still and peaceful. A notice by the village green announced, 'The yew tree which stands in Ashbrittle's St. John the Baptist Churchyard is reputed to be 3800 years old and to have been visited by Coleridge, Southey and Wordsworth'. I went and had a look at it and it certainly seemed pretty ancient. Not feeling too ancient myself I kept down the lane to Tracebridge, following the West Deane Way. A shady valley gave way to the warm village of Appley. I drifted gently down through open fields for a mile to Cothay Manor then along the line of the Grand Western canal again. The water has long since disappeared along this stretch but the line is obvious. The next mile was more difficult. It looked quite easy, still following the West Deane Way, but I made a complete hash of my map-reading and got snarled up in a wood, scrabbling up steep banks and ducking under low hanging branches and generating quite a mucksweat while doing so. I still haven't been able to work out where I went wrong.

I soon found myself in Langford Budville. I had previously been advised by today's B and B hostess, Susan, that I would be unlikely to find an evening meal in Milverton on a Sunday, so I went in to The Martlet Inn and had a substantial meal. I had plenty of time to wander my way by fields and tracks before joining a road down into Milverton. The B and B was in an elegant town house full of antiques which Susan seemed to deal in. I took my own food up into the back garden and sat on a bench eating my evening meal. This garden was exquisite and dominated by a beautiful magnolia tree in full bloom. Wonderful!

My notebook tells me I have come 195 miles already in seventeen days.

Monday 6th April
Milverton to Cothelstone Hill - 9.3 miles

Today was cooler than the previous couple of days and I made steady progress, mainly on tarmac. Somewhere near the village of Halse a lady in a car pulled up behind me and in a very county voice announced, "I see you're hobbling, can I give you a lift anywhere?" I explained that my limping was a fairly permanent condition and that I hoped, despite it, to walk all the way to John O'Groats, so I declined her offer and she drove on. I hadn't really realised that my limp was so obvious.

I carried on and made my way over Ash Priors Common and through Bishops Lydeard. After a rather enclosed bit of track there was a two mile stretch of lane, pretty well straight, which took me into West Bagborough. I arrived at my cousin Julian's house at about one o'clock, just in time for lunch. Julian and his wife Pat have been taking a keen interest in my progress and I was able to share my experiences with them, knowing I had an eager audience.

My walking for the day was not over. I took only a light pack with me in the afternoon and climbed up the lane and onto Cothelstone Hill where splendid views can be had. On the way up the lane I met three immaculately be-jacketed, be-helmeted and be-booted gentlemen on horseback. The pale green cloth of their jackets was, I discovered later, the uniform of the West Quantock Staghounds. As they came cautiously down the hill I stepped to one side so as not to disturb the horses. There was barely a flicker of acknowledgement to me as they passed by. I thought, "What must it be like to be high up on a horse and feel so superior that you don't even raise a hand to thank us inferior pedestrians". I guess I felt sorry for them, 'stuck up' on a horse. At the top of the hill there were horse boxes parked and a group of other hunt people. They were seemingly waiting for something or other; I gathered the 'hunt' was some distance away at that moment. I stopped to chat to them and they were much more approachable. I even took a photograph of them and they didn't mind. My End-to-End credentials had perhaps relaxed them into thinking I wasn't a hunt saboteur or some such.

Coming down off Cothelstone Hill I made a special visit to Tim's Tree. Tim was the second of three children of very special friends of ours, Michael and Margaret Stocks, who used to live not far away in Kingston St. Mary. Jo and Tim and Elizabeth were very similar in age to our Bryony, Beth and Caroline. Tim was a sportsman and adventurer and stood well over six feet. He and some friends took part, some years ago, in a Human Power adventure, sea-kayaking and cycling from London to Sydney. There were about six of them I think, though only a couple of them did it all. Tim joined them part way through and kept with them from Tibet down through the islands to East Timor. They had 400 miles of ocean to cross and managed to charter a sailing boat with a fairly unskilled 'captain'. They got caught by the tail-end of a typhoon, had various disasters, the captain gave up on them, the Australian coastguards took a couple of the team off, the compass gave out and they had to use the tiny compasses on the bikes. They eventually got stranded on a reef just off the giant-crocodile infested Australian coast. It was Tim who waded ashore to seek help, early in the morning. They eventually got sorted and carried on with their ride down to Sydney.

In one job that he was in, Tim and his colleagues had to write a sort of resumé about themselves. Whilst others wrote reams Tim wrote three words: 'Tall. Determined. Surprising'. He was the most likeable and lovable character one could ever wish to meet. But sadly he got cancer and died at the age of 35. This book is dedicated to Tim. I was very pleased to visit Tim's Tree, which his family and friends planted in his memory. It looked in good nick. I took the opportunity to ring Margaret, to tell her where I was. Julian came and picked me up in the car park and took me back to his house. The rest of the day was spent talking and talking and talking ...

Tuesday 7th April
Cothelstone Hill to Cossington - 13.2 miles

There had been overnight rain and the grass was a bit damp at first but everywhere soon dried up. It was very fresh first thing, which was delightful, and by the afternoon it was bright and sunny. My goodness - I have been lucky with the weather! This is the tenth consecutive day without rain. In fact I have only had four hours of rain since leaving Land's End. Julian drove me back up to the car park on Cothelstone Hill and I started walking at nine o'clock.

My recording of wild flowers has continued and by the end of today the overall count had risen to 72. Today's 'new' finds included cowslip and false oxlip. Along a lane just short of Lydeard Cross I came across what I reckoned was the first big tree in full leaf that I had seen. This was a sycamore and stood out boldly - and very green - against other trees whose buds were still waiting to burst open. Distant views opened up across Bridgwater Bay and the Mendips were very obvious. I came down through fields and into Goathurst. On the way I passed a building called a 'Temple of Harmony'. I did not investigate, but it sounded intriguing. The next three miles or more were very level through an area known as The Meads. Once or twice I thought I was going to lose the path but it kept on coming up trumps and I reached the outskirts of Bridgwater without any difficulty. I came across a café and went in for a coffee.

I picked up a local paper and found a news item about two young men who were just about to set off from Land's End on motorbikes, hoping to reach John O'Groats in 16 hours. Each to his own, say I.

Knowing I wasn't going to find an evening meal I made a substantial lunch in 'Prezzo', with pasta and salad and ice-cream. I bought some blueberries and carried them for my evening snack. Visited a cash machine then plodded on over the M5 and through fields to Bawdrip. Here I paused to look at some rather good specimens of yellow archangel and a lady approached me. She wanted to know if I was something to do with a Bath and Wells Diocesan Youth Pilgrimage, which was supposed to be in the vicinity and which she was supposed to meet. I had no information to give her - but she did seem a very nice lady. A stretch of disused railway track took me into Cossington and I found my way to the farm B and B, right on the edge of the village.

In the absence of his Nan I was welcomed very politely by Will, aged 13, although I thought he seemed younger. Nan arrived later and I was welcomed all over again. I later enjoyed coffee and cake with her. This was probably the friendliest and most laid back and easy-going B and B so far.

Wednesday 8th April
Cossington to Chapel Allerton - 9.2 miles

Today involved a major change in scenery. After the ups and downs of Cornwall and Devon and the Quantocks, a day of flat walking lay before me. The Somerset Levels are correctly named! A lot of the day was on tarmac, albeit on unfrequented lanes, but I managed a little bit of field and track. The weather was cool to start with and warmed up later. It was dry underfoot except for one horrendously muddy bit for a few yards that I almost circumvented.

The roads here run very straight for long stretches and then have right-angled bends. The roads are often almost like causeways across the peatlands, with a rhine (pronounced reen) alongside, sometimes on both sides. These are often unfenced. The road sometimes dips up and down where subsidence has occurred.

I have been very pleased with my camera and managed a shot of a chiffchaff high in a willow tree. I had been hearing chiffchaffs since my second day out but I hadn't often seen them. I generally expect to hear them for the first time when we go to Sidcot at Easter - the Mendips being a little earlier for migratory birds than Buxton. I think some are starting to overwinter nowadays, but I am not sure how widespread this is. When hearing one for the first time I really feel that spring has arrived. Anyway, the zoom worked and the focussing worked and I have a reasonable picture.

I crossed the Huntspill River at Gold Corner Bridge and there was a surprising difference in water levels on each side of the bridge as there are sluice gates here. I went along Gold Corner Drove and found tied bundles of osiers lying on the ground. The willow hedge had just been reduced in height and the cut 'crop' was waiting to be collected. The word withe (pronounced withee) is a more general term for a cut twig but osier is more specific to willow. I suspect the two terms are used interchangeably. I would have loved to have found someone to talk to about this local industry, but no-one was around. Pollarded willows are a common sight on the levels. The map named an adjacent track as 'Shaking Drove'. This, I surmised, refers to the ground trembling underfoot.

The long straight bits were not daunting at all. I found I was just accepting the terrain as it was. There is no point in trying to fight it or wish it wasn't there. I wasn't just 'accepting' it, I was really enjoying it. I don't think I was trying to kid myself that I was enjoying it. Every day, every mile, every yard, every step is a newness. How can one not enjoy the excitement of the newness?

I sat on a grassy bank at Westham and ate a simple lunch, before moving on through Blackford, which was looking quite delectable in the sunshine. After Ashton the ground rose slightly and I came out by Ashton Windmill, which was undergoing repairs to the sails. It was then only a few yards to the home of Patrick and Enid, with whom I was to spend the night. I arrived at about two o'clock and was pressed to a second lunch. Patrick was in my form at Sidcot and is an old friend.

Another friend, John, was staying with Pat and Enid. Pat and John and myself spent most of the afternoon working on the preparations for hanging a five-barred gate to an old stone gatepost in one of Pat's fields. We did manage to sit around in the evening and have a good old chat.

Thursday 9th April
Chapel Allerton to Sidcot - 5.8 miles

I set off on a rather damp morning at 1000. Within the first mile I saw a fox. Half a mile later I didn't see, despite the most diligent of searching, the entry into a field which was clearly marked on the map as a right of way. The hedge was completely grown over and I could find no sign whatsoever of an old stile or gap. It didn't really matter because it was hardly any further to go down the lane. After the little ridge of hill where I had spent the night I was back on the levels again for a couple of miles, crossing the River Axe at Cradle Bridge and the Cheddar Yeo a little further on. I arrived in Axbridge square at about half past eleven and went in search of some elevenses and wondered if it ought to be lunch as well. I found a café near the church steps and had something reasonably sustaining. I climbed up a familiar route onto Fry's Hill. This is a lovely spot, with increasingly wide views across the Levels, and a haven of wild flowers growing in the short limestone turf. It was a bit early in the season to find much in the way of flora and besides it had come on to rain and it was misty. The views never arrived and the emerging rock-rose flowers I found had curled their petals up again - I guess they thought it wasn't really spring yet. I kept over the top of Callow and down the combe to Sidcot, arriving before half past two. This had indeed been a short walk, but I managed to record thirty-five flowers seen, the rock-rose being the only new one. Ann tells me it wasn't a rock rose, having looked at the photo I took.

I have mentioned Sidcot several times already. Sidcot School is a Quaker co-educational boarding school in the village of Winscombe about 15 miles south of Bristol, 8 miles from Weston-super-Mare and about 5 from Cheddar. The A38 trunk road runs down one side of the school grounds. The school is situated in a delectable fold in the Mendip Hills and is splendid place in which to be educated. It has been there, in one form or another, since 1699. I was there from 1952 to 1958. Ex-pupils can join the Old Scholars Association. I have been an Old Scholar (OS) since leaving and have often been involved in the administration of the Association. If I continue to refer to "OS" I probably don't mean Ordnance Survey.

The main delight of the Old Scholars' year is attending the OS reunion at Easter. This event is a great escape from the workaday world and attracts OS and their families for a long weekend, Thursday afternoon to Tuesday morning, staying in the school, with full board provided. There is a full programme of events including a swimming gala, mixed hockey, nature trail walk, an Easter lecture by a prominent OS, a barn dance, a disco night, an Annual Meeting, games for young children, a Sunday Evening meeting with hymns and an address, which is followed by 'Music after Meeting' where a high standard of performance is usually attained. A scratch choir performs after a few rehearsals and on the Monday evening there is an entertainment on the stage with sketches and the like. And much more. There is always a 10 mile-or-so walk on the Monday, and for the last 15+ years it has been planned and led by my friend Alan and myself. Alan lives in Shipham, just up the road from Sidcot and was also in my class.

The reunion is very much a must on the Evens family calendar. The year after Ann and I took our young daughters for the first time, we asked them if they wanted to go again. We were immediately informed that there was no question - they had to go. They, like Ann, were not OS themselves, although they have since become Associate Members and attend the reunion as often as they can. They have made lifelong friends with other children of OS since those early days.

The reason I explain all this is that I had to consider whether I was going to start from Land's End a few weeks earlier than I actually did, and miss the OS reunion altogether, an almost unheard of occurrence. I know I had wanted to 'start in the winter', but in the end it turned out to be the last day of winter when I set off. The clincher was that my elder brother, Nick, was to give the address at Sunday Evening Meeting and there was no way I wanted to miss that. The family all turned out in force to support me during my Presidential Year in 2006, so it seemed only fair to reciprocate. So I timed my departure from Land's End so that I would arrive, all being well, on the Maundy Thursday, along with all the other OS. I then would spend four days having a 'rest day'. I wondered whether it would be 'cheating' to have such a long gap in the middle of the walk, but fortunately there are no rules, except the ones you make up yourself.

Alan and I had researched the Monday Walk as far back as the previous June and I was a bit rusty about where it went. Alan, who is usually tremendously healthy and doesn't really know how to be ill, was convalescing after a spell in hospital and wasn't going to be able to lead the walk. I spent odd bits of the weekend familiarising myself with portions of the walk, with help from Ann with the car.

On the Monday I led the ten mile walk with several dozen folk trailing behind me. So the four day 'rest day' turned out to be only three.

Having arrived and found my room I hung around waiting for Ann to arrive from Buxton. She was bringing Belinda, as we do most years. Ann had to dash off to Yatton to meet Bryony (eldest daughter) and Caroline (youngest daughter) off the train. Beth (middlest daughter) arrived later in the weekend in time to hear Uncle Nick give his talk.

Thursday 11th April to Tuesday 14th April - at Sidcot

10 miles walked on Easter Monday (not counted in overall mileage)

The weekend continued in its usual fashion with all its variety and fun. Various folk I had already stayed with in Cornwall and Devon turned up and wondered how I was getting on. To be honest I felt pretty chipper and my ego basked in the attention it received.

It had been a great weekend as usual, but come Tuesday morning I had to re-think myself back into 'OK, let's get on with it' mode. I didn't quite know how I would feel, or how long it would take to re-acclimatise. There was only one more rest day planned and that was to be in Fort William, many weeks away.

It took me three weeks to walk the Cambrian Way some ten or so years earlier and that was the nearest match I could find to measure how I might be managing on the 'big one'. After three weeks walking from Land's End and then four days 'off', I felt I would have to start again, physically and psychologically. I then felt that I would have to walk for another three weeks after the 're-start' to find out whether I was up to it, or whether I might conk out.

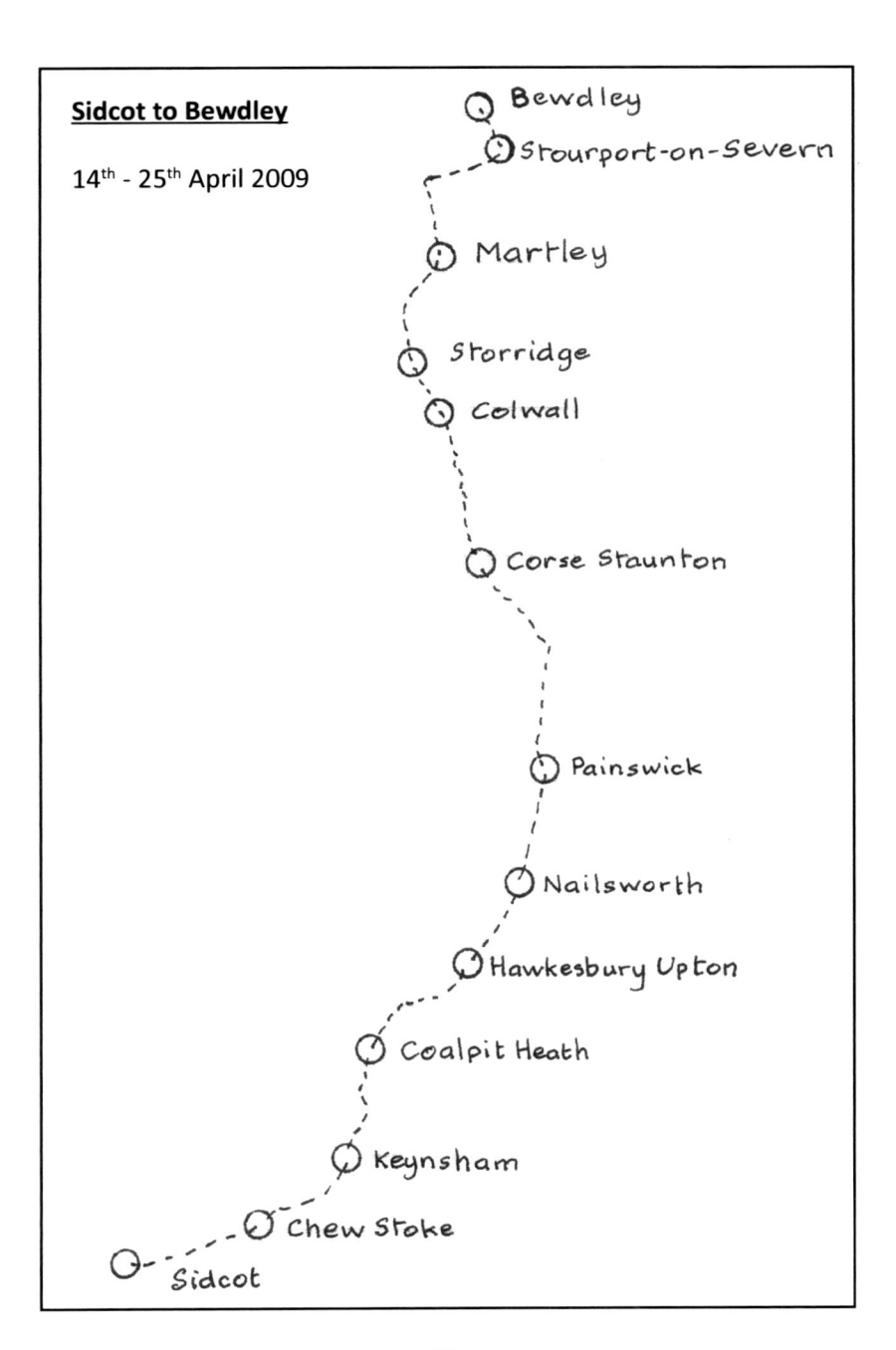

Sidcot to Bewdley

14th - 25th April 2009

- Bewdley
- Stourport-on-Severn
- Martley
- Storridge
- Colwall
- Corse Staunton
- Painswick
- Nailsworth
- Hawkesbury Upton
- Coalpit Heath
- Keynsham
- Chew Stoke
- Sidcot

Sidcot to Bewdley

Tuesday 14th April
Sidcot to Chew Stoke - 10.7 miles

Having said my goodbyes to family and friends I set off at about 1045 and walked up to Shipham and called in on a convalescent Alan and had a mug of coffee. He had missed most of the goings-on at the weekend and particularly wanted to hear about the walk.

I carried on, crossing Water Valley and along to Burrington. At Rickford I settled down for my lunch on a seat by the pretty little brook. Soon after, I went somewhat trepidaciously down a farm drive, because that was the line I wanted to take. I hadn't seen a footpath sign but I had assured myself that, according to the map, this was the right way to go. I entered the farmyard and there was a sleepy old dog there who didn't pay me any attention. At the far side of the yard I went through a big metal gate, rather the worse for wear and was confronted with a sign that said 'Keep Out - Restricted Area'. I found this somewhat daunting. The area ahead of me was pig sheds, old elder trees, nettles and brambles and muck. A stream at one side prevented escape that way and I was just wondering whether I really ought to be there when I spotted an old circular disc with a footpath arrow on it, so I thought, "OK, here goes". I had my map out and was still pondering, when the farmer came out of his kitchen with a washing basket. He seemed not to be cross at my presence, although perhaps a little surprised. Our conversation went something like this.

"Am I alright to be coming through here?" I asked.

"Yes, there is a right of way, but nobody do come down yere much nowadays," he replied in a lovely North Somerset accent.

"I couldn't see a footpath sign at the top of your drive, but I see there is a little sign over there".

"The path does come through, but my new sheds is in the way, but I can show you how which way to go, and then you'll be back into the field, then down to the lane".

"Well, that's very kind of you. Actually I'm on my way from Land's End to John O'Groats".

"As I said, we don't often get folk through yere, in fact we 'aven't 'ad no-one through yere for a few years. In fact, the last fellow that come through yere was that there naked rambler? Seein' you standin' there with your map in your 'and was what reminded me of it. 'E was doin' what you're doin'. He was stood there like you 'is. I were up in the other yard and I sees this feller stood there, with 'is map in 'is 'and, and I says to myself, 'What the bloody 'ell's that then?' I comes over to 'im and says to 'im, 'What the blimmin 'eck's this all about then?' Well 'e told me. 'E told me all about it for quite a long time, all about 'is reasons for doing it and why 'e 'ad to do it. 'Well, I said to 'im, you won't want to go through there, it's all nettles and brambles.' He said to me, 'I'm pretty hardened to it by now'. And off he went. About three minutes later 'e cum back sayin', 'Them bloody stingers!' So he went back down my drive and went round by the lane".

He then told me which way I could go and I made my way through his 'stingers' without any trouble and found my way out onto the lane. The dog continued to pay no attention.

The lane was delightful with an excellent crop of lady's smock along the damp verges. I passed through Aldwick and on to Butcombe. I saw three deer in a field but they seemed to be feeding quite contentedly. I don't know what sort they were. I paused at Butcombe by an entry into a field. A sign indicated that it was the route of the Two Rivers Way. Another sign said 'Bull Beware'. Just at that moment a farm pick-up pulled into this entry and started reversing. The farmer got out and I had a chat with him. It turned out he was the owner of the land ahead of me, and the owner of the bull and the originator of the 'Bull Beware' sign. I asked him if the bull was in the field at the moment and whether there were cows there as well. He said there were cows but that the bull might be in the back field, so I might not see it. I pointed out that this was a right of way, and the Two Rivers Way to boot, and that people should be allowed to pass freely along it. I asked about the sign and he said that it was there so that people could choose whether to go there or not. I told him that I had planned to go that way and that his sign would make no difference to me and I would go anyway. He told me that he was 'covering himself'. I wasn't quite sure what he thought he was covering himself against. He is not allowed by law, such as I understand it, to put dangerous bulls, such as Friesians, in a field where there is a right of way. He told me that his bull was not a dangerous variety, but you never knew. I thought that if a 'non-dangerous' bull was to attack me or in some way upset me enough to make me want to sue him, his 'Bull Beware' sign would not 'cover' him at all. I don't know whether my reasoning convinced him; I don't think it did because he kept on about covering himself. I left him and struck up across the field. I saw some cows but never saw the bull.

After a second field I came to a stile. This was the most God-awful stile I had met since Land's End, if not for many a long year. It was a crude stile with another rough and ready structure just beyond it. The space between the two bits was neither use to man nor beast. It was almost too wide to stretch one's legs across both bits but not wide enough to climb down into and then up the other side. I knew it was going to need some careful manoeuvring so I approached it with greater caution than usual in such fixes. Coming off the far side I contrived to fall rather than climb down and landed in a heap with my right knee, the silly one, underneath me and twisted where I didn't want it to be with my weight upon it. I was a bit shaken and swore comprehensively. I was in some pain, mostly coming from my knee. As I sprawled on the ground, trying to recover my equanimity I found myself looking at the stile upon which was a sign - another one - 'Bull Beware'. I wish the farmer had put up a sign that said, 'Crap Stile - Beware'.

I picked myself up, somewhat gingerly, and limped my way tenderly on up the hill. I was pleasantly distracted at the top of the hill by the sight of another deer, this time leaping away in great bounds. A little way further on, I found a lamb in the lane, when it should have been in the field which I was about to enter. I don't know how or where it escaped, but I thought I had better see if I could help it back to its mum who was answering the bleats of the lamb. The gate into the field was a new-ish metal field gate. The sheep in the field were quite some way away, so I opened the gate and tried to stand inconspicuously out of the way, hoping the lamb would have the sense to come through this wide gateway. It made tentative approaches but was never quite daring enough to take the final dash through. I should have given up then, but twenty five minutes later, the wretched thing was still charging about. It had contrived to evade my carefully considered schemes and had been up the lane this way and down the lane the other way. Because of its mother's bleatings in the field it tried to take a direct line, through the hedge, only to be held up by the fence alongside the hedge. It rammed itself against the fence over and over again, cutting its face on the wire. I gave up. I had met two farmers earlier in the afternoon when I didn't really need to, but when I really did need one to help me, there was no-one to be seen.

A couple of miles later at about half-past five, I was at Chew Stoke and eventually found my B and B. I went to the Stoke Inn and had a vegetable lasagne and chips and salad and then retired to the B and B to nurse my mild bruises, my painful knee and my injured pride. Stupid lamb!

Wednesday 15th April
Chew Stoke to Keynsham - 10.5 miles

I set off from Chew Stoke at about a quarter past nine on a grey, overcast day and followed tracks and fields into Chew Magna. After my fall yesterday I felt a bit the worse for wear. I'd only come two miles but felt in the need of a sit down and luckily there was a café where I nursed my knee a little. I may have visited a chemist to stock up on painkillers, but this is not a firm memory. After a while I crossed the River Chew and almost immediately took a wrong turning and proceeded for a way before realising. I trudged up a field of long wet grass and found the correct line again. Before long I was in Stanton Drew and went to have a look at the stone circle there. It is nowhere near as impressive as Avebury, say, but at least as old, I think. I followed a pretty little lane down into Pensford, passing under the old railway viaduct. I sat on a bench beside the quaint old lock-up with its domed stone roof and ate my lunch. It wasn't quite the weather for lingering too long, although it never actually rained all day. Publow church with its well-proportioned tower soon came into view and I joined the Chew again. Walking along its bank I met a lady walking her dog and I asked her if she ever saw kingfishers on the river. She said that they were around and that she saw one occasionally. I kept my eyes well peeled for the rest of the day, but never saw one.

At Woollard I talked to an old man tending his allotment by the river's edge. We talked about the great floods of July 10-11 in 1968 which caused so much devastation here and all the way down the valley to Keynsham, where the Chew joins the Avon. I had thought to continue along the bank to Compton Dando, mainly for the purpose of seeing the weir at Woollard Mill where we had paddled and bathed as children, but my friendly allotment-man warned me of the 'black dog that nips' at the Mill so I changed my plan. I don't think I was feeling very brave just then, despite having my faithful cherry-slasher in my hand. Instead I found a lovely little covered path that led me up the hill and then down through a bluebell wood near Peppershells. I had been seeing bluebells ever since my second day out from Land's End but this was the first 'proper' bluebell wood I had met, and a great delight it was too. Compton Dando is a pretty little village, often the target of boyhood bike rides. I kept along by the river again to Chewton Keynsham, all the while moving into increasingly familiar territory. I took my time over the last mile into Keynsham, savouring sweet memories of childhood. Much, of course, has changed, but I nevertheless enjoyed a nostalgic few moments.

I lived here with my parents until I was 22. Ann and I were married at the Quaker Meeting house here in 1966, the only Quaker Wedding in Keynsham, we understand. I stayed the night with Roger and Janet, who are Quakers, although I didn't know them as well as my parents did. They were very hospitable and kindly. In the evening I walked over to call on David and Adeline to have a coffee. I had known these delightful people since my childhood, David being a Quaker. However, I hadn't dared to invite myself to stay with them as this would have been too much of a burden, particularly in view of Adeline's poor health. But ... it was good to have a bit of a clack. David in particular was very eager to know of my route and my progress.

So this had been a grey day weather-wise but the sun shone out of David and Adeline's eyes.

Thursday 16th April
Keynsham to Coalpit Heath - 9.8 miles

Leaving Roger and Janet's house I went round the corner and stopped outside the house where I was born. This house used to be a 'nursing home' but is now a private dwelling. I paused and wondered whether I might dare to take a photograph of the front of someone else's home, when a builder appeared. I told him that I had been born here (and probably that I was on my way to John

O'Groats) and that I rather fancied taking a photo and he replied cheerfully that this was his sister's house that he was working on and she wouldn't mind a bit. So I took my photo and made my way to the station. I spent many a happy hour here as a youngster collecting engine numbers, always on the lookout for King Class locos, especially King George V with the bell on the front. The station staff were a mixture of friendly and fierce. Sometimes we were allowed free run of the platforms but if 'Grumps' was on duty he would rather we were not there at all. I waited on the up platform for a few minutes and a train came in and picked up a few passengers. No whistles, no escaping steam, no clattering of semaphore signals, no sense of majestic power - just a common or garden diesel multiple-unit. Very ordinary.

I went down the hill to the 'County Bridge', alas no longer since the floods of '68. Instead there is a smooth, wide, straight modern affair with not much to commend it except its smoothness and straightness. I lingered long enough to check that the Chew was still faithfully joining the Avon a few yards away. It was. Notwithstanding the loss of the old stone bridge, which had had plenty of character, I still managed to pass from Somerset into Gloucestershire. Three counties down, goodness knows how many to go. I turned left into the meadows and after about a mile rejoined the road and went through a back lane towards Bitton. Along here I was surprised to find a garden centre café, so I sidled in and idled away some pleasant moments with a warm drink.

I made my way up to Bitton station where there is a preserved railway line. Almost immediately a steam train obligingly came past. This is the old Midland line from Bath to Bristol and Birmingham. I didn't immediately fall in love with it as I am really a GWR man at heart. The old prejudices die hard! I came past some old metal casings on which had been written in white paint: 'RUST IN PEACE' and 'THOMAS CAUSES GLOBAL WARMING'.

I followed the railway for a while on a walk-cum-cycleway. This was pretty level walking but not soft underfoot. I came across an unusual piece of sculpture, seemingly carved out of cement, with a rather larger than life male figure reclining with a water bottle poised above his lips. Going round to the end you find the button to press to make the water flow out of the bottle and into his mouth. Of course passing cyclists and walkers can place their own bottles under the flow and obtain refills. The inscription referred to the figure as Gaius Sentius and the sculpture was sponsored by Wincanton Distribution and ABSA. The sculptor was Gordon Young and the date was MDCDXCII and the whole thing had been commissioned by Sustrans. Well done them all, I say, I thought it was splendid. At Warmley I came away from the track and eventually found myself at lunchtime in 'The Horseshoe' at Siston. I availed myself of a pensioners' special fish and chips dinner as this was to be my main meal of the day. Moving on to Rodway Common I enjoyed the slight rise and its pleasant open space, with a view out across Bristol.

One of the things I noted was that for the last day or two a feature seemed to be the patterns of tiny white blackthorn petals, fallen from the trees above, covering the ground in mini-snowdrifts. My notebook also records, "You can't keep on expecting amazing things to happen - you just have to make the most of what presents itself". I did have these odd philosophical thoughts occasionally, and so I scribbled them down in case they seemed important later. I think this thought was indeed important. In a way I tried to make everything I met 'amazing'. This sometimes meant scaling down to something quite small, rather than, for example, a full-flung view of great grandeur. It might have been stopping to appreciate a pussy willow bud opening into fullness, the warm colour of an old brick wall or the curve of the path ahead of me. Amazing may be too strong a word, but satisfying - yes.

Unsatisfyingly, I became tangled up in a housing estate as I was trying to escape from Mangotsfield, but then it was alright as I hit the old railway track again. The day had been overcast, much as the day before, but warmer. However, by mid-afternoon it had got cooler and the clouds looked more threatening. Leaving the railway track I dived under the M4 and across flat meadows and along a lane to Box Hedge Farm B and B. It seemed to be quite a busy place for the white van type clientele. As soon as I arrived it started to rain in big heavy gobbets.

Regarding housing estates and, for instance, unpleasant bits of main road, I would sometimes put up with walking through or along them, if it meant that I would then be on course for a more suitable line to take further on.

Friday 17th April
Coalpit Heath to Hawkesbury Upton - 10.9 miles

It must have rained quite a bit in the night as the fields I walked through were pretty damp. It wasn't raining when I started walking but before I had gone a mile it was 'put your over-trousers on' time. It may have been because of the dismal weather, but during this first hour of walking I felt really rather low. My knee was still hurting rather more than usual from the stile incident a few days before and I had a sense of the enormity, or even stupidity, of the whole venture. I was thinking, what are my options? I could keep going and suffer the pain and hope that it would gradually disappear. I could keep on dosing myself with painkillers, but, I said to myself, there is no way I'm going to take painkillers all the way to the north of Scotland. I could apply elastic bandages etc to my knee and see if that works, but it didn't seem to when I tried it in Devon. And - truly ghastly thought - I could give up.

Ann had passed on to me a message from our friend Simon who had said, "If you give up you will never forgive yourself". I had had many positive expressions of support, not least from folk at the Old Scholars weekend, and this particular message seemed to have a negative ring to it rather than a positive one. But I knew it to be true and this message played itself back to me quite a few times before reaching Scotland. I thought, "Bother it, or words to that effect, I am *not* going to give up"! One possible solution did present itself, however. Buy some walking poles. I had never used walking poles and had been prejudiced against them for quite a few years. I am not quite sure how this prejudice arose, but prejudices are often due to incorrect information or sloppy thinking. So I wrestled with these thoughts as I walked along.

I came to a bridge over the main railway line from London to South Wales, just outside Yate. Well, as you may have realised by now, I am not averse to stopping and waiting for trains to come along, even if they are only diesels. A signal light shone green up the line, but nothing came. I thought I would wait and see at least one train. After a few minutes a very pleasant young man came over the bridge and he stopped and we had quite a good old natter. I mentioned my adventure and he was a good listener. He seemed happy to join me in my vigil - waiting for the next train to come. After quite a few more minutes he realised that he really ought to be getting on and he disappeared down the path. A moment later a train did come into view. I shouted, "Goods train" and he came running back and together we watched it pass underneath us and on down the line. Then he went on his way again. What a dear man!

This little incident lifted my spirits to somewhere back above par. I was aiming for the centre of Yate, hoping to find elevenses at least. I found it quite hard making my map fit the terrain, it being seemingly endless housing estates. There were walkways and cycleways and green patches but nothing seemed quite to fit.

I ended up doing a vast detour, adding over a mile to my intended route. I think my spirits dropped below par again. Eventually I found the town centre and came in out of the dampness and into the Boswell Café. I dredged myself up above par again with the help of hot food and drink. I then found a convenient Millets store very nearby and went in there and enquired about walking poles. I was pretty sure that if one is to use poles properly one needs to have a pair. The kind lady in the shop told me they were £24.99 each. I gulped a bit. Can I afford fifty quid? Then she added that they were on special offer, two for the price of one. She fetched a young man assistant to teach me how to use them. The length was adjusted and I walked up and down the shop a few times, watched critically by the very helpful young man. I passed the test and bought the poles. My cherry slasher graciously allowed the two shortened poles to join it in my rucksack and I went back into the Boswell Café and had some lunch.

I was now feeling much more at ease. Decision made. Prejudices overcome. I didn't think my poles were going to solve all my problems overnight but I felt they would help. I kept to little walkways along the edge of Chipping Sodbury and followed the Monarch's Way across some damp meadows to Little Sodbury where I joined the Cotswold Way. It had stopped raining. With only eleven hours of proper rain since Land's End, nearly a month ago, I really couldn't complain. So I didn't.

It was here that I met two lady walkers who were walking south along the Cotswold Way. I reckoned these were the first real 'proper walkers' that I had met so far. A mile or so further on at Horton I got into conversation with a chap who, it turned out, was, like me, a member of the Long Distance Walkers Association. He lived nearby and was just pottering about.

Shortly afterwards I came across a splendid, recently built stone building. It was a bit like a folly, a bit like a fat round tower but was in fact a specially built home for swallows and barn owls. I ascended the scarp, without really noticing the climb and carried on along the edge of the plateau on a quiet lane into Hawkesbury Upton. On the way I was surprised to see some amazingly dark blue comfrey flowers. I found my way to Di and Brian's house in the village where I was greeted most warmly. Di was in my form at Sidcot and has been particularly interested in my adventure.

After a meal Di took me to the village school where the Local History group holds its monthly meetings. Di always goes if she can and she thought I might be interested in that evening's talk, which was about Shire Horses. The be-whiskered and smartly groomed gent giving the talk was 'a bit of a character'. He seemed to be more interested in telling us 'humorous' anecdotes about his experiences with shire horses and going to shows and judging and the like, with some Prince Philip name-dropping along the way, rather than telling us about shire horses. Anyway it was all decent enough entertainment, but it delayed my evening routine of writing up my notes. So ended a day of mixed emotions. The 'low' was just a blip. In fact, looking back, this was my 'worst' day of the whole trip.

Saturday 18th April
Hawkesbury Upton to Nailsworth - 11.9 miles

I have been familiar with the countryside in this area since childhood, but I have never walked all of the Cotswold Way. In order that it can include all the best bits it winds around and goes up hill and down dale at frequent intervals. I used lots of long distance trails on my journey north, but there was never the intention to follow them faithfully from end to end, but just to use them to suit my convenience. (The exception to this was to be the West Highland Way.) So, I set off from Hawkesbury Upton with the intention of using bits of the Cotswold Way where it suited my purpose.

After a mile I passed the tower/monument and turned into fields. A cool, almost fresh breeze made itself felt on the plateau but it wasn't long before the path led me down into a wooded valley. On the way I was pleased to find some good specimens of toothwort under some hazels - a typical habitat. The going underfoot was what I call sticky-to-wet in the fields but there were occasional stretches of tarmac. From Kilcott Mill in its sheltered valley there was a long pull up to Tresham. I was now following the Monarch's Way up on the plateau again. In a very large field I was pursued by scores and scores of Friesian cows. They wouldn't take 'Go Away' for an answer. I had to turn and 'Shoo' them three or four times to keep them from getting too close, but they kept coming on and coming on. I wasn't especially bothered by this, but young stock can be a bit of a nuisance. They come barging along inquisitively and get up quite a speed. As they come closer the front ones decide they have come close enough and brake suddenly. The ones behind crash into the stationary ones and the front ones are pushed forward again. This can be a little awkward at times and I tend to be more wary of such situations than I might be of bulls. I eventually reached the gate into the next field and left eighty or so beasts to ruminate over lost delights.

I was soon down into the woodland of Ozleworth Bottom and then climbing up and along Scrubbet's Lane. I gentled my way along with oodles of time in hand and found myself at the Hunters Hall Inn at Kingscote. This was just what I wanted as it was now lunchtime and I needed to eat a main meal as there would not be a convenient place near the B and B in Nailsworth in the evening. I entered this 16th century coaching inn and found a cosy corner and took my time over some very good lamb shank followed by Exeter Pudding. Across the small alcove were three retired gentlemen. My notebook refers to them as 'three posh gents - not quite old buffers'. I think this part of the world is probably fairly full of 'posh old buffers'.

I could easily overhear their conversation which seemed to include something about Hockey Internationals (a son? a nephew?), the Daily Telegraph Crossword and Rolls Royce cars. After a while they seemed to think it prudent to enquire about myself. I told them what I was up to and they showed some interest. One of them jokingly said, of one of his companions, "He'll give you a lift, he's got five cars". I thought to myself, "I live in a different world"! They departed in high good humour leaving me to dawdle with my dessert.

Because my B and B hostess was going to be at work it had been arranged that I wouldn't arrive before six o'clock. I had masses of time to kill with not much more than three miles to go. Although the afternoon was brightening up a bit, I thought it was rather too cool for sitting around. Along the edges of fields I went and was intrigued to discover a badger latrine. Badgers have definite set routes whereas foxes roam around more freely, so I have always understood. This was obviously a territorial marker. Perhaps the three old boys at the inn mark out their territory by digging themselves into regular corners for their Saturday lunches?

Looking across the next valley I could easily see the tops of trees and the caption I have given to the photo I took, which is now pasted in my walk Scrapbook, says 'Trees tentatively waiting to join the spring'. The sheltered understorey at the fringe of the wood, maybe a hawthorn, was green with leaf, but the tall trees were clearly finding it slower going. Down in the valley I followed a lovely track and found wood spurge and woodruff. I love woodruff, but Ann doesn't like it in the garden because it tends to swamp everything else. I climbed up into the village of Horsley with fond memories of my first visit there, when I was a participant in the regional heat of the British Cycle Touring Trophy competition. I think I gained points on the hill climb there because I dugs my heels in, didn't get off and walk and I kept my bum on the saddle. I came sixth when it was the first five to go through to the national finals. Golly! That was years and years ago. When I were a lad.

The evening light was now pretty good - quite idyllic really - as I crossed yet another valley at Downend and up to the western outskirts of Nailsworth where I eventually found my B and B at about half past six.

Sunday 19th April
Nailsworth to Painswick - 10.1 miles

The B and B was pleasant enough but I had been left to my own devices most of the time. I crept away at about 0920 and found a decent little path that slanted down into the valley. I had just paused momentarily at the top and a nice lady came along, going my way, so I walked down the path with her. She used to live at Saltford, the next village to Keynsham, so we found some things in common to chat about. It has been a continuous delight to be able to talk to folk along the way. Many people wished me good luck after only the briefest acquaintance.

I found my way through the centre of Nailsworth and onto the old railway track. This runs up the valley and is well sheltered by trees. Just at the same time that I started along the track there was a group of about twenty people, of all ages and genders, setting off as well. It didn't take me long to discover that this group was the vanguard of a much larger group, all taking part in a sponsored walk in aid of Breast Cancer research or something similar. I kept pace with them and a certain amount of overtaking and re-overtaking took place, either while I stopped to look at a flower or whatever, or when for some reason a group waited for an errant child. After several miles of easy level walking we came to the outskirts of Stroud. Here there was a refreshment stop with drinks and buns for the weary walkers. I hadn't really intended to beg a drink, but a dear little old lady offered me her 'ration'. My experience of checkpoints on Long Distance Challenge Walks is that there is no specific number being catered for and Open House is the order of the day. This kind soul must have felt that her need was less than mine and that she had to go without in order that I could have a drink, when in reality there would have been plenty for twenty thirsty Bens. I protested that I wasn't officially on the walk but drink was pressed upon me. I gave a donation to the cause nevertheless. I then followed my own route, still on the old railway, for another mile into the centre of Stroud. It was early lunchtime and I found a caff and had a snack.

I had plenty of time in hand and sauntered out of the town and at the top of a sloping field I just lay down and soaked up the sunshine for about a quarter of an hour. Sauntering on, just before I reached Painswick Old Road, I had a good view of Hawkwood College, embayed by surrounding woodland, nestling in a fold of the hill. This brought back many fond memories, as I had worked there for four months during the spring and summer of 1964. I worked as an assistant gardener under the eye and tutelage of the redoubtable Armine Wodehouse, sister of P G Wodehouse. Hawkwood College is a Rudolf Steiner establishment and my time there was enchanting. I worked hard and ate excellent healthy food and my belt had new holes put in it, to accommodate my decreasing girth. I also spent time with the 15 or so students, who came from a variety of different, mainly European, countries. They were mostly between school and university and had come to learn English language and culture. When it came to the end of the term in July, there were many fond farewells with hugs and kisses all round. Two of the girls were cousins from aristocratic German families with a well-concealed 'Graf' somewhere in their names. I occasionally have cause to tell friends that I once kissed two princesses - affectionately, not formally. But all that, as I seem to keep saying, was when I were a lad.

The day that had started off overcast and cool had now brightened considerably with just a smattering of small white clouds, the delicate cumulus fractus. The next two miles or so were absolutely magical. The weather was warm, the going was easy underfoot, I felt good, and the scenery was great. What made this mid-April Sunday afternoon absolutely idyllic was the blossom. I came upon an old orchard where old pear trees were overflowing with fullness. There was a dell of tall cherry trees also in bloom with blackthorn, an even brighter white, at its fringe. The whiteness all around was incredible. I just felt so privileged to be there at such a time. Awesome. This afternoon ranks as one of the most perfect moments of the whole walk and will stay with me. I wanted to say 'will stay with me for ever', but that seemed a bit too definite. But actually, I guess it will.

Arriving at Painswick I soon found my way to the home of Natalie and Glynn. Natalie was in my year at Sidcot and Glynn, another Old Sidcotian, was two years our senior. I was given a very warm mid-afternoon welcome and we had a cup of tea together. I dumped some of my baggage and Glynn and I walked on another couple of miles up onto Painswick Beacon. This is a splendid viewpoint with views across Gloucester and up to the Malverns and over to Wales. It was bit hazy in the far distance but we stood there for a while just taking it all in. We dropped down to the lay-by on the Gloucester road where Natalie picked us up in the car and whisked us back to a fine macaroni cheese and a wonderful evening of reminiscing. My observations lead me to believe that at Painswick I was as far *east* as I was going to be on the whole of my walk.

Monday 20th April
Painswick to Corse Staunton - 14.8 miles

In the morning Glynn dropped me off at the lay-by on the Gloucester side of Painswick Beacon where we had finished the day before and I started walking at about 0840. After a few hundred yards of busy road I turned right down a decent track, much overhung with trees and bushes. This took me quickly onto little lanes which led me into Upton St. Leonards. Various suburban streets led me to the bridge over the M6. I can remember 'Good Morninging' several people, dog-walkers and folk out shopping but no-one seemed very anxious to return my cheerful greeting. This seemed out of kilter with my experience so far when meeting people. I guessed it might be something to do with the nature of living in a city where you don't expect to be greeted by all and sundry. Perhaps I didn't look respectable enough. It was quite a contrast to the quiet lanes of Devon, where my presence, I fancy, was at least a nine-minute wonder. I found little cycleways and paths between the houses, a long short-cut through a park and eventually hit the centre of Gloucester. I dropped off some maps at the Post Office, stocked up my purse at a cash machine and visited a café to enjoy a Chelsea Bun with butter. Yummy.

I would have been happy to have walked the Severn Way but it ran along the 'wrong' side of the river and there appeared to be no convenient crossing further upstream to suit my purpose. I had left the town centre knowing I had to negotiate Ring Roads, slip roads and the East Channel of the Severn. The map showed quite clearly that a path went up the west side of the East Channel and I found myself in Pool Meadow and no obvious path. I was in a large lorry park-cum-fairground vehicles park-cum-containers park with added rubbish. I walked round the perimeter of this yard, feeling pretty out of place and still found no exit. I went back to the entrance and scouted around there again to no avail. I re-entered the yard, almost guiltily, and made my way over rubbish heaps and found a place where I could escape over barbed wire and between overgrown bushes. I was then in a grotty field and no obvious path presented itself. I kept along the water's edge, under the railway and then under the A40 trunk road. I came across a notice nailed to a willow tree which said 'Path Diversion'. I don't know how whoever it was managed to nail this notice up. They must have risked life and limb, fighting through nettles to the river bank and then had to lean out perilously over the water to fix the notice. I didn't attempt to read the details. I cut away from the river and crossed a large ploughed field, thankfully dry, and across another field to join the road at Maisemore Bridge. I felt I had had a bit too much adventuring since leaving Gloucester and wasn't anxious to cultivate more just yet. The day was now pretty warm and sunny and I had generated just a little bit of a 'muck sweat'.

I regained my equanimity by enjoying some time at the White Hart pub at Maisemore, which serendipitously presented itself at just the right moment. I did justice to a very good ploughman's. I see that my notebook records what I had seen written on the side of a van in Yate some days earlier, 'Give us a quote and we'll beat it'. Spout poetry at them and they will disappear quickly. On another van in Gloucester I wondered at the lightning efficiency of the 'Mobile Tyre Fitting' service.

Refreshed and renewed I kept to lanes along a delightful shallow ridge, just sufficiently elevated to give me views back to the Cotswolds and ahead to the Malverns. At Ashleworth I made my way into fields which led me eventually onto Corse Wood Hill. I occasionally met little signs that informed me I was on the 'Three Choirs Way'. These were adorned with a treble clef and the words 'Blessed is the Eye between Severn and Wye'. I half recognised the words and thought it might be Housman, but I couldn't find the reference when I got home. I have subsequently discovered that it is an old adage. I certainly have great solidarity with the sentiment, with the exception of that terrible bit on the outskirts of Gloucester.

During April my average daily wild flower count was about 36, but in the ten days since leaving Sidcot I had only seen ten 'new' flowers. I had had my fill of a Cornish Spring when the rest of the country was still feeling winterish, but now I felt I was in a bit of a lull while the spring was perhaps just behind me. The spring was gradually going to overtake me and thus I hoped to find, as I proceeded, not just spring flowers but early summer ones as well. The overall total of different flowers seen was by this time standing at 83. Today I saw my first may blossom, a sure sign that something is moving along.

I was drifting along a field edge and I was pleased to see plenty of clumps of cowslips. To my utter surprise I came across a clump, and it was this clump only, where the yellow petals were rimmed with a rich red colour. I have never seen anything like that before and I was quite amazed to find such a treat. I can imagine it was some sort of cross but why that clump only and not any of the others? The mystery of it added to my enjoyment. I took several photos.

Within the next couple of miles I had reached my B and B at Corse Staunton, arriving at about 1820 after quite a long day. Carole and Jasper made me very welcome.

Tuesday 21st April
Corse Staunton to Colwall - 11.3 miles

The day dawned bright. It stayed bright and became very warm. I have often said to myself, "Beware the April sun", which was a way of reminding myself that using a sunhat would be wise.

I was away by nine o'clock and was soon on a quiet lane and then into fields. The grass was a bit dewy but that didn't last long. The paths I was trying to follow were not very pronounced and despite keeping a pretty close eye on my map I managed to miss a concealed stile and wandered up a large field and eventually back down the same large field once I'd realised my mistake. Then there was another stretch along beautiful lanes through Lowbands with peaceful, flowery gardens and fruit trees coming into bloom. I zigzagged my way through some more fields and crossed over the

M50. I soon left the road and went up past Eggs Tump and up to a lovely path along a woodland edge. I was starting to flirt with the southern extremities of the Malvern Hills. I arrived at the A438 at Hollybush in the strong hope that I would find at least a pub. I walked up the main road and into Herefordshire, but there was no pub, no shop and no café. I think I have become too used to having it all my own way! I sat in the sun at the edge of a car park and ate a very meagre lunch of whatever little driblets I had in my pack. This was probably the least organised and tiniest lunch I had on the whole journey.

I climbed along the western edge of Midsummer Hill and then up onto Swinyard Hill. It was good to have a bit of climbing to do after a flattish day or two. This was as near the top of the Malverns that I got, and I had hazy glimpses of the Black Mountains and the Sugar Loaf away to my left. The woods were absolutely delightful, with leaves starting to spread and giving that dappled light that you only get before the leaves are fully grown. The rutted track through the woods could have been very muddy in wet weather but it was as dry as dry and my passage was gratefully easy. Near British Camp I heard my first cuckoo of the year. I was to hear several more on my way north. This cuckoo must have been a learner, just starting, because the first note was clear but the second was a fudged, smudged sort of affair. I suppose that is what happens being brought up by foster parents who aren't singing from the same hymn sheet. The track led me down to the A449 and I had to contend with traffic for nearly half a mile to the 'pass' through the hills. Here were choices a-plenty. I chose a snack bar where I bought a bacon sandwich and a coffee, a sort of cheating second lunch.

I was to spend the next two nights at the home of my friend Susanna, who lives in Hereford. The arrangement was that she would pick me up at Ledbury Station at about five o'clock and she would drive us to her home. My plan was to walk to Colwall Station and catch the train to Ledbury, about an eight minute journey. I knew there was a train at 1450 and another about an hour later. The later train would have been more than adequate as regards timing, but I got it into my head that I had time to catch the 1450. From my second lunch point I had about two miles to go so I dived down the hillside and across fields to reach Evendine. Then I set off across more fields with the railway in sight in the distance. I was soon in one of the most horrible dilemmas of the walk so far. I was trying to be quick (unnecessarily) to catch the train; it was hot; I was hot *and* bothered and the path just disappeared under a ploughed field. Maybe I am an innocent abroad, but this ploughed field was like nothing I have ever met before. There was a team of machines working in an adjacent field which were probably doing something similar to the field I was trying to cross. The 'furrows', if one could dare to call them that, were at least three feet deep and the crests of the ridges were too far apart to stride across. One had to descend into them and then climb up the other side. I was crossing the field diagonally and had to cross dozens and dozens of the wretched things. I am not a farmer but I couldn't imagine what the rationale was for such deep digging. I presumed this was preparation for growing potatoes but I had no way of verifying that and I wasn't going to stop and ask. Luckily the clods were dry - if they had been wet I would probably still be there now. I eventually escaped and hurried my way through another field or two and arrived at the station at 1453. I hadn't seen a train go by, but I was quite prepared to believe I'd missed seeing it due to being so flustered. Two minutes later the train arrived, five minutes behind schedule.

In next to no time I was in Ledbury with nearly two hours to go until I was to meet Susanna, who was coming from Birmingham or somewhere, having parked at Ledbury Station in the morning. I strolled into town and found a rather glitzy coffee shop and enjoyed an iced mocha in a glass mug. I pottered about and then

Rare red-rimmed cowslip

Malvern woods - Swinyard Hill

sauntered back to the station. Susanna duly arrived and she drove us to Hereford.

Susanna was also at Sidcot, and had walked from John O'Groats to Land's End a few years previously. I referred to her earlier when I was staying in Launceston. She had taken a keen interest in my plans and was eager to hear all my news, so over a meal and into the evening she heard all about it.

Wednesday 22nd April
Colwall to Storridge - 5.9 miles

Susanna wanted to accompany me today so we walked to Hereford Station and took the train to Colwall. We then sauntered along tracks and fields below the western slopes of the Malvern Hills. Susanna told me about birds and I told her about flowers. We had a picnic lunch on a pleasant rural bank near West Malvern. We came down to the fringes of Storridge and Susanna went down to the main road to find a bus stop. I hastened on for another mile or so to join the Worcestershire Way and then almost immediately the A4103, at the New Inn, about a mile north-east of Storridge. I waited for the expected bus and Susanna rejoined me a stop or two further along. In Hereford again Susanna went off shopping. As I made my own way towards her home, two teenage schoolgirls saw me and called out across the street, "Like your pink rucksack!" Remembering my brief conversation with the Crediton schoolboys I immediately responded by asking, "Is it a 'man thing' or a 'girlie thing'"? The girls replied, "Both!" This seemed to settle the matter once and for all. This had been a very short day of less than six miles. I hadn't planned to have rest days except at Sidcot and Fort William, but I guess these occasional short days, especially if with a light pack, helped my overall feeling of general wellbeing.

Susanna, being a bird person, told me of the 'Red List' of endangered species. She wondered if I would be kind enough to record the grid references of the locations wherever I heard or saw yellowhammers, skylarks and willow warblers and to forward these to her. I was indeed 'kind enough' to agree to this task and by the time I reached John O'Groats I had recorded several hundred locations. The willow warblers were by far the commonest of these three and yellowhammers the fewest. I wrote down in my notebook the Grid Ref each time I heard or saw, usually heard, one of them. At the end of the day I transferred the information from my notebook to my logbook. After a few days the business of stopping and working out a Grid Ref and noting it down each time I heard a bird became tiresome. Instead, each time a bird was heard I would deface my map by scribbling on it either a W or an L or a Y with a circle round it. This was more straightforward unless it was one of those rare days when it was raining and the map was inside a map case. Then in the peace and quiet of a B and B bedroom I would work out the Grid Refs and note them in my big log book. I had started off by texting the information to Susanna but this became too burdensome so I sent her a bulk load of data after my return home. She passed the information on to the RSPB or whoever. All this was quite time-consuming but I felt it was in a good cause and was a thank you for Susanna's kind hospitality and help.

Thursday 23rd April
Storridge to Martley - 10.8 miles

In order to get back 'on route' I had to go on the train to Ledbury, then take the bus to the New Inn. I started walking at about ten past ten. I had wanted to include the Worcestershire Way on my route because it passed through an area of country that I had only driven through previously. If, for example, you are driving north up the M5 north of Worcester you might glance away to the left and glimpse an intriguing cluster of wooded hills. These have always looked inviting, seen from a distance. I wasn't disappointed. The path winds up and down hills, affording, as Gerard Hoffnung might say, 'delightful prospects'. This time of the year was just right for appreciating the spring flowers, but I would be happy to go there again at any time of the year and expect to enjoy it.

Setting off I immediately passed apple orchards, with regimented rows of fruit trees, usually no more than six feet high. I was plodding up a steepish bank, but stopped to take a photo of what seemed to be a little speedwelly/milkworty thing. I wanted to take a close-up picture so I stretched myself out on the slope and was happily engaged in being technical for a minute or so. A man was coming down the hill and he stopped to talk. He asked me how far I was going. Something about his speech and his manner led me to think that he was probably a person that lived locally. My reply, therefore, did not mention Kidderminster or Scotland, let alone Land's End or John O'Groats. I said I was hoping to reach Martley and his response was that that was going to be quite a walk. He did seem quite relieved that I was having a conversation with him, because he had seen me lying on the ground and he told me that he thought I might have been dead; and he wasn't sure what he would have done if I had been. We continued on our separate ways.

The day was a bit overcast to start with but soon became sunny and warm. The going underfoot was dry. I bobbed in and out of woodland, down bits of track, onto lanes for short distances, into fields, down into valleys and up and all over again. I came down into the village of Longley Green and was 'fell-on-my-feet-pleased' to find Suckley Post Office, which was offering hot drinks. The postmistress bade me sit outside under the garden umbrella and she brought me coffee and a muffin. It was just perfectly idyllic sitting there in the morning sunshine in a sheltered nook in a colourful garden without a care in the world.

Despite this rather rosy-glow account I have to admit that I had written in my notebook a rather more sobering thought. It said,

"The whole venture seems quite daunting and I am not sure if I am determined enough to complete it." I guess my knee had just about recovered from the fall off the stile about nine days earlier, but the 'normal' achey pain/discomfort from my arthritis was with me every day and there were not many steps taken when I was unaware of it. The poles helped a bit. Nevertheless that was one factor that made me feel, in the back of my mind, that I might conk out before the end. I suppose I was by now about a third of the way - about 330 miles - but the miles stretching ahead of me were still unconquered. Another 'worry' was not being totally booked up with accommodation and there were certainly a multitude of factors concerning the unknown-ness of Scotland. These niggles were, in a sense, ever-present but not too often in the forefront of my mind. I tended to be pretty faithful in writing down the occasional philosophical thoughts that I had, and I usually stopped immediately to do so. This morning, this day, was perhaps one of the loveliest and most attractive of the whole walk so far and so this thought, arising from the depths, seemed contrary to my outward feelings. It perhaps was just a momentary expression of deeper anxiety, and having recorded it in writing I probably didn't think about it again for a while. As the walk went on these 'anxieties' gradually receded as there was less and less to worry about. I think I recognised there *were* unresolved problems ahead of me, but I didn't let them overpower me and make me feel gloomy. I just kept on living for the moment and dragged the problems to the surface when a suitable opportunity arose and I could do something about solving them. Things often got sorted with the help of Ann who, for example, might have been researching a distant B and B for me.

I carried on through really captivating scenery. The path was a delight, the trees were starting to come into leaf in real earnest, the flowers were just everywhere and kept me busy with my notebook. I counted 46 different wild flowers today, the highest daily total so far. Seen for the first time were bugle and early purple orchid.

Reaching Crews Hill I looked back at the Malverns and they seemed very close. My notes record, "I don't seem to have come very far"! but I told myself to stop fussing by reminding myself that many years ago I had seen the Malverns from the top of the Arans in North Wales, when they did indeed look pretty tiny, but unmistakeably Malvernish. A little further on at Round Hill I had my lunch sitting on a lovely wooden seat, one of several similar ones along the Worcestershire Way, with good views out to the west.

I made my way down to Knightwick where I ate a strawberry ice-cream, which I must have bought in the butcher's shop that I found there and where I was addressed as 'Young Man'. We shop at a very good butchers in Buxton, where the bouncy young lady addresses all and sundry as 'Young Man'. Ann used to teach her in the infant school. Is this a common feature of butchers' shops? I crossed the River Teme and up through blissful woods, the path winding carefully between tumbling swathes of bluebells and ramsons. After more lanes and fields I came to Martley where I found my B and B at The Chandlery. This house was full of character and John, the proprietor, was a fine character too. He was very interested in my progress and his receipt for my payment says 'Good Luck and well done'. I ate an evening meal at the pub. There seems to be a much more Midlandy/Birmingham accent from the local folk.

Friday 24th April
Martley to Stourport-on-Severn - 12.2 miles

I was away by nine fifteen, looking forward to another day like yesterday. It was rather more overcast with a moderate cool breeze blowing. As I climbed over Rodge Hill the view towards Brown Clee Hill gradually opened up. I have climbed nearly all the County tops in England but, strangely, Brown Clee has eluded me so far. Titterstone Clee, its neighbour, provides, in my opinion, one of the finest 360° viewpoints in England. It would have been good to have included both those in my route north, but along with so many other worthy places, it wasn't to be. They haven't moved away, of course.

Before leaving The Chandlery, John had told me to look out for peregrines in a quarry a few miles along the way. I found the quarry, I looked out and I saw at least one peregrine. That was good, my first of the trip. I remember being on the top of Pendle Hill some years ago, and some men were flying radio-controlled model aeroplanes. I was surprised and delighted to see a peregrine chasing one of the aeroplanes. I didn't find out if this was a regular occurrence and whether they chased the planes just for practice.

The woods continued to provide much of interest in the way of flowers. At one point I found a clump of False Oxlip, which is a kind of cross between a primrose and a cowslip, but these were very big and dwarfing some cowslips growing nearby. I'd seen a small specimen in the old railway cutting in the Poldens before Easter and I think I saw no more after this. They don't seem to occur very often. I came down off the hill and passed beside Abberley Hall, a private school. It has a tall and distinctive clock tower, near which I sat to eat my lunch. I climbed up through the woods of Abberley Hill but not getting much of an opportunity for views out. I came down off the hill, still following the Worcestershire Way, and joined a lane.

The Worcestershire Way has been well waymarked and has been a joy to follow. However, it let me down in the coming minutes. Maybe there had been an official diversion not recorded on my map, but there seemed to be no indication of the Way leaving the lane where the map said it should. I hunted up the lane; I came back along the lane; there was no stile, no sign, no trodden field path. I gave up. I had already decided that I was going to cut away from the Way about a mile or so further on, so that I could make my way to Stourport-on-Severn. Going back to a bend in the lane I went down a footpath I had previously noted, but which had no waymarkers on it. Within half a mile I came to a farm and having not roused any dogs or farmfolk I tried to follow the right of way across several paddocks. On the map the path led easily towards Wordley Dingle, but I was frustrated by enclosures with horses in, and guarded by, electric fences. I entered one of these and I reached the wooded edge of the rim of the dingle, but there was no exit through the fencing. I tried an adjacent paddock, still no luck. I came back near to the farmhouse and tried a way through another field. There had been no signage or indication of a right of way. Farmers and landowners do themselves no favours by not putting up sensible signs indicating a way through their territory. Asses like me can go blundering about, frightening the horses not to mention frightening myself.

The way I had chosen did in fact lead me to the dingle where a meagre stile suggested it might even be about in the right place. It was pretty clear to me that I was a rare visitor to Wordley Dingle, as no 'trod' presented itself. I crept about and eventually found a sort of path which descended steeply down the bank. There were several sections of rope, tied to trees and bushes, which provided a cautious handrail for the slithering pedestrian. At the bottom there was a stream to cross which was managed with some judicious leaping. The path was a little stronger up the other side and I climbed to join another footpath, which looked in rather better condition. I kept along this path for a short way and it was apparent that I had reached another farm. There was a sign which seemed to be referring to a path leading away at a right angle to the line I wanted to take, so I kept on. I was probably at fault for not interpreting this notice more thoroughly, because I should have realised, as I subsequently discovered, that there were some painted yellow splodges on fences and gates indicating a way through yet more paddocks and enclosed fields with numerous electric fences.

The weather had become quite warm, nay hot, by now and this was how I felt. Not to say bothered as well. I wasn't observing the yellow splodges because they were not the line I felt I wanted to take. I tried a be-fenced path up to some barns, but there was no way out. I came back and followed another path that led into a lawned area not as big as a tennis court completely surrounded by high thick hedges, except for the gap I came in by and a gap leading into the farmhouse garden. I retraced my steps. I then struck off across a paddock or two, following the line I thought I wanted, using the well-maintained gates, only to find myself again with no useful exit. It was at this point that a woman came out of the house and wanted to know what the h-ll I was doing, or words to that effect. I explained that I was trying to find the right path and she berated me for not noticing the yellow splodges, indicating to me where they were. I said that that was not the line I wanted as indicated on my map and she said that that was the only way there was. This interchange was not conducted at particularly close quarters and so my usual affable nature wasn't cutting much ice. She exhorted me to get away as quickly as possible because her husband was going to be coming out and that he was not a well man. I had visions of an irascible nature or worse. Luckily he did not appear in time to be within earshot of me and I retreated over another gate and found the yellow splodges and eventually escaped from this unpleasant situation. The path I found led me down into another arm of the blessed dingle, but this time not so overgrown and difficult. I at last rejoined my intended route. Why on earth do I do this??? Why didn't I go round by the road earlier??? Why am I so stupid??? After a mile or so my heart stopped pounding so violently, metaphorically speaking, and my usual equanimity started to return.

Some pleasant enough fields took me to the A451 a long mile out of Stourport. I trudged along the pavement, feeling just a little sorry for myself as my knee was quite painful. I crossed the River Severn, found a bus stop and caught a bus almost immediately which took me to the centre of Kidderminster. Within seconds I was on another bus that took me to within a few yards of my sister's house at Wolverley on the outskirts of Kidderminster. This has been a good day until I got to the bloody horses - twice, separated by the bloody dingle. All part of life's rich tapestry.

My sister, Juliet, is married to John and they were to put me up for three nights and Ann as well. This meant some to-ing and fro-ing in cars and trains, but it was good to have family around, especially Ann. I realise that it has taken me eleven days to walk from Sidcot and an easy day tomorrow seems in order. Ann has brought me changes of clothes and I was able to leave my cherry-slasher with her to take home. Despite having my walking poles I hadn't wanted to lose my faithful stick, so it had been sticking out of the top of the rucksack since Yate.

Saturday 25th April
Stourport-on-Severn to Bewdley - 5.0 miles

You must be familiar with those nightmarish dreams where you are trying like mad to get something done, but progress is only inch by inch and you never get to where you intended. I think my main task on this Saturday morning was to be well organised and be in control of getting rid of dirty clothes, receiving clean replacements etc from Ann. I also needed to get on with phoning B and Bs further along the route and feel that I had accomplished at least something. But I couldn't *concentrate*, everything seemed to be in a muddle. It was lovely seeing Ann again, of course, not to mention Juliet and John, but I felt on edge and couldn't settle to anything coherently. But that gradually sorted itself and things *did* get done and I felt a bit better. After lunch Juliet in her car led Ann and myself in our car to

Bewdley Quaker Meeting House, where we parked our car and Juliet drove all of us to Stourport-on-Severn. Then Juliet went home and Ann and I walked back to Bewdley.

We set off at about a quarter to two. After about a mile we came upon a noisy, dusty and exciting spectacle. Some fields and woodland had been taken over by Motocross activity. There was a course laid out up through the trees and with several loops and circuits in the fields above the woods. The place was buzzing with people and participants. This, we learned, was the National Motocross Championship event for 8 to 13 year olds. It was amazing to watch these tiny people whizzing around on what looked like modified quad bikes. There was a high edge of competitiveness, we thought. There were older teenagers on light motorbikes who acted as marshals. The dry red earth flew up in clouds of dust every time a competitor came speeding by. It was all very exciting. We eventually escaped onto the top of Stagborough Hill and had a cooling walk through the upper parts of Ribbesford Woods. At some point we saw and heard a goldcrest. We joined the Worcestershire Way which we followed into Bewdley, arriving at the Meeting House soon after four o'clock. We then drove back to Wolverley for a relaxing evening.

I guess part of my trouble of the morning was having to fit around other people. As I walked along I *was* happy to stop and talk to folk I met and I never felt anti-social or hermit-like, so in that respect I shouldn't have been lonely. But I did feel that I was lonely as I walked along. It was the lack of a like-minded companion that made it lonely. Mind you, I am not complaining because that was the way I wanted it to be. It was lonely, but I didn't *mind* it being lonely.

I am a fan of the works of Robert Louis Stevenson, not least his 'Songs of Travel', particularly as set to music by Vaughan Williams. In his 'Walking Tours' he says that a walking tour should be gone on alone and that you should have your own pace. With this sentiment

I am in reasonable agreement., especially about going at my own speed. My daily overnight stops were pre-determined and the open-endedness and spontaneity of an uncertain destination was not to be. I was certainly not a Stevenson, and I wish I had the poetry of Laurie Lee, but, for me, tame though it was, my journey was an adventure.

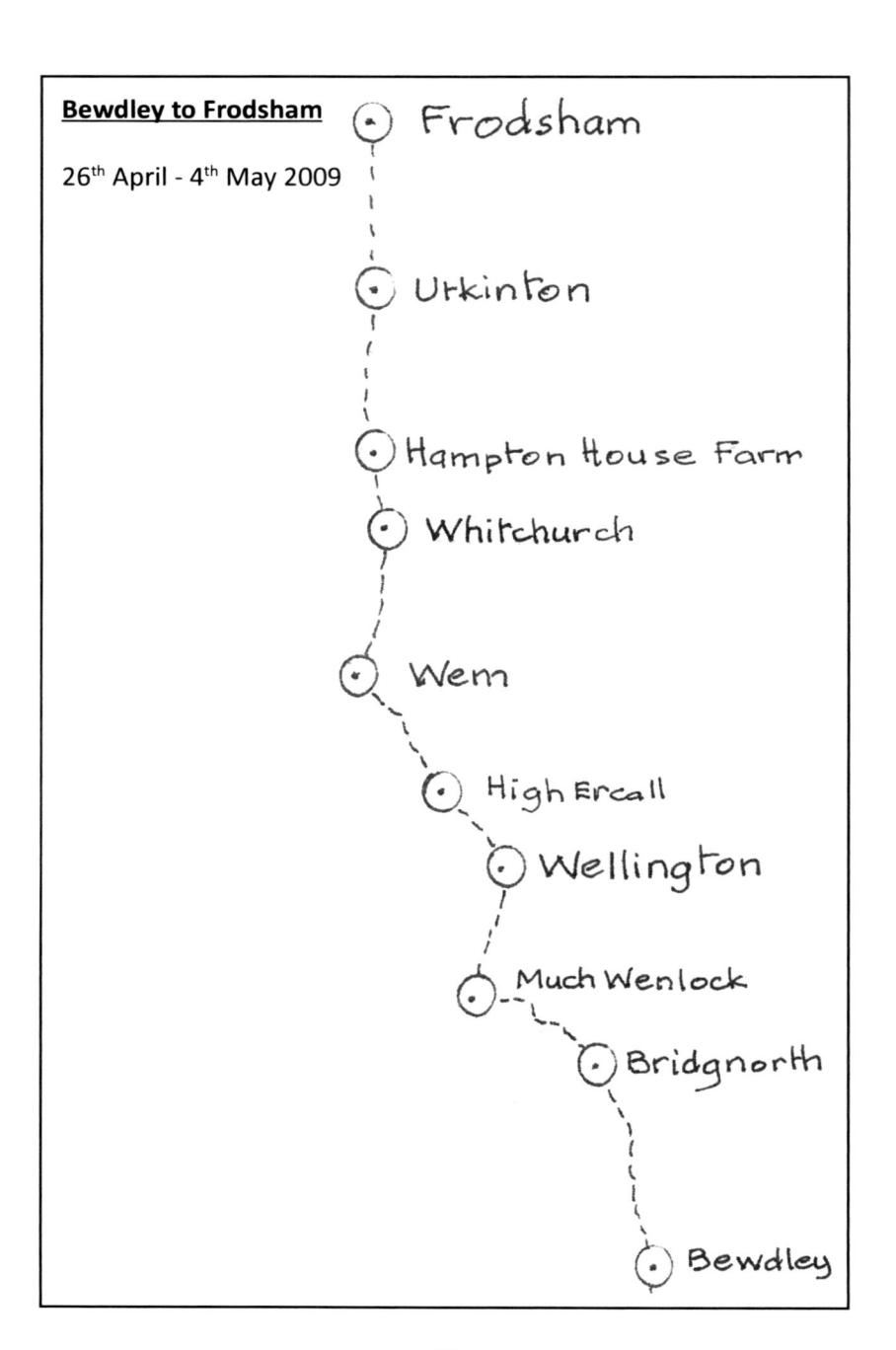

Bewdley to Frodsham

26th April - 4th May 2009

- Frodsham
- Urkinton
- Hampton House Farm
- Whitchurch
- Wem
- High Ercall
- Wellington
- Much Wenlock
- Bridgnorth
- Bewdley

Bewdley to Frodsham

Sunday 26th April
Bewdley to Bridgnorth - 14.6 miles

Ann and I drove back to Bewdley and we parked our car again. We then started walking at nine-fifteen and followed the west bank of the River Severn on the Severn Way. This was delightfully easy walking on a sunny day and the going underfoot was dry. There were other walkers around with whom to exchange greetings. Ann helped me with my wild flowers. The count today was up to 55 with heartsease, sweet cicely and broom appearing on my list for the first time. We made good time to Arley and went up the hill to the station to see if the refreshment room was open. It wasn't, but it did open up within a few minutes. We watched a steam train come and go, this, of course, being the Severn Valley Railway. We carried on and arrived at Highley in time for an early lunch. There was a splendid new museum-cum-information centre-cum café here with a balcony overlooking the railway, from which we watched another train chugging up the line.

I left Ann here and I walked on. I was in a bit of a quandary for a while because I wasn't quite sure how far I should walk. If I stopped at Hampton Loade I would have to get there in the morning to continue my walk to Much Wenlock. It felt a bit awkward. As I progressed, carrying only a light pack, I decided the easiest thing to do was to carry on to Bridgnorth. So that is what I did. Ann was to join a Bridgnorth-bound train at Highley wherein John and Juliet and their friend Gottfried were expected to be. They were. At some point this train went past me but I was screened by trees from the line so mutual waving of hands never happened.

At Hampton Loade there is a fascinating foot ferry. The ferry consists of a floating platform to which is attached a cable with a ring on the end. This ring runs along another, fixed, cable which runs across the river and is anchored at both ends. When the ferry wants to go, the operator casts off from the bank, the cable tightens and the rudder is put into a certain position and the platform moves into midstream and then to the far bank. The current pushing against the rudder provides the motive power and the taut cable prevents the ferry moving away downstream so it just goes across laterally. To return, the rudder is put into the opposite position and the ferry glides gracefully back again.

There were interesting-looking caves in the soft red sandstone at Lower Forge, which I chose not to investigate. There were marvellous clumps of ground ivy, the bluey-green effect I found quite enchanting. About half a mile short of Bridgnorth I left the river and joined the road to reach the railway terminus, arriving just before half-past three. That was quite quick going for me as I reckoned it was over fourteen miles. Here I met the four others and we travelled back to Bewdley on the train. Ann and I collected the car and drove back to Juliet's. I felt relieved that I had made it all the way to Bridgnorth because it will make tomorrow that much easier.

Monday 27th April
Bridgnorth to Much Wenlock - 9.0 miles

I looked out of the bedroom window at Juliet's and the rain was pouring down. Starting the day's walk in the rain was a bit of a rarity, but in the grand scheme of things I suppose I was due to have some such days occasionally. However, it wasn't time for kick-off yet. We said our farewells to John and Juliet and Ann and I drove to Bridgnorth. Ann then drove home to Buxton and I was left standing in the rain. I made my way up into the town and thought a very early elevenses might be in order, partly because the route ahead looked pretty rural and elevensesless and also I hoped the rain might ease up. I dawdled over a coffee and then with my over-trousers on set off along a quiet lane leading towards Haughton. The rain was neither fierce nor bothersome and I whistled my way placidly through gently undulating countryside. After a few miles the Jack Mytton Way slid in on my left and this was to be my companion for the next few miles.

Life is full of surprises and along this stretch I noticed something I've never seen before. I had passed quite a few isolated cottages and farms and each dwelling had a 'house' number. I seem to remember seeing one or two seventy-somethings. I suppose I have always assumed that in a rural area house names would suffice. These numbers stretched over several miles. What limited observations I made led me to believe that these numbers covered an *area* not just one road. Either I am singularly unobservant, generally speaking, or this phenomenon is rather unusual.

I turned off the tarmac road and climbed up a dinky little sunken lane leading over Round Hill. I had trees for company and I was sheltered from the diminishing rain. I stopped to watch a robin feeding in the gutter of what had now become a metalled lane. Pine needles that had fallen had been swept by the rain into little ridges lying at an angle to the side of the road. Occasional open stretches gave me views back at the Clee Hills to the south-west while ahead of me The Wrekin started showing its top above the hedgerows.

I have long understood that oak trees can lose their boughs without much warning and I have tended to shy away from pausing long under them in case I was to become a victim. I arrived at a T-junction near Shirlett Farm and there was an oak tree on the grassy bank. Although the rain had now stopped the verges were pretty damp. But lo and behold! sitting prettily immediately under the oak tree was a quaint and ancient wooden seat. It was time for lunch so putting aside all childish fears I bravely sat upon the seat and ate my picnic. Moving away after a while I felt no great sense of relief. Perhaps I'm cured.

The lane led me to the B4376 along which I poddled for a couple of miles into Much Wenlock, where I arrived at about two o'clock. I had time to kill so did some necessary purchasing and some almost unnecessary extra feeding and sheltered from a sudden April shower in a convenient hidey-hole in the main street. The second hand bookshop was an attraction, but swinging a rucksack around in a confined space is not conducive to good relations with the proprietor; also I didn't want to carry the weight of a book with me. Eventually it seemed to be time to make my way to my B and B. This was about half a mile along the way I would want to go tomorrow and was easy to find. I was very warmly welcomed by Merle and Reg who offered uncomplicated but homely facilities. They were lovely and wanted to hear all about my walk both so far and into the days to come. Reg was very much a bird person and we discussed what I might have seen and what I might yet see on the morrow.

I walked back into town for an evening meal before returning to the friendliest B and B so far. Some months later Ann and I were passing through Much Wenlock and called in at one of the several cafés for a mid-morning coffee. I had thought there was an unlikely chance that we might bump into Merle or Reg. We had barely sipped our drinks before in came a horde of ramblers and amongst their number were Merle and Reg. They had been on one of these 'oldies go for a healthy walk for an hour every week' jaunts. I think there were some strict rules about having a drink but only one bun or the effort would be wasted. Anyway there was mutual recognition and we had a good old natter for a little while. I keep meaning to go back with Ann and stay at their B and B again, but haven't managed it yet.

I may have alluded previously to my evening routines. I was kept quite busy with various matters which included doing my washing of 'smalls', transferring the list of flowers seen that day from my small pocket book into my Log Book and writing up the Grid References of Susanna's 'endangered birds' from map to Log Book. I looked through the day's photos and recorded the location or subject. I phoned Ann and perhaps booked a B and B or two. I would study the maps for the next day and plan the detailed route. All these activities took quite a lot of time and I didn't really relax until I hit the sack.

I filled two pocket notebooks with my daily notes. Once the first one was completed I felt it was so full of essential details that I didn't dare to post it home for fear of it going astray. I was always trying to find ways to lighten my rucksack so I spent several weeks of evenings copying my notes from this first book into some spare pages in my Log Book. When that was done I posted the notebook home. It arrived safely.

Tuesday 28th April
Much Wenlock to Wellington 10.8 miles

Reg was keen to tell me which way I should go and his suggestions largely coincided with my plan which was basically to follow the Shropshire Way, at least for part of the day. A few yards up the road from the B and B I was able to take to the fields and through some woodland and then onto the Shropshire Way. It was a bit overcast but the fields were not too mucky and it was good to feel some softness underfoot. A little winding lane took me up to Wyke. On the way up to The Vineyards a bird flew out of a tree nearby. I didn't recognise it and I pretty well convinced myself that it couldn't be a nightingale, but some other bird of similar size and colouring. It didn't stop to sing to me, which I am sure would have clinched it. My limited knowledge of nightingales led me to believe that they are mostly to be found in the south-east and East Anglia, but a little niggle just made me wonder ... what if??? I rang bird-expert Reg that evening and he said it probably wasn't. I was happy for that to mean a no.

Leaving the Shropshire Way I picked my way carefully down a rather muddy slope by Banghams Wood and then on to join the main road at Buildwas Bridge. Already today I had crossed the Jack Mytton Way at right-angles and now I crossed the Severn Way similarly. The River Severn looked dark and uninviting and I didn't linger on the bridge. The Ironbridge Gorge Power Station dominated the valley scene. I found a byway that climbed up towards Braggers Hill. This was a long steady climb, which I found most enjoyable. I think this was probably the longest continuous climb since ascending the Quantocks and perhaps even before that. Cornwall and Devon were certainly pretty hilly, crossing the deep valleys. Halfway up the hill I met a fellow walker. It was quite a rarity to find anyone else out for a 'proper walk', especially on a weekday, and so we stopped and compared notes. He was out for a 'practice walk' as he was soon to set off to walk from Wolverhampton to Sunderland in twenty days. I think he had family in the north east and he himself lived in Wolverhampton and dreamt up the idea of walking the whole way. I tried to think what stretches of interesting country he could contrive to include but we didn't get into that much detail. I admire people who plan these unusual routes. I wished him very hearty good luck and I guess he did the same for me. I have read Joyce Tombs' books which were about journeys from Beachy Head to Cape Wrath and another from the Norfolk Coast to St. David's Head. Now there was certainly someone to admire.

At the top of the hill I decided it was time I had my lunch (look no elevenses), so I sat on a grassy patch beside the track and took my time. There were loads of white dead nettles growing all around and I watched a bumble bee visiting many of them. I tracked it from flower to flower with my camera and it eventually stayed in one place long enough for me to take a picture.

The weather was perking up a bit as I strolled, for a short mile on the Shropshire Way again, into Little Wenlock. The views had opened up a bit and the hills around Church Stretton were dimly seen back the way I had come. I stopped at the Huntsman Inn and had a coffee, before following lanes to Huntington and New Works. I had planned to take the path through the woods to Steeraway but for some reason I changed my mind at the last minute. I can't remember, but I think there may have been a blocked entrance or a diversion sign or something, so I stayed on the quiet enough lane that took me down gently towards Wellington. I crossed the M54 and soon found a suburban shop where I bought a bottle of flavoured milk which I consumed sitting on the wall outside.

I thought the town centre of Wellington looked a bit rundown, but this didn't stop me re-stocking my purse at a cash machine, re-filling my mobile at an Orange shop and re-filling the larder section of my rucksack with lunches for the next day or two. I also located a Chinese restaurant which I visited later that evening. I made my way to the Guest House where I was to rest my head for the night, conveniently situated for getting away in the morning. Later, in the restaurant the piped music was playing a poor arrangement (pan-pipes) of 'Hold the Door'. The version by Clannad is much superior. I came to realise that with all this walking lark I was missing listening to good music. I miss having access to it. I do not own an ipod and do not desire to do so. I wish to experience the sounds around me and not be cocooned inside an aural prison, however good the music might be. But I do miss it. A gentle day today and tomorrow looks to be even shorter.

Wednesday 29th April
Wellington to High Ercall - 8.6 miles

I think I may have mentioned already that I had had three weeks walking from Land's End to Sidcot, then after three rest days I felt I was starting all over again. I had had it in my mind that I would need another three weeks walking to prove to myself that I wasn't suddenly going to collapse with tiredness. Well, here I am 15 days on from Sidcot and feeling pretty OK. I was gradually realising that the 'three-weeks twice' rule that I had invented for myself was not worth pursuing any longer. The original 'don't overdo it' rule was working fine. However I found it hard to ditch the idea of avoiding 'unnecessary' detours. I still kept telling myself that I was aiming, somewhat single-mindedly, for John O'Groats and that deviations were out. It would have been fun to have re-visited the top of The Wrekin, but, for whatever reason, I didn't.

I knew I was having a short day in pretty flat countryside so I took every opportunity I could to slow myself down. It is quite hard *not* to go at one's normal cruising speed. I dawdled away from Wellington and then down a lane to Wrockwardine. The weather was cloudy/bright with the sun popping in and out all day. I tried two different benches in the churchyard but both seemed to attract draughts and I couldn't really feel comfortable enough to have a mid-morning nap. Round the corner was a large grassy triangle where roads met and this was comfy enough but I still didn't stick it for long. Down a pleasant lane a sycamore - query - maple tree dangled its pine-cone shaped flowers into my face. It had a beautiful honey scent, so I enjoyed breathing that in for a few moments. My flower haul today was fifty flowers and I was surprised enough by one to write in my notebook, upon seeing it, "Bloody 'ell, crosswort." I think of crosswort as a summer flower and it's still only April, and Cornwall it is not.

The Wrekin was now starting to disappear behind me, and I was thinking that the flat area ahead of me was going to be devoid of significant landmarks, when I was proved wrong by glimpsing the Breiddens away to the left, way beyond Shrewsbury, nearly to Welshpool. I wasn't going that way, but they are old friends in that we occasionally see the three distinctive lumps from the western fringes of the Peak District. Not only that, but was that the Berwyns lurking dimly even further away? Less than a mile out of Wrockwardine I rejoined the Shropshire Way. Perhaps it was a bit early in the season, or perhaps ramblers choose not to come this way very often, but my re-acquaintance with the Shropshire Way was somewhat inauspicious. I had to locate the overgrown stile, push my way through a tangled section hemmed in by a paddock fence and a rampant hedge and then enter a large field with no obvious trod through the crop. I then reached a railway line, Shrewsbury to the left, Wellington to the right, and so I sat on the adjacent stile in the sunshine and had a very slow lunch. I was able to enjoy watching several trains pass by. I don't think anybody waved back.

The cumulus humilis was gentling north-west-ish on a moderate southerly-ish breeze and it was all very peaceful. I crossed the railway line and passed through the settlement of Allscott. I left the road at Allscott Mill, still following the Shropshire Way and walked for a short distance beside the River Tern. At Marsh Green I was fascinated to observe a sparrow with a beakful of feathers, plucked from the breast of a recently dead pigeon lying in the road. I presumed that it was nest building. It seems that nothing in nature is wasted. One can look at dead flower heads at the end of the flowering season and think, "Oh! they're not so pretty now they're dead". But of course, as they contain the seeds of new life for next time around, how can they not be pretty?

A little further on I had a better view of the Berwyns with what I took to be Cadair Bronwen, detached towards the eastern end.

Passing on through arable fields I kept to the Shropshire Way into the village of High Ercall (pronounced Arkle, I believe), hearing a cuckoo near the sewage works. For some strange reason I had not established the location of my B and B at The Mill House and had to ask in the village where it might be. After one or two blank looks I got a sensible answer in the Post Office. I then had to walk over a mile out of the village along a busy road to find it. I could have taken a short cut earlier straight to it and saved myself about two miles, but if I had, I would have arrived too early and it would have meant a longer walk the next day.

I received a warm welcome from Chris and Judy at The Mill House, who were very kind. The accommodation was excellent and the River Roden running by outside was almost like a fairy tale, or straight out of *The Wind in the Willows* or *The Little Grey Men*. It was not too big and it curved gently and the willow trees hung gracefully beside it. I had been thinking as I walked along that I was too near Wales to feel that I was in 'Middle England'. I had always associated BB's book *The Little Grey Men* with 'Middle England', which I had imagined to be Warwickshire or thereabouts.

Chris ran me in his car to The Bull at Rodington a couple of miles away and came to fetch me back when I rang him after my evening meal. Well, that *was* an easy day.

Thursday 30th April
High Ercall to Wem - 11.5 miles

Judy gave me a lift back into High Ercall as she was going that way anyway. The day was a bit grey, but after only a couple of minutes I was able to bandy cheerful exchanges with three elderly ladies waiting at a bus stop, which kept gloomy thoughts at bay, despite looking back and seeing The Wrekin wreathed in cloud. I was conscious, as on some previous occasions, of a following wind, which all goes to help a positive feeling. My way was along quiet country roads, virtually level to start with. After Muckleton, where I rejoined the Shropshire Way, it seemed better to put my over-trousers on as the light, occasional rain seemed to want to occasion itself more frequently. This is only the sixth time since leaving Land's End that I have needed to put on wet-weather gear. The morning was dominated aurally by the continuous flying of helicopters from Shawbury RAF base nearby, but despite these noisy beasts I was pleased to see and hear a peewit. What beautiful, odd birds, with their plaintive cry and their erratic, lunging, dropping flight. A short field or two took me to the busy A53 north-east of Shawbury and more field paths led me to Stanton upon Hine Heath. I scouted around for a mid-morning coffee but I came away empty-handed.

The Way led me through more open, dampish fields and then for a short distance along a lane with curiously high hedges. In the vicinity of Papermill Bridge the flat terrain gave way to tiny hills and rises which added more interest to the scene. I crossed over the A49 and made my way into Lee Brockhurst village, again on the lookout for a (warm) lunch spot, ie a pub. There may have been one there, but I didn't find it. I made do with the (cool) church porch to eat my picnic. There is always something to compensate for life's little discomforts. On this occasion it was a magnificent Japanese cherry in full bloom in the churchyard. The camera came out.

Setting off again I crossed a field where plastic strips were laid to protect the young crops. Luckily, the path went parallel with the way they were laid so my heart rate subsided. The path led down into a deep little valley and after crossing the stream I ascended a flight of well-constructed steps, which seemed to be quite a deliberate feature, presumably, I guessed, to assist the locals in the old days to get to and from their work or from village to village. I think there was a sign at the top referring to The Hundred Steps, or some-such.

By now the rain had cleared away and the day was becoming pleasantly brighter. As I walked along the quiet lane a blackcap kept me company in the hedgerow on my left. I am not very familiar with blackcaps and their behaviour, so I don't know whether what I noticed was typical. As I walked along it kept pace with me, but always in the hedge. It was making continuous tut-tutting and squeaky door noises as it went. It sounded like a sort of alarmed/distressed noise, because it was quite persistent. If I paused it didn't go on along the hedge, but waited to see what I was going to do. I suppose it could have had young nearby, but it may just have been marking out its territory. After a hundred yards or so the hedge petered out and the bird no doubt felt that it had 'seen me off' and we parted. Another couple of miles of gentle road-walking took me into Wem. I don't quite know why, but I thought of it as 'Sleepy Wem' for no valid reason that I could think of. I paused by the railway level crossing in case a train came by. I didn't see a train just then but I did notice a large wagon hauling tree trunks. The map showed that there were bits of woodland here and there - the logs looked like large deciduous trees, rather than boring old 'forestry' softwood.

Ann had rung me with a worrying problem to do with our bank account earlier in the day, and I was lucky enough to find a branch of our bank still open. I was able to sort out some of the problem and was later able to re-assure Ann. While I was in the bank there was the most tremendously loud BANG! outside in the street. I don't really know what a bomb going off sounds like, but this was far bigger than the largest firework you could imagine, and it was more clean-cut than the noise of a car crash. I couldn't leave the bank immediately, but as soon as I was able I, as with many others, was out in the street to see what on earth it could have been that caused this huge noise. The answer was that a large timber wagon had burst a tyre. I don't remember ever hearing a tyre burst before - what a sheltered life I lead. The glass in a window two floors above where the bang occurred had shattered and broken shards littered the street. Strangely, shop windows nearer to the blast seemed unaffected. I would have hated to have been alongside it when it burst. Although there were quite a few people about, nobody seemed to have been hurt, as far as I could tell, but there was dirt and debris scattered about. Some minutes later, after an exploratory 'evening meal reconnaissance' down the street and back, I spoke to a group of lads watching the sweeping up operations. I had been thinking that this would be a bit of a nine days' wonder in the town and would outpace the Women's Institute cake bake or the darts league results in the local newspaper. One of the lads said, as if to confirm my thoughts, "That'll keep us going for a while"! Later in the Chinese Restaurant I overheard a lady telling, well, quite a few people, I suppose, "I was only two cars behind it"! Sleepy Wem!!

My B and B was managed by a dear sweet couple, Anne and Ivan, who couldn't quite steel themselves to the idea that they really ought to stop running a Bed and Breakfast and retire instead. They were lovely and despite a rather old-fashioned feel to the place I had I everything I wanted and was very comfortable. When I arrived and mentioned that I had, indeed, walked from Land's End in six weeks, Ivan said, "You don't look tired"! I felt pleased, because that was the whole idea.

Friday 1st May
Wem to Whitchurch - 9.6 miles

I came back into the town centre and did some food shopping and was on my way properly by about half past nine. I was still following the Shropshire Way which started off along a narrow alleyway and then between back gardens and eventually into fields. The day was fine and bright but my feet became a little damp for a while from dewy grass. After Parkgate the Shropshire Way became less obvious and seemingly less well-used. The path became overgrown with all sorts of foliage and progress was not very easy. I passed a very large industrial site, plonked down in a really rather rural bit. There were large sheds and plenty of fences, but I never really found out what went on there. After the 'overgrown' bit I came to the 'field full of interested cows' bit. This, combined with the disappearance of the path, too many electric fences and the uncertainty of exactly which way to go made me slightly uneasy, or even flustered. I made such judicious progress as I was able to muster, which meant moving fairly swiftly, hopefully in the right direction, in order to evade the pursuing cows. I finally made it to a lane, with my dignity almost intact, but also feeling rather relieved. Wimp!

I came to a T-junction in the lane and a signpost had one arm pointing to both Wem and to Whitchurch. I had started the day in Wem and was aiming for Whitchurch, so this was slightly disconcerting. I knew what it meant really, but I took a photo of it. At Whixall, the Way became a yucky, mucky, mud-filled horror. After one glance at it I decided to stay on the road. Anything for a quiet (and mud-free) life. I passed through tiny settlements and stopped to eat my lunch on a bench at Hollinwood Common. As it was yet another short day, I was in no real hurry and my notebook records, "I stop quite often and often stop between stops". Well, I supposed it seemed funny at the time.

As the afternoon progressed the sky clouded over a bit and I experienced a few speckles of rain, but not enough to make me need to shelter or unpack my over-trousers. A feature of this rather flat countryside is the presence of quite a few pools and little meres. Today was probably as near as I got to Wales on the whole walk - I saw a sign leading to Welsh End and passed not far from Cambrian Farm. From the occasional rise I could see some hilly bits away to my left which were probably Ruabon and/or Llantisilio Mountains and I maybe even glimpsed a corner of the Berwyns.

As I crossed some more fields I could see ahead of me a farmer in his tractor spreading slurry. One can just about tolerate walking through freshly spread farm-slurry, but not have it flung in one's face. I was pleased when the farmer obviously saw me coming and waited for me to pass by before carrying on with his spewing. I waved my grateful thanks.

I carried on along lanes now, passing Alkington and then on into Whitchurch. A mile or so out of the town I received a phone call on my mobile from Margaret Stocks, Tim's mum, previously referred to on my day in the Quantocks. She and Michael were driving from their home near Kirkby Lonsdale to Devon, and at that moment were in the immediate vicinity on a main road. They had been taking a keen interest in my progress and I was due to stay with them in about ten days' time. Margaret was anxious to know how my knee was holding up, so I said it was still holding me up. As I walked through a 'tunnel' under the A41 Whitchurch bypass they may have been whizzing over the top at the very same moment. It was good to have friends giving me moral support - I did feel genuinely encouraged.

I found myself in the town centre by about a quarter past three with bags of time in hand. The B and B was just a little way out of town and the road I walked along was lined with Japanese cherry trees making a magnificent showing. Out came the camera again. I walked back to town for a Chinese meal at The Swallow and after that went to find the station. It was all rather quiet. Many years ago, in the late sixties, I had put myself and my bike on the train here on my way to Bolton, having cycled here, in several days from Southampton. I remember that as I waited on the platform two silly teenage girls were larking about and one climbed down to the track, but luckily came to no harm. As I stood there, in my late sixties, there was no sign of them.

Saturday 2nd May
Whitchurch to Hampton House Farm - 8.8 miles

I left the B and B at about 0945 and walked back into town. I did some bits and pieces of shopping, which included a short chat with a pharmacist in Boots who recommended Ibruprofen Gel to rub into my right ankle, where the tendon had been giving a tiny bit of trouble. Two years on, as I write this, I don't remember anything untoward happening to my body that I haven't already mentioned. This tendon bother can't have lasted long, perhaps only a day or two.

I was having another short day so I had a lazy time in a nice olde worlde café, with a window seat on the first floor, looking out over the busy street. I *do* like Saturday mornings. This morning was reminiscent of my Saturday morning in Tiverton, only this time I don't think I bought a Guardian to give away - sans crossword. As the days went by I only kept up with the news in a vague sort of way. I certainly didn't buy a paper every day and I didn't always watch the news on the telly at the B and B. I didn't mind 'escaping' from the news and I certainly didn't feel deprived because of the lack of it.

After a street or two I found a pleasant path that led me to the Llangollen Canal. There was a fair bit of boating activity which gave interest to the walk. Making my way to the towpath proper I thought I would take a photo of one of the lift-up bridges with a canal boat passing through 'underneath' it. There were two couples on the boat and the two ladies disembarked and came along to 'open' the counter-balanced structure by pulling on chains, or whatever. The men, still on the boat, saw me taking the picture with their wives also in it. One of them called out, "Your camera's broken!" This caused there to be some continuing, shall we say, friendly banter, from the ladies. I strolled for several miles along the towpath, meeting several more boats, and they all gave friendly good-natured greetings as we passed each other.

At Grindley Brook the place was crowded with folk out for the day enjoying the sunshine. I popped into the little café and had a toastie and a pressé. Soon afterwards I passed from Shropshire into Cheshire. The Sandstone Trail starts in Whitchurch and it was my plan to follow it, near as dammit, to Frodsham. I left the canal at Willeymoor Lock and rambled through pleasant fields, for a while in the company of four other walkers out for the afternoon. At one point the five of us passed through a paddock with llamas in it. They were very inquisitive and came quite close. I did take a photo of one of them, but only after I had put a stile and a fence between it and me.

I left the others behind when they detoured to visit a little isolated church or chapel. Near Chads Farm I had to go through a field which had longhorn cattle in. Some of the horns were amazingly twisted, and dangerous looking. None of them looked particularly interested in me except for one youngish beast, with rather straighter, but just as spiky, horns. This one was a bull. I didn't feel too bothered
because I have always understood that when the bull is in with the cows they tend to be placid. And anyway farmers are not allowed to put dangerous bulls in fields with a right of way through them. This fellow was standing right in my path. I stopped and we did some eyeball to eyeball stuff for a couple of minutes. He was close enough to me for me to have poked him with my walking pole, but I thought it best not to. I eventually decided to break the impasse and went even closer to him and he backed off and let me through. A few more fields and a lane took me to my B and B at Hampton House Farm. Richard and Helen were lovely. They took a keen interest in my walk, and if I remember correctly, Helen did a small amount of washing for me. Richard had booked me in to a pub a couple of miles away and he dropped me off there so that I could

enjoy an evening meal. The arrangement was that when I was all finished the landlady would run me back to the farm. Which she did. In her pink sports car.

Sunday 3rd May
Hampton House Farm to Utkinton - 13.8 miles

It had rained in the night and I was expecting there to be showers on and off all day, but they never materialised, and by the time I set off at about ten to nine the going underfoot was dry. I had spoken briefly with another walker yesterday who had told me of a private horse-racing track he had seen along the way. I soon came across it within the first mile. I understood from what I had heard speculated, that it, and the nearby large house, belonged to a famous footballer. I guess it might have been a Manchester United player. I don't think I want a racetrack in my back garden. Several more fields took me to the skirts of the south-western extremity of the Peckforton Hills. A delightful woodland path led me round the base of the hill and then up a little valley to the top of Maiden Castle. This sandstone outcrop rises quite sharply from the Cheshire plain and the top has pleasing amounts of birch and heather and bilberry amongst other things.

This was probably the highest point I had been on for several days and possibly the finest look-out point for distant views since Painswick Beacon a fortnight earlier. From here and from Bickerton Hill a little further on the views to the west were very good. I drank my fill of the Clwydian Range with Moel Famau showing up well. The Berwyns still made their presence felt but they were not going to be seen much more after today. It certainly gave me a feeling of northward progress now that I was 'leaving Wales behind'. I descended to Gallantry Bank and then abandoned the Sandstone Trail and survived a short stretch of busy main road to go up a lane leading to Bulkeley Hill. I hadn't been on Maiden Castle before but I had been on the muddlingly-named Bickerton Hill, a different one, before. This time I chose the short cut while the Trail waltzed round the rim of the hill, going round three sides of a square. There were more people around now, out for the day. Near the top of Bulkeley Hill I came to a good look-out point, facing roughly south-easterly. A family were resting there and looking at the view. They were not sure what they were looking at, or which direction, so I was able to fill in a few gaps for them. I stayed talking to them for ten minutes or more while the two children aged 5 and 4 clambered about and played with the two dogs, Holly and Chester. They were a very pleasant family and took an interest in my adventure. Anybody who takes the trouble to take an interest in my walk has got to be an absolutely splendid person!

I left the Trail again to go down the lane to the Cheshire Workshops where there are candlemaking workshops and such like. There was, I knew, a restaurant and I made use of this for an early dinner. I call it dinner because it was to be my main meal of the day, the evening meal possibilities being a little uncertain. After plaice and chips and ice-cream I continued along the Sandstone Trail to Beeston Castle, but I did not feel the need to re-visit the castle perched magnificently on its abrupt sandstone cliff. One only has to travel a few miles westward out from Buxton to find oneself on the edge of the Peak District. On our journeyings west from Buxton we often look out across the Cheshire plain in the hope of seeing Snowdonia, but a sighting once a year is about as good as it gets. Beeston Castle, thrusting up from the lowland, is a good marker for orientation purposes. A very distant prominence could be described as being just north or just south of Beeston Castle. The radio telescope at Jodrell Bank serves a similar function. For years I have been meaning to write a book called *Viewpoints of Western Peakland*, which would describe the view that could be seen, on a good day, from about twenty different locations along the western fringes of the Peak District. My efforts to write this charming little book have reached no further than the title.

My notebook, somewhat inexplicably says, 'Big Bang Theory Exploded'. Was this some Sunday newspaper headline I glimpsed at lunch-time? Or was this the product of my overworked imagination remembering the burst tyre at Wem? I remained content with the universe as I found it day by day. I realised that I am into my third month of walking now that I am into May. Day 45, in fact. I really do find it quite hard to believe.

As I write this account, and looking back and knowing that I *did* complete the whole thing, I am overawed by the immensity of the undertaking, even before I had got halfway.

I made my way gently downhill and crossed a railway and the Shropshire Union Canal to reach Pudding Lane. The Trail led on through rather level fields to the A51, then in another mile or so I was at the B and B just short of Utkinton village, arriving at about ten to five. This had been a rather longer day, the longest since the valley walk along the Severn Way from Bewdley to Bridgnorth. The B and B was a bit 'do-it-yourself' and not particularly homely, but the bed was comfy enough and I wasn't complaining.

Monday 4th May
Utkinton to Frodsham - 11.2 miles

Today is Bank Holiday Monday and I had the great pleasure of being joined on my walk by my second daughter, Beth, and her partner Andy. They had driven over from their home in Altrincham and had arrived at my B and B in good time. They had arranged to leave their car parked there to be collected later in the day. Beth and Andy are both used to walking in the hills and this was to be quite a tame day for them. They have both been very interested and supportive of my journey and it was very good to see them. We set off soon after nine o'clock following lanes and tracks, still on the Sandstone Trail.

Lee Brockhurst Churchyard

With Beth at Woodhouse Hill

It came on to drizzle a bit but it never came to very much, although the day stayed rather overcast. We stopped for coffee at the Summertrees Tea Room where we heard of another long-distance journey, a charity event, which involved a convoy of vintage tractors taking seven days to travel from Liverpool to Whitby. We carried on, a lot of the time in Delamere Forest, which by now was buzzing with walkers and cyclists and runners. The ground was dry underfoot and made very pleasant walking, where pine needles had fallen or where it was soft and sandy. Soon after Manley Common we sprawled under a hedge and ate the lunch that Beth had brought. The Trail goes up and down and in and out and there is never a dull moment. We reached the top of Woodhouse Hill, where the ground drops away abruptly, and Andy took a fine photo of Beth and myself looking out over the Mersey Estuary. We were looking north-west, which wasn't quite the direction I would be taking on the morrow, but there is a good sense of adventures yet to come.

It was only about another mile to go to my next 'staging post' at the home of my dear friend Rose, where I was to spend the night. Rose and I had been Young Friends together back in the sixties. Young Friends are Quakers aged approx 18-30. She is one of the most splendid people I have ever had the good fortune to know. Her outlook is positive and her principles unshakeable. Her enthusiasm for life, her energy and her caring attitude towards others is beyond compare. She has always been a great inspiration to me and supported me on my walk with occasional happy mobile phone texts. I write of her in the present tense, but it was with a great shock and sadness that we learnt of her unexpected death a year after our visit.

It had been arranged that Ann would come and spend the night, bringing me clean clothes etc. Beth had been busy on her mobile and it was with great delight that we saw Rose and Ann coming towards us. They had climbed up to meet us from Rose's house just under the hill at Netherton. We all walked down together and had a splendid meal and loads and loads of catching-up. Ann drove Beth back to Utkinton to pick up Beth's car. What a splendid day!

You may have noticed my mileage reference in the heading at the start of each day. To find my daily mileage I measured the route on the 2½" map each evening, using a length of very fine string. The length of the string in inches was then multiplied by four and divided by ten which gave me the distance in miles to the nearest tenth of a mile.

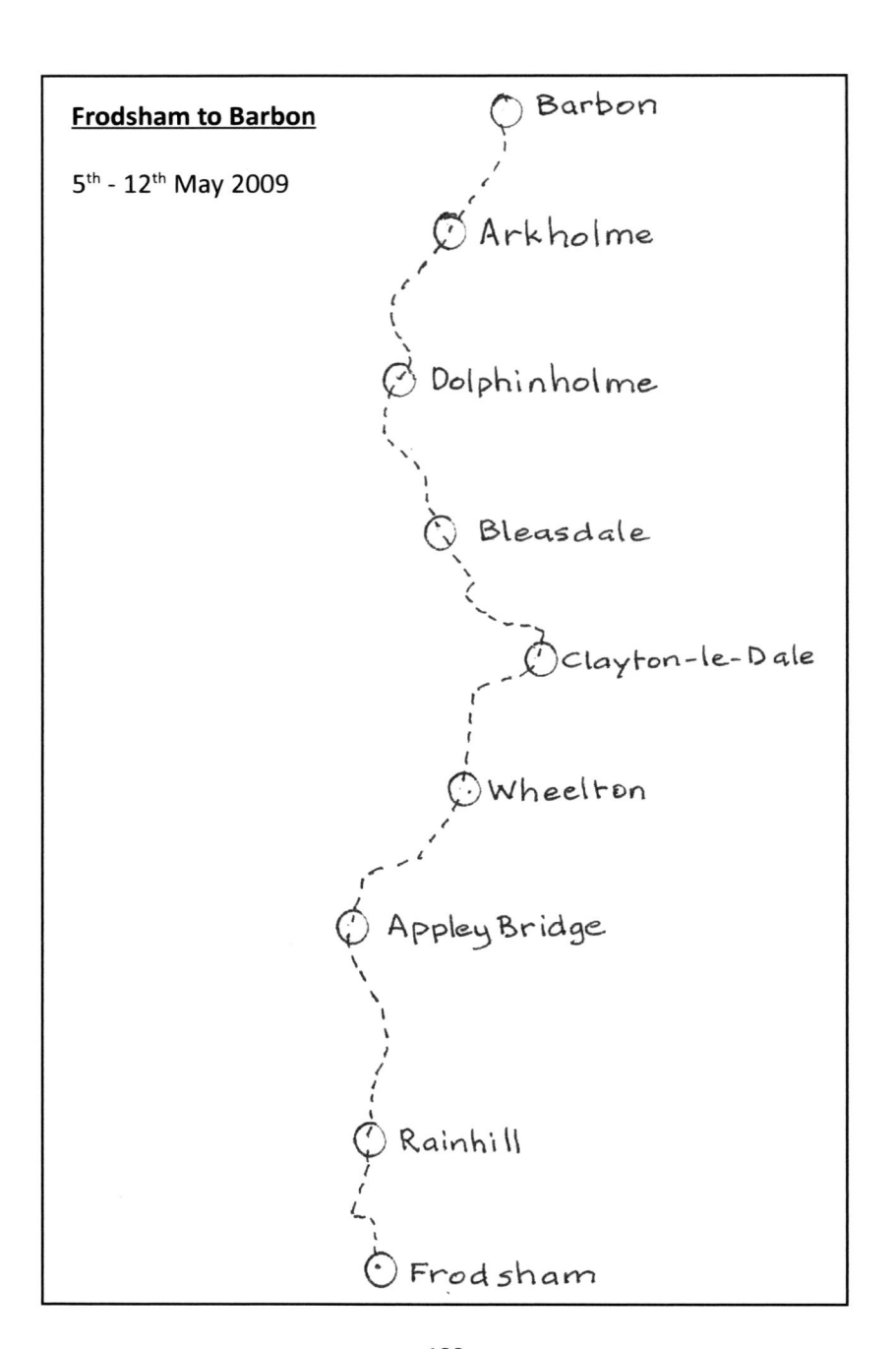

Frodsham to Barbon

5th - 12th May 2009

○ Barbon

○ Arkholme

○ Dolphinholme

○ Bleasdale

○ Clayton-le-Dale

○ Wheelton

○ Appley Bridge

○ Rainhill

○ Frodsham

Frodsham to Barbon

Tuesday 5th May
Frodsham to Rainhill - 13.0 miles

It was a bit of a wrench leaving the delights of Rose's company, she is such good fun. I shall be seeing Ann again in a week's time at Michael and Margaret's, but there was a somewhat poignant moment as she drove past me, a few yards down the road. The day was rather overcast with speckles of rain, which I was able to shrug off until lunchtime, when the rain came on rather more heavily. I had the best part of three miles of pavement along a main road to contend with before turning onto suburban streets and then some pretty good walkways/cum cycle-tracks which led me, without *too* much confusion towards Runcorn.

I then got onto a quite pleasant tree-lined suburban road, with decent front gardens with blossom and flowers making a good showing. This went on for a mile and a half and brought me to a T-junction and to a point where, most unusually, I had no map to assist my progress. It was my intention to buy one in Runcorn. I have never been to Runcorn town centre before and had no clear idea of which direction to take at this blessed T-junction, except that it felt as though it ought to be straight on. There were no helpful signs, so I eventually plumped for going left, and then taking the next available right. After a street or two of older housing I asked a woman which would be the best way to get to the town centre. She looked at me a bit oddly, much as if to say, "Are you sure you want to go there"? Having confirmed that I did, café/map shop in mind, she said, "Go down here, take a right turn by the church, and then straight on, but there's not much there when you get there!" Feeling somewhat chastened by this dismal news, I did find my way, and went over an elegant footbridge which spanned the Bridgewater Canal and made my way down into the 'town centre'. There didn't seem to be many what I would call 'civic' buildings, just a few streets of shops. I entered with gladness the Market Hall and sat down in Lil's Café and had some cheese on toast and a milky coffee. Rose had given me a hugely generous package of sandwiches, but I decided to leave these for an evening meal. At some point I must have bought the map I wanted, because I now knew where to go. Even without the map I knew I had to cross the Widnes-Runcorn Bridge, the huge structure which dominates the area.

By now the rain had come on rather more determinedly, so I struggled into my over-trousers before re-crossing the canal by the elegant footbridge. I looked back, with no regrets, and found myself agreeing with my informant, that there was, indeed, 'not much there'. The Widnes-Runcorn Bridge spans the River Mersey and is a busy main road. The pavement alongside has a more than adequate fence to prevent you falling into space. Many years ago, when I was on my way to the start of the Offa's Dyke Path, I walked across the Severn Bridge to Chepstow without any qualms, probably because it was a sunny day. Today, for no rational reason, I felt scared. Cars were rushing by on my left. The rain was coming down from above me. To my right the almost non-existent view was dull, gloomy and murky. Beneath my feet the solid tarmac did not prevent me knowing there was a great deal of space between me and the cold, steel-grey depths of the Mersey. Behind me the hounds of hell were racing to catch me and toss me over the barrier into oblivion. Ahead of me the path stretched away endlessly, as in a bad dream where steps forward leave you standing in the same place. Then, horror of horrors, somewhere near the middle, a soggy, decaying wreath of wilted flowers, attached to the fence. Oh my God! someone jumped ……

This turned out to be the worst few minutes of the whole walk. Quite irrational.

At last it was over and I found my way into Widnes, which seemed to have rather more 'oomph' about it than Runcorn. I left the town centre and joined a road leaving the town to the north. After a while I turned left and went along residential streets before stupidly going round three sides of a rectangle in a new housing estate to reach Sandy Lane. This was a narrow, potholed road which seemed to be being used as a rat run. It was rather like a causeway, crossing low-lying fields. Anyway it led me to Cronton where I followed a track up to Pex Hill. This slight eminence afforded me a view of the tower of Liverpool Cathedral. This is one of the features to look out for when using my non-existent book, aforementioned, as you peer westwards from the rim of the Peak District. However, today it was much closer, probably only about ten miles away. Pex Hill has at its centre a disused quarry. I was struck by the clean, smooth verticality of the sides of the quarry and wondered how it could have been thus. I only had about a mile to go now but this was across some rather straggly unkempt fields, much frequented by dog-walkers and their dogs. Despite the urban nature of most of the day's walk, I managed to see 41 different wild flowers and also added a coot to my bird list.

I then emerged from the fields onto the junction of the A557, the A57, the A570 and the M62. Earlier in the day I had had my scariest moment of the whole walk and now I experienced the most dangerous moment. This junction was a huge roundabout and the rush hour traffic was, indeed, truly rushing. There was no let-up in the flow, to allow a poor pedestrian to have his turn. After several minutes of waiting, a minuscule gap appeared and I fled across two lanes of the slip road to safety. A roadside sign informed me that I was now in St. Helens Metropolitan Borough at 'Rainhill, Home of the Locomotive Trials - 1829'. I could have told them a thing or two about the pedestrian trials of 1729, approx, trying to cross the blessed road. In a few more minutes I arrived at the Premier Inn at Rainhill Stoops. This was an expensive place to stay, but I occupied a large room with decent mod cons and I thought never mind the crumbs as I tucked into Rose's packed lunch.

Wednesday 6th May
Rainhill to Appley Bridge - 16.6 miles

The day started overcast and there were spots and speckles of rain on and off through the earlier part of the day, but not anything really bothersome. My route was essentially urban/industrial to start with, but I tried to find green bits where I could. From Rainhill Stoops I passed through Micklehead Green, all industrial estates and wide new roads. Sherdley Park gave me a mile of softer walking, then a stretch of woodland was very welcome. Back to the streets through Peasley Cross and on towards Parr Stocks.

I had been carrying some maps that I wanted to post home, and was waiting to come across a Post Office to buy a padded envelope. My map said PO at Parr Stocks, but with so many Post Offices closing nowadays I wasn't holding my breath. I stopped by the side of the A572 and asked a passing old gent if there was a Post Office just round the corner, but he replied that there used to be, but that it had closed in the last year or so. I thanked him and stood there puzzling which was the best way to continue. It either meant a left/right or a right/left. Having decided on the latter, I waited to cross the road at this busy traffic-light controlled junction. I was feeling it was time for a little something, but I had no high hopes of finding anywhere. As I waited for the lights I could see a little row of about four shops, but my impression, from a distance, was that they were unlikely to be the kind of place I needed. They were something like a fishing-tackle shop, a ladies' hairdressers or a betting shop. Not quite my scene I am afraid. I eventually reached the far pavement and to my surprise and delight one of these seemingly unpromising premises turned out to be a little snack bar. I went in.

There were two smiling ladies behind the counter and one of them said, "We've been watching you! We think you need a nice hot coffee". I didn't disagree and ordered a bacon butty as well. It wasn't long before I told them my tale and they expressed great interest in my achievement so far and wished me well for the rest of the walk. Everybody in that little café was friendly and lovely and it did me good to be there. Not least because when I came to pay they waived any payment because of what I was doing. I did put some money in the charity tin. I took a photo of the two kind ladies. Cockles truly warmed, I pressed on.

Soon I had a pleasant half mile along the banks of the disused St. Helen's Canal. There was a clump of tall reeds and I heard the most beautiful bird song coming from it. I could not see any movement and could not identify the song. I pointed my camera hopefully in the right direction and pressed the button but I have not been able to distinguish from the picture any birdlike shapes amongst the reed heads. I guessed it must have been a reed warbler or a sedge warbler but cannot be certain. Amidst all this industrial dereliction one finds little unconcerned pockets of wild nature. To be fair, it did seem that the local authority or who-ever, was doing quite a good job dealing with re-developing the area.

I walked through the suburb of Haresfinch and stupidly, as yesterday, went round three sides of a rectangle because of lack of attention to the map. I crossed the East Lancs Road and for a mile escaped into a rural bit near Carr Mill Dam. I came into Billinge and found a little café called 'Buttylicious' where I sat and had my lunch. I got talking to one of the other customers and found out that he was a cyclist. He takes people out on bikes for short rides around St. Helens, who might not otherwise get the chance to do so. I didn't quite fathom all the details, but it sounded like he was performing a useful social service.

I walked up through Billinge and turned left to go over a corner of Billinge Hill. It was here, with the weather improving, that I had one of those occasional moments when I felt I was making progress. On slightly elevated land I could see ahead a little and I had a sense of moving into new territory. The tall masts on Winter Hill came into view for the first time. I was well out of Cheshire, I had crossed the Mersey and was into Lancashire. It felt different. I had known that I would have to come through some industrial bits on my way north and this morning was one of those times. Now I was enjoying at least a little stretch of green countryside. After Longshaw I made my way through Orrell Water Park and then on to cross the M58 and back to urban streets again.

I may already have referred to 'the promise over the next rise' somewhere else in this narrative, but it won't hurt to repeat it. I loved the sustained anticipation and the gentle excitement of what might appear 'over the next rise', however slight that rise might be. I was always eager to see over the next hill, but not so eager that I wanted to ignore the just here and now. Sometimes, coming over a rise, I would be surprised by the realisation of a new and different vista from that which I had imagined.

Leaving Orrell I tried to remember a particular path that I had used once before when taking part in a Long Distance Challenge Walk quite some years earlier. I found what I thought was the right place (it was) and crossed a deep little wooded valley and then onto Dean Wood Golf Course, to join Lafford Lane. I was planning to reach Appley Bridge railway station, on the Southport line, by a particular time - one of the very few deadlines that I set for myself. I was booked to spend two nights with Beth and Andy in Altrincham, which meant a big detour away from my route. I had noted times of trains from Orrell and Gathurst, but Appley Bridge seemed like a good target to aim at to shave a few miles off the following day. In fact, with various little unscheduled diversions, this turned out to be the longest day's walk of my whole venture. So, unusually, I had a target to aim for, and instead of my oft repeated afternoon sauntering, I found myself pressing on with some urgency. I joined a main-ish road at Roby Mill and scurried along to Appley Bridge which I reached with time to spare. The train took me into Manchester and then I used the Metrolink to Altrincham, where I had a warm welcome from Beth and Andy. With staying two nights in the same place I was able to leave a few of my belongings behind and have a lighter pack the next day. I was able to sort out some of my overnight stops during the evening. Although I had a few main 'staging posts' booked, my intermediate stops had still to be worked out and thus my route, even only a fortnight ahead, was not always certain.

Thursday 7th May
Appley Bridge to Wheelton - 11.3 miles

I took the Metrolink tram into Manchester and went in search of a map shop. I used to work in Manchester and knew that the Stationery Office, which always had a full range of maps, had closed down, so I sought out Stanfords, but was dismayed to discover that they were no longer there. I had rather been relying on them. Somewhat thwarted I found some of the maps I wanted in Waterstones and felt a little relieved. On my way through the streets I came across an A-frame outside a hairdressing establishment. I regretted later not taking a photo of it. It said, '25% off on first visit'. I was slightly tickled. I caught the 1046 train from Victoria and reached Appley Bridge at about half past eleven.

I crossed the A 5209 and shortly afterwards went over a bridge to reach the east side of the M6, never to be crossed again. The day was warm and bright with sunny intervals and the ground was dry. The gardens were looking lovely with colourful flowers and blossom. After I had crossed the A49 I took to the fields, passing Langtree Hall. The West Pennine Moors were becoming more obvious and there was a sense of space as the fields were open and there were hardly any hedges. I sat in an open space at a spot where tracks crossed and ate my picnic.

Moving on northwards I came to a little brook beside which I found a stone marking an old well on which was inscribed 'Hic Bibi'. My rusty Latin suggests that this means 'Drink Here'. I didn't search for the well or spring, and even if I had, I guessed the water might have been as rusty as my Latin. I had thought I might take a particular route through fields and woods towards the south side of Chorley but opted instead, I can't remember why, to continue along the road passing the west edge of Yarrow Valley Country Park. In the end it was a bit of a hot trudge into Chorley along a main road. Once in Chorley I sought out the bus station and found a very friendly and helpful lady at the Information Desk, who was able to tell me about bus times and bus-stop locations for my use today and tomorrow. The sign on the bus station said in big letters, 'Lancashire - where everyone matters'. For a moment I thought it said 'natters'. I guess they do that as well.

I found my way through a residential area and reached the towpath of the Leeds and Liverpool Canal. I kept along this delightful path for a couple of miles. There were bluebells along the banks adding beauty to the scene. A little way south of Wheelton I left the towpath and found the recommended bus stop and after a few minutes, along came the promised bus, which whisked me back to Chorley. I then caught a train back to Manchester and the tram to Altrincham to spend a second night with Andy and Beth. I am reminded that I am supposed to mention the 'fantastic cuisine' at Beth and Andy's!

I felt that Wheelton was at a kind of gateway into new territory. The hills are crowding round a bit more and the flatness of the Lancashire plain is now behind me.

Friday 8th May
Wheelton to Clayton-le-Dale - 11.0 miles

Leaving Beth and Andy for the second time I travelled by tram back into Manchester and caught the 0919 train from Oxford Road back to Chorley. I walked around the town for a short while and then took the bus back to where I had left off yesterday. I walked along beside the main road for a little way then slid off to the left into Wheelton village and then cut down a track to rejoin the towpath beside the Leeds and Liverpool Canal. I kept on that for the best part of three miles. The weather was overcast with very short sunny spells. It was very windy, but luckily coming from behind me. There were one or two rather exposed places along the canal after Withnell Fold and I felt quite pushed along by the wind. I watched two drake mallard ducks fighting over a female - well, I suppose it is springtime.

Looking back I could see the Jubilee Tower above Darwen. I left the canal near Riley Green and descended a hillside on a grassy track to reach the River Darwen. I sat on an almost dry river bank and ate the lunch that Beth had made for me. A young man came along with his dog. He was walking cum jogging and seemed quite a fit person. He stopped for a minute or two and we passed the time of day. He was an 'outdoory' enough sort of person to understand pretty well the size of the task I had undertaken.

I had now joined the Witton Weavers Way which led me into a wooded gorge. This was delightfully unexpected. The damp woodland gave me a chance to become quite undecided as to whether I was looking at Bog Stitchwort or Marsh Stitchwort or something else altogether. If I had been carrying my usual wild flower book, which is quite a hefty tome, Marjorie Blamey + Fitter + Fitter, I might have stopped and sorted the matter out properly, but I wasn't and I didn't. I had similar trouble in the Eden valley later on.

Features of the gorge were a viaduct carrying a railway high above me; a rushing river which cascaded over a waterfall, below which there was deposited a significant amount of rubbish including a wheelie bin and a traffic cone. This point is just a few miles downstream from Blackburn, where, no doubt, much of this junk had originated. After a short while the valley opened out at Hoghton Bottoms. I sat on a convenient seat and took my trainers off and changed my left sock to my right foot and my right sock to my left foot. I had almost nil trouble with my feet all the way along and this manoeuvre must have been prompted by some slight discomfort. Slight discomforts not attended to can sometimes develop into blisters and I didn't want this to be the start of one. I had learnt this trick of swopping socks many years ago and I have used it to good effect on a few occasions. It must have worked this time because I had no more bother. While I sat there two men and a lady appeared, all well retired I guessed, and they stopped for a chat. One of the men was quite a jokey kind of gent and I think he was making some sort of comparison between me - (walker - thus - mountaineer) and himself - (hard done-by overworked domestic kitchen slave) with a remark about 'the North Face of the Aga'. They were decent folk and interested in what I was doing and their presence provide a pleasant interlude.

Leaving them to saunter back to their car I climbed up a hillside through fields to reach Close Farm. I had intended to take the bridleway from here and descend to Arley Brook and then wend my way to Mellor. I was dismayed, therefore, to find a heavily blocked entrance to the bridleway and a notice proclaiming 'Bridleway Closed Ahead At Alum-Scarbridge Please Find Alternative Route'. Another sign warned of 'Danger Deep Excavations'. There wasn't really any choice in the matter. I felt I could probably have managed to skirt any deep excavations I might have come across, but it was so well fenced off I didn't spend too long deciding it was a no-no. This meant more than a mile of unanticipated tarmac. This led me to what appeared to be a village, nestling under the lee of another

Billinge Hill, but it had no name that I could see and no name on the map. I met a lady wearing a big, pink woolly jumper taking her dog for a walk and we discussed briefly possible footpath routes to Mellor. I am afraid I didn't get much in the way of a useful response. You'd think dog-walkers would *know*.

The map indicated a series of paths leading the way I wanted to go. The tarmac alternative did not seem attractive, with too much main road, so I sought out the footpaths. In retrospect this was not a wise decision. For the next half hour or more I had some of the most frustrating and demoralising walking of the whole fourteen weeks. The badly maintained stile into the field was not signposted and the field itself was horrible, wet, pitted and alarmingly uneven and I sympathised with my ankles. At the bottom, which was well soggy, there was plenty of determined looking fencing preventing me entering the wood as the map indicated I should. I made my way towards a farm and I spoke with a young man who obviously worked or lived there. He pointed out a particular way I should go, saying that was the only right of way, but it led away at right angles to the line I wanted. I felt I was obliged to continue that way but was then surprised to find a series of arrows and little notices indicating a diverted path going the way I wanted. This was fine while I skirted the farmhouse and gardens, but soon the signs gave out and I was left to sort out my own salvation again. I took what I thought was an obvious way but got cul-de-sacked in amongst pig and poultry pens. Retracing my steps, all the time expecting irate shouts from behind me, I found a way that meant some fence climbing and pushing through tangled undergrowth until I reached the comparative sanity of an ordinary field. Looking back on this unhappy episode from the bedroom of the B and B my notebook says, "Madness"! Why *do* I plough on, getting more and more mired in cockeyed situations? Why didn't I turn back at the very beginning at the unappetising stile and go round by the road? Bloody stubborn I suppose. Or stupid.

After another field or two I came to the main road which I followed for a short way then struck up a sensible grassy slope with a respectable path to reach Mellor. This seemed a happy, blossomy, tulippy little village, perched on the hillside in the afternoon sunshine, and I would gladly have spent more time there. There was a lovely path round the rim of the hill leading away from the village, with good views across to Bowland Forest and a glimpse of Pendle Hill. Then I missed the correct line briefly and joined a lane further up than I had meant to. I took a right through the yard of a private residence with the intention of doing the last mile and a half through the fields. The prospect ahead looked unappealing and there was no sign to indicate precisely which line to take. It looked as though nobody went that way much and I decided to give it a miss and went back through the yard to the lane. I didn't fancy another episode of mud and mishap.

I kept on down the lane to the main road at Osbaldeston, where I went into The Bay Horse on the corner to enquire of the whereabouts of my B and B at Rose Cottage. I had assumed that it was going to be roughly where it eventually turned out to be, but I wasn't absolutely sure of the precise location. The advice from various locals was conflicting and unhelpful except that it was 'along that way somewhere'. So trudge, trudge, trudge, along the A59, thankfully on a pavement. I eventually reached Rose Cottage at about five past six. I had only walked 11 miles, but I had had a late start, and this was probably one of the latest of all my arrival times. Marge, who runs the B and B, had told me there would be an evening meal nearby and there was, a restaurant just across the road.

Ann says it was Bog Stitchwort, no doubt with the telephone in one hand and the Blamey in the other.

Saturday 9th May
Clayton-le-Dale to Bleasdale - 16.0 miles

I left Rose Cottage by about 1000, which in retrospect seems a bit late considering I had quite a long day ahead of me. I crossed the A59 and zigzagged my way by little lanes with high hedges on both sides to reach the Ribchester road near Eden Holme. I walked down to Ribchester Bridge, enjoying views of Pendle Hill on my right. There are precious few crossings of the Ribble upstream from Preston and this bridge had for a while been pivotal in my plans. At Ribchester village I found a convenient little snack bar and whiled away some more time with warming elevenses. The day was overcast and the blustery wind continued to strengthen as the morning went on.

I found a lane which took me up to Parsonage Farm where I took to the fields. This being a Saturday I was not too surprised to find that there were a few other walkers around. I followed one group for a while, which was quite useful because the path wasn't always clear and I could see them casting about for the right line, which meant I could correct my course accordingly before reaching the same spot. I know from experience that it is not always wise to follow others blindly because they might not actually be going the same way as you want to go. However they stopped for a snack and I was back to making my own wrong decisions. After a mile or two I was back on a lane before taking to the fields again. As I approached the three Alston Reservoirs I had another encounter with some frisky frolicking Friesians. They seemed very intent on a close investigation so I detoured off-route into an adjacent field and climbed a fence, probably where I shouldn't have, but there was no harm done to either the fence or my person.

Alongside the easternmost reservoir I was amused to find the first of several notices that said, 'North West Water - DANGER DEEP WATER - No swimming or unauthorised boating'. Now I know that reservoirs can be dangerous places and I also know that it is possible to drown in only a few inches of water, but this sign was adjacent to a pool about twelve feet long and about six feet wide. OK - keep your toddlers on the safe side of the fence but make sure you are properly authorised before organising a regatta in this reed-fringed puddle. I know I shouldn't mock but this was a good antidote to meeting the fr---ing Friesians.

Equanimity thus restored I walked up into Longridge. I then wandered down the main street looking for a place to have a main meal as there wouldn't be anything available in the evening. The place was quite busy with Saturday shoppers and I found a fish and chip type café which suited my mood and need admirably. I had hardly been in there a few minutes when there was a torrential rainstorm outside. By the time I was ready to leave it was still pouring down but I needed to get on. I crossed the road and 'sheltered' (ha ha ha!) under the canopy of a filling station, which was no protection to speak of, while I put my over-trousers on. Once I had started walking again the rain slackened off almost immediately and it cleared up altogether within less than an hour, so my progress was not at all unpleasant. I was keeping to quiet lanes, which led me via Lower Cockleach, Moss Gate Farm and Loud Bridge. The ground began to rise as I made my way towards Beacon Fell Country Park. There were very good views of the western edge of Bowland, clear after the rain.

As I was passing Carwags I met a Countryside Ranger and stopped and had an informative chat with him. I asked him about the best route to take in the next mile or two. I had two reasonable choices ahead of me, both crossing the deep wooded valley through which runs the River Brock. I couldn't have asked a better person because he was able to tell me that the route I had virtually decided upon was not suitable because of a broken footbridge and strongly advised me to take the other way. He also listened politely to my telling him of my long trek. No, I think he *was* genuinely interested. He was a nice man.

I carried on up the lane and passed the by now deserted car parks and decided I would come back again one day and climb to the top of the hill proper. I then entered a sloping field and just had to stop and take in the beauty of the scene around me. The rain had long gone and the sky was bright blue with a scattering of cumulus fractus drifting eastwards on the breeze. The views were superb. I could see the Blackpool Tower, Preston, Parbold Hill, Winter Hill, Great Hill and far away, across Liverpool Bay, the Clwydian Hills in North Wales. I think this was to be the last time I was to see the sea until somewhere in Scotland, probably Fort William. With this splendid sight before me I thought it was time I rang up Geoffrey, my younger brother, as it was his birthday. I stood and chatted with him for a few minutes, soaking up the sunshine.

I carried on, as directed, along Snape Rake Lane passing the ominously named Boggy Wood and down into the lovely valley to cross the river by a footbridge that was quite eminently passable. A steep pull up the other side took me onto a track which led up to a road where I turned right. After half a mile I turned left up the drive to Broadgate Farm where I received a very warm welcome from Brian and Anne. This was an excellent and friendly place to stop for the night. Having said yesterday that that was one of my latest arrivals I realise that today was even later - not arriving until twenty to seven. Today I became aware of curlews for the first time since Land's End. This is certainly their sort of territory and their plaintive calling was a delight to hear.

Sunday 10th May
Bleasdale to Dolphinholme - 7.6 miles

Brian and Anne have a Caravan Site as well as doing B and B and are also developing other features around their estate, which includes disabled access to a bird hide. I had hardly left the farmyard when I heard that magical and unusual, for me, sound of a snipe drumming. I have only heard this sound once or twice before in all my life, and I was instantly captivated by it. It is hard to describe the sound, but it is perhaps a bit like a sheep bleating faintly on a falling cadence, and is definitely eerie to the untutored ear. I think the sound is made by air passing through the tailfeathers of the snipe as it flies quickly, perhaps as it dives. Anne had helped me plan my route for the first half mile which took me past their bird hide from which I watched an oystercatcher which was standing and giving me a good view of its red legs. I did just wonder whether it might be a redshank, a bird I am not familiar with. I usually identify oystercatchers by their black and white backs when flying and the call that they make, but this one was not doing any of that. Anne had told me to look out for some young whimbrels in their top field, so I did look out and I did see some young whimbrels, and although they flew away pretty smartish, I am pretty sure that that is what I saw.

I came out onto Delph Lane, from which point I had a decent view out over the Fylde area and saw just a vague outline of Lakeland mountains. I was in no hurry, with only a short way to go today. I had stopped to look at my map or blow my nose or something, when I found, resting on my left fleece jacket sleeve, a most gorgeous insect. I have never knowingly seen one of these before and I felt honoured that it should settle so obligingly on my sleeve. The body, with its wings folded on its back was orangey-brown and about an inch or so long, but the most dominant feature were its two antennae which were two or three times as long as the body. The antennae seemed quite disproportionate to the rest of it and I gazed in wonder at it for some seconds. My camera was around my neck as usual and this wonderful creature stayed calmly resting while I managed to manoeuvre my camera with my right hand and I succeeded in taking a picture of it. I have not identified it yet. That was a joyous and yet humbling experience. I couldn't expect such a thing ever to happen again.

I carried on to reach the turning for Calder Vale and I realised that this was the spot where there was a checkpoint on the LDWA Lancastrian Hundred, which I had completed about eighteen years before in 42 hours. I stayed on the lane down into Oakenclough and up the other side. I knew I was approaching Grizedale Bridge, again with memories of another LDWA challenge walk, the Winter Wyrecock. As I came down the hill towards the bridge I could see a few parked cars in the little carpark near the bridge. The road becomes unfenced after the bridge and the moorland stretches on both sides of it. To the right of the bridge and just north of Grizedale Brook I could see someone moving between the gorse bushes and other scrub. The person seemed to be moving erratically, to and fro, in and out, sometimes bending down and then stopping for a few moments. It looked rather odd and I couldn't puzzle out what this person was doing. What I was seeing didn't seem to fit any kind of rational explanation. As I neared the bridge I could see that it was a young woman, but then I lost sight of her.

I had barely crossed the bridge when I was greeted by a rather boisterous and over-friendly dog. Then the dog's owner came up and started to apologise to me for the dog's behaviour and, with some difficulty, he put it on a lead. This was slightly odd as the dog hadn't really bothered me at all. He said that it was a rescue dog and was now seven years old. It had been found in a skip in Lancaster when it was five weeks old. He said that it was not always obedient, and he had, indeed, had some trouble getting it to come to heel to put the leash on. "I can't do nowt with 'im", he told me. It did strike me that he can't have trained the dog very well over seven years if he still was having a problem with it; not that I know much about training dogs. This man rather button-holed me with repetitious comments about the dog and kept on apologising. He wasn't the slightest bit interested when I told him of *my* venture but kept on about himself and his blessed dog.

I eventually escaped and made my way across the grass to where there was a rather good seat built of stone and timber. It was shaped like an S with a seat in each 'bay' so that you could shelter from the wind or whatever. I don't think it can have been there very long, only a year or so, perhaps. I saw that the man had packed his dog into the car and driven off. While I sat there, the young lady who had been darting around near the brook came up to me. She told me how she liked walking and that she often came this way, on her own, perhaps as often as twice a week. I guessed she was in her thirties. After some minutes she asked me about the man with his dog. I explained what had happened to me and that he had apologised rather overmuch and that he seemed to quite like the sound of his own voice. This young lady agreed and said that she often met him up here and that he would come up to her and talk to her for twenty-five minutes at a time and that she didn't know how to get him to stop. She obviously didn't welcome these meetings and I could see what she meant, having had a small dose of his garrulity. Then it became clear why she had been doing all this dodging about among the bushes - she had been *hiding* from him. "He's so *boring!"* she explained. I couldn't work out why she didn't go for a walk somewhere else, or choose a different time of day. After talking to her for about ten minutes by the stone seat, a group of walkers emerged from the woodland having come up Grize Dale. My acquaintance saw them coming and exclaimed that she couldn't be doing with people, or some such remark, and dashed off. She obviously seemed shy of company except that she spent quite a sensible, friendly time talking to me. Perhaps I have a kind face.

So, she went and the ramblers arrived. They stopped at the seat for a snack break. They were out for a Sunday walk and soon discovered my plans. I happened to mention the oystercatcher-cum-redshank I had seen earlier, guessing that amongst their number there would be a bird specialist. One of the ladies dived into her pack and produced a little bird book and we soon established that it must have been an oystercatcher. As the party was preparing to move on another woman was talking to me about Land's End to John O'Groats adventures. She told me how some (many?) years previously she had cycled it with friends. I asked how long it took her. With great feeling she replied, "For ever!" It had obviously been quite a trial for her.

They moved on and I did so too. As I walked along the road with gorse bushes on either side, the air cooled and I felt it might rain. I kept on to the end of the moorland bit and then down a short hill with sheltering trees. I perched on a bank under a hazel tree and ate my lunch. It didn't come on to rain. False alarm. I descended gradually to the River Wyre at Street Bridge and then sat in a meadow on the river bank and, using my rucksack as a pillow, tried to laze and doze. I had masses of time to spare, but I couldn't quite do this lazing lark properly. It was warmer than earlier but not quite full-blooded blazing sunshine and I didn't feel quite comfortable with myself, despite the pleasant surroundings. After about twenty minutes I gave up and sauntered on. The river seemed like a good place to look out for a kingfisher, but I had no luck. I wandered up in to Dolphinholme and pottered about in case I found a Sunday afternoon tea room. It turned out to be as rare as the kingfisher.

I made my way slowly along the Abbeystead road and before long found my excellent B and B at Greenbank Farmhouse. Simon and Sally were friends of Brian and Anne of the night before and I received a warm welcome. Sally later ran me to The Fleece Inn a couple of miles away where I enjoyed some roast lamb. When I rang up after my meal, Simon came to fetch me back. All very friendly and obliging.

What a wonderful, yet strange day this has been, with a snipe, an interesting insect, an unnecessarily apologetic man and a shy lady. I feel I am accumulating many colourful memories as I go along.

Monday 11th May
Dolphinholme to Arkholme - 15.4 miles

I was away before eight-thirty with a fresh north-easterly breeze sweeping away any cobwebs. It was invigorating and I made good speed along quiet lanes with good views of the surrounding countryside with Clougha Pike a prominent hill on my right. I suppose I could have taken field paths but I stuck to the roads via Yeat House Farm and then along to Quernmore. This morning I was charmed to be audience to several peewits playing with the wind. Perhaps one should call them peewits when you hear them and lapwings when you see them.

At Postern Gate I could glimpse a corner of Ingleborough and I was reassured that I really was, unbelievably, in the north of England. The road was rather busier now and I had to practice my jumping sideways trick a few times. I kept hearing lots of willow warblers. I arrived safely in Caton and made a raid on the tiny sandwich shop and came out with a coffee and an iced bun plus. I sat across the road on a municipal bench in the Memorial Gardens enjoying my late elevenses. A very friendly man from the nearby garage spoke to me and he very helpfully told me of a short cut to the far side of the river. The map indicated 'Waterworks Bridge' and I hadn't been sure if this was actually a right of way and he was able to reassure me that it was perfectly passable. I could have gone a mile out of my way to a crossing downstream, but I was not over-anxious to have to do this.

I kept along the old railway track for a half a mile or so and then cut down another track towards the River Lune. With few crossings of the Lune just around here I was surprised to see a tractor and trailer moving through the water from the far bank towards near where I had just been. It was taking a long line rather than crossing at right angles and the river was pretty wide so presumably fairly shallow. I scrambled to take a photo but intervening trees prevented a decent shot. I passed over the Waterworks Bridge without incident and joined the Lune Valley Ramble. I could have added another extra mile if I had kept to the bank as the river made a huge curving loop, but I cut across a meadow and rejoined the Way upstream. At times the path was across flood meadows, which were not always easy underfoot because of hard-dried hoof holes from the ever-present cattle. To relieve this, the path occasionally dived uphill through woodland, but here one had to survive tree roots and budding brambles. But it was all quite lovely. I sat and ate my lunch on a little knoll beside the river, which remained calm and blue in the sunshine.

As I progressed up the valley Ingleborough and its companions became much more full blown. I reckoned I was seeing Gragareth, Great Coum, Whernside, Crag Hill and other parts of the Barbon Fells. During the latter part of the walk the wind got up a bit and became more northerly. I was to spend two nights with Michael and Margaret at their home in Casterton. Ann was coming to stay as well and this was to be a major staging post as it was just about halfway. With the help of my mobile phone I was able to arrange a rendezvous in Arkholme for four o'clock or thenabout. I arrived there on time and sat waiting for only a few minutes before Margaret and Ann arrived and I was whisked back to Casterton for welcome rest, refreshment and excellent company. I was to meet Ann only one more time, north of Glasgow, more than 200 miles further on.

Just a gorgeous, gorgeous day along the river.

River Lune and Ingleborough

Bluebell wood near Sedbergh

Tuesday 12th May
Arkholme to Barbon - 8.5 miles

Ann and I drove back to Arkholme and then Ann returned to Casterton. I rejoined the riverside Lune Valley Ramble. There was a cold breeze against me but the ground was dry underfoot. I again had some trouble with over-inquisitive cows and hard-dried hoof print holes. In places walkers were forbidden, by little notices, to walk immediately alongside the river bank, but were obliged to pursue their way on the wrong side of a low embankment so that the river wasn't always seen. The river scenery was too nice for me to pay *too* much attention to this restriction. It wasn't very long before I found myself at Devil's Bridge at Kirkby Lonsdale. This is a picturesque spot and a favourite rendezvous for numerous motorcyclists, who seem to meet there at almost any time of the day or year. Mind you, the snack van does a very good bacon butty and coffee.

Although I was only a mile or so from Michael and Margaret's I wanted to 'borrow from the morrow' if I could. I made my way through the nearby caravan site and then across fields and along lanes to pass through a sun-blessed High Casterton with its pretty gardens. The countryside around here is very walkable with decently signed footpaths and good views. More lanes and fields took me via Langthwaite and Fell Garth to Barbon, where I arrived soon after one o'clock. I waited by the Village Hall for a few minutes and Ann and Margaret came to pick me up.

I had visited Barbon Village Hall on one previous occasion, in April 2007, when I took part in the LDWA Challenge walk 'The Barbondale Round'. This was a 24 mile walk which 10 years earlier I would have carried off with a flourish. This was to be my longest walk for eight years and I was ill-prepared for it. I had done a couple of 15 mile walks in the previous fortnight but this was not enough to put me in really good trim. The Barbondale Round is a great walk visiting some splendid tops but gradually I fell further and further behind schedule and was obliged to be kept company by the sweep-team from Calf Top and back to the Village Hall. I came in last, the first time that has happened to me on a challenge walk, and I felt pretty weary but not absolutely knackered. Having had my first experience of LDWA events in 1989 I felt I had had some cracking good times on numerous walks. Since the ignominy of the Barbondale Round I have not attempted any Challenge Walks since.

But what the heck am I doing here, as far north as Cumbria already?

Barbon to Innerleithen

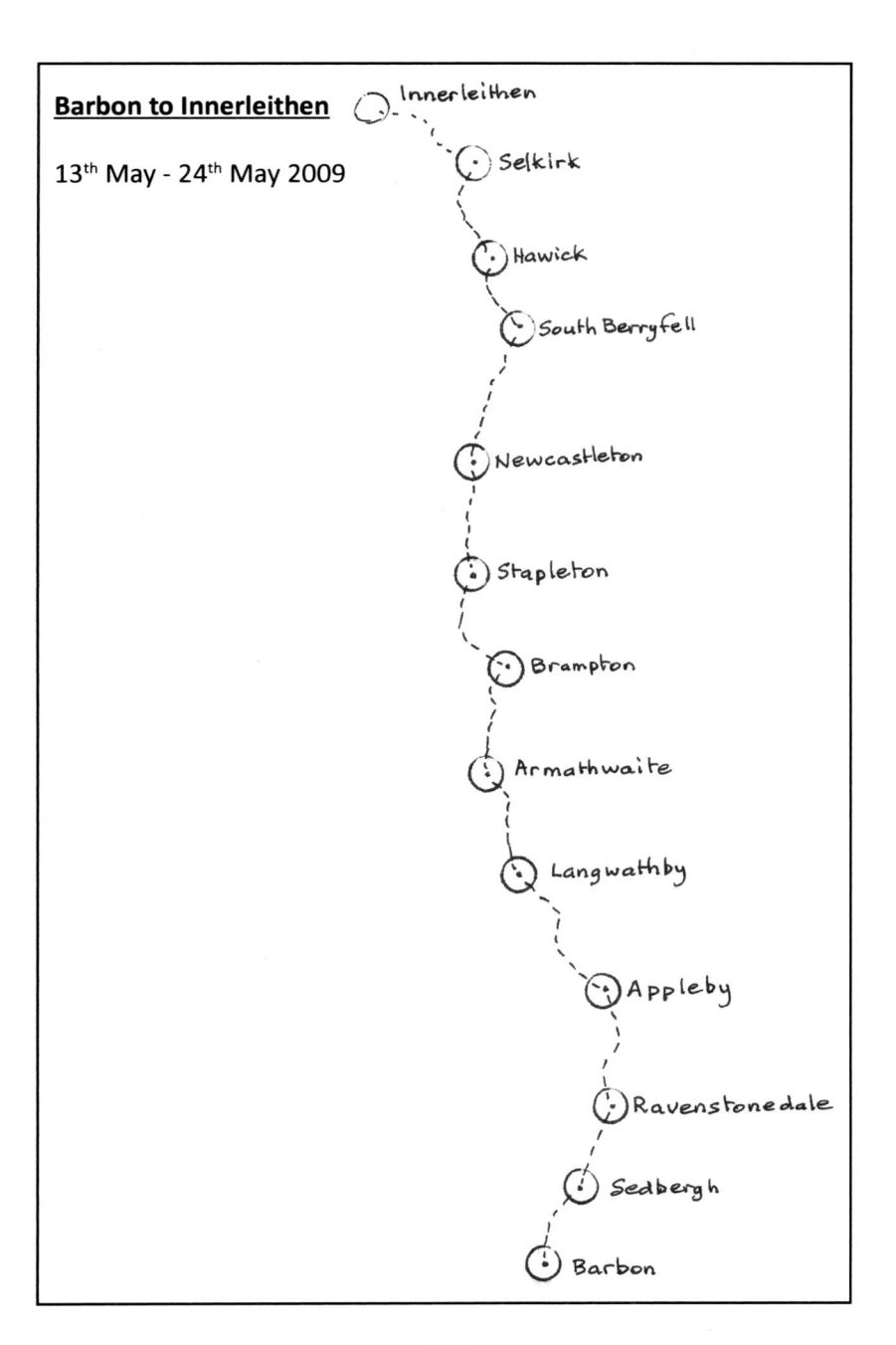

13th May - 24th May 2009

- Innerleithen
- Selkirk
- Hawick
- South Berryfell
- Newcastleton
- Stapleton
- Brampton
- Armathwaite
- Langwathby
- Appleby
- Ravenstonedale
- Sedbergh
- Barbon

Barbon to Drymen

Wednesday 13th May
Barbon to Sedbergh - 7.6 miles

I was driven back to Barbon Village Hall, said goodbye to Ann and set off along the lane that runs parallel to, but a little east of, the main road that leads to Sedbergh. It was a bright morning but was to become cloudier later. A strong wind made it rather cool. However, the lane was absolutely delightful. Very little traffic disturbed me and wild flowers were plentiful. A cow parsley lane - feel the fullness. I stopped by a field entrance to watch a farmer bringing water to his small flock of sheep. He was using large plastic drums which were on a trailer behind his quad bike. It seemed odd to me that sheep needed watering. I don't think I have noticed the business of fetching water to them before. In conversation with the farmer he told me that there was no stream or ditch in this particular field, hence his task. He told me the sheep were properly referred to as Rough Fell sheep, but he called them Kendal Roughs. A ewe and two lambs came running up to the farmer as he waited by the gate, and he explained that he, "Sometimes gave them a bit of 'cake' and that they were coming to be 'opeful".

After a few miles of lovely lane I crossed the main road and went down a couple of fields to the bank of the River Lune, which was still looking quite charming. I came through an excellent bluebell wood - with added ramsons, and there was a sense of the repetition of the spring such as I had experienced on the Worcestershire Way three weeks earlier. I then re-crossed the main road and went along Jordan Lane and then across the fields and down the lane to Abbott Holme Bridge. The place is full of rivers! I had now 'lost' the Lune but I crossed the River Dee and a few minutes later I was beside the River Rawthey. I sat on the bank near the footbridge and ate my lunch. It was a bit draughty and I was glad to move on. During this period no kingfishers appeared.

It is hard to describe the sheer loveliness of walking through spring woods with sunlight filtering through the trees, with all their different greens. This was almost a daily occurrence.

I then followed the Dales Way for a few hundred yards and very soon I was entering Sedbergh. It was still very early afternoon and I found myself passing the sports grounds of Sedbergh School, a public school. A cricket match was in progress so I stopped to watch. I probably stayed the best part of half an hour enjoying the game. I asked another spectator, a pupil, who the visiting team was and was told it was Kwegs Penrith. I interpreted this to mean Queen Elizabeth Grammar School, Penrith. It seems it was a 20/20 match. I thought the quality of the cricket was good. I wandered on into the town proper and went into 'The Sedbergh Café' where I consumed two buttered crumpets with raspberry jam and a milky coffee. I had had high hopes that there would be a superfluity of map shops in Sedbergh so that I could easily purchase various necessary maps for the days ahead, but was only able to find one. I was killing time rather and when I was in the Post Office I found that it housed a little café as well. Unfazed by this superfluity of places of refreshment, I consumed a mocha coffee and wrote postcards.

I was to stay the night with Alison. Michael and Margaret are members of the Quaker Meeting at Brigflatts, a mile across the meadows from the town. I had long ago asked Margaret if she could find someone from Brigflatts Meeting who could put me up in Sedbergh and she very efficiently found me Alison, whom I did not know. I found my way to Alison's house and she was very hospitable and we got on very well. She fed me and we chatted for much of the evening.

Being in the proximity of Brigflatts I was reminded of another adventure I had been part of in 1999. Every four years, in recent decades, the Society of Friends, Quakers, hold a Summer Gathering, which is a week-long event with speakers and discussions and fun and games, worship and fellowship, with about 1000 participants. In this particular year the gathering was to be at Canterbury University and somebody had had the idea of making a pilgrimage, on foot, from London to Canterbury, á la Chaucer. Then somebody else came up with a much grander idea, why not walk from Firbank Fell (near Sedbergh) which has strong connections with the beginnings of Quakerism in the 1650s to the Gathering, with its latest manifestations of Quakerism. So a group of us did, in fact, undertake this long trek. Some stayed the whole distance and others joined in for different lengths of time. We had a support vehicle to carry our bedding and gear. We mostly slept the night on Meeting House floors all the way down through England. We took 23 days and during that time we had about two hours of rain. We arrived in Canterbury in time for the start of the Gathering. We had slept our first night on the floor of Brigflatts Meeting House, which is one of the oldest in the country. As an 'adventure' it was pretty tame for me, with only having to carry a light pack, despite walking, on average, 16 miles a day, but others struggled with tiredness and blisters. Nevertheless it was a grand jaunt, even though it was north to south. I find walking 'north' preferable to going the other way as the sun is usually behind you and even, possibly, the prevailing wind.

Well, this has been a lazy day, but it doesn't seem to matter ….

Thursday 14th May
Sedbergh to Ravenstonedale - 9.9 miles

The sky was overcast and there was a blustery cold wind against me most of the day. Had the weather been better I might *just* have persuaded myself to get up into the hills on my way to Ravenstonedale, but I decided not to tempt providence. I love the Howgills and I haven't yet visited every corner of them, but the 'get to John O'Groats single-mindedness' prevailed. I was away by just after nine o'clock and was soon into fields and little lanes via Underbank, Stone Hall and Ellerthwaite. Somewhere around Ellerthwaite I caught up with a party of walkers who were staying at a nearby Holiday Fellowship establishment and who were out for a day's walk. There were eight of them, as I remember, and they were a very pleasant bunch of knowledgeable people. I really enjoyed their company as walking with other 'proper walkers' was a rarity.

The lane became a path which contoured along just below the access land boundary. This was a splendid sort of 'shelf' walk with nice views ahead up the valley and across to Baugh Fell. There were plenty of gorse bushes - all clad in bright yellow, so what with the gorse and the scenery and the company, the day didn't seem as grey as I feared it might have been. Further brightnesses were to come! Upon reaching Cautley Beck my companions sat down on a bank by the river and got their flasks out, so I bade them farewell and carried on a little way. Just below the footbridge to the Cross Keys a school party was carrying out river studies of some sort. I guess they were sixth-formers but they seemed to be having a grand old time bobbing about in the water, no doubt doing some work as well.

I had been aware of the existence of the Cross Keys Inn for some years but had never visited it. First of all - was it going to be open for elevenses? Luckily it was. I had hardly set foot over the threshold when I was warmly greeted by the proprietor, Alan Clowes. The Cross Keys Inn is a temperance inn with an interesting reason for being so. It is apparently the only inn in England without a liquor license. In 1902 a visitor became drunk and fell into the river. The landlord tried to save him but perished in the attempt. The drunken man survived and his guilt-ridden family bought the inn and the deeds state that it should never sell alcohol again. I was ushered into what you might otherwise call the bar, but it is furnished like a sitting room with comfy chairs and a settee - very homely. It was easy to announce that I was doing the 'big one' and Alan asked me if I was being sponsored. When I replied that I wasn't he flourished a collecting box in front of me for a charity in South Africa. It turns out that Alan is a Quaker and is connected with the meeting at Brigflatts. I understand that he spends some part of the year in South Africa helping with this charity and its work. Alan lit the fire and brought me coffee. It was certainly very snug in there on a cool morning. Other folk came in and it was all very friendly.

Alan seemed to be fond of using the somewhat archaic, but nevertheless meaningful, Quaker language. A neighbour popped into the kitchen and Alan greeted her with, "Good morning, Shirl, how art thou?" I got to talk to Shirl before I left, because she lives at Narthwaite just up the valley and she was able to advise me about the detail of the route I would need to take through her farmyard.

I eventually tore myself away from the cosiness of the inn and made my way outside. I had hardly gone a few steps when my mobile rang - it was my old friend Andrew, enquiring how I was getting on. I had probably sent him a postcard and this may have prompted his call. Andrew and I were Young Friends together in Bristol. I introduced Andrew to long distance walking on the South Wales Marathon in the early sixties. This marathon was a 45 mile walk over the Brecon Beacons and Black Mountains going over the seven peaks over 2600' high, to be completed in one day. Andrew was my best man when Ann and I got married in 1966 and he and my brother Geoffrey broke off from a group who were walking the Pennine Way, to be in Keynsham in time for the wedding. Afterwards they dashed back to the far north to carry on but there was a three day hole in their achievement. In 2004 Andrew invited me, along with other like-minded friends, to join him on an attempt to do the whole of the Pennine Way in one go in order to celebrate his retirement and his 60th birthday. Luckily he managed to do it all and I did it all with him bar a gap of a few days when I had to be at work. It was really good to hear from him, a rare treat, and we had a good old clack for a few minutes.

I re-crossed the footbridge over the Rawthey, without being drunk and without falling in, and made my way to Narthwaite and successfully navigated my way through the farmyard. From here there were terrific views of the surrounding hills and I half-wished I had taken the upland option. Only half, mind. The track ahead was less well frequented but still kept pretty level along the side of Wandale Hill. I stopped and perched against a stone wall and ate my lunch and then descended to Adamthwaite. This seemed an isolated spot and despite being less than a mile as the crow flies to the main Kirkby Stephen road, there didn't seem to be any access to it. The only way in and out was the lane I took, which climbs to 1350' before descending to Ravenstonedale. This high point was the highest altitude that I attained in England. The second highest, 200 feet lower, was on Bodmin Moor above Minions.

I enjoyed this steady climb and I kept wondering what I would see at the top of the pass. I knew I would see the northern Pennines, but I was excited because I was entering a new section of the walk, leaving behind the water that drained into the sea at Lancaster and moving into an area where the water drains into the Solway Firth. The Solway Firth has definite Scottish connotations so I felt I was making good progress, although it was to be the best part of a week before I was to set foot in Scotland. There were views of Cross Fell and the Great and Little Dun Fells and I thought I glimpsed Kidsty Pike in the eastern Lake District before I lost them as I descended into the pleasant village of Ravenstonedale. I found my B and B and later went to the hotel in the village for an evening meal. Three more flowers today: Good King Henry, Queen Anne's Lace and English stonecrop.

Friday 15th May
Ravenstonedale to Appleby - 13.3 miles

The weather was uninviting. The sky was very dark and overcast with a definite promise of rain. I walked down into the village and bought some items in 'The Village Store'. Here was another example of a community-run enterprise. I think there was some mention of an initiative by Prince Charles about starting village shops next door to, or in, pubs, or something. I may be muddled about this. I followed paths out of the village and under the big main road, the A685, and along the hillside to reach an old railway track. I crossed this and was then on access land which at this point was what I would call rough pasture. I climbed gently, with occasional hastenings, as the blessed cows were after me again. Underfoot was just rough grass, but I was intrigued to discover wood anemones growing in the open field. I always associate wood anemones - windflowers - with ash woodlands on limestone, although I am sure they grow elsewhere, but I don't ever remember seeing them way out in the open in such profusion. There were no trees or woodland nearby, although this was limestone country with a vengeance. But, in the years since this walk I have kept on seeing wood anemones out in the open ……ah well!

Another treat was seeing my first mountain pansies of the walk and I also found some spring sandwort, a lover of dry places and old spoil heaps. I kept along the edge of the moorland on a good level track and it wasn't long before I was in Crosby Garrett. It had started spitting with rain and I took a short rest in a convenient bus shelter, mainly so that I could turn my double-sided map over. At the same moment the local bus pulled up - the Upper Eden Plus Bus. I think this must have been the end point of the route because the driver had a few minutes to spare, so we had a chat about this and that. What struck me most was not the content of our conversation but the quiet, gentle, soft-spoken nature of the driver's voice. It indicated a different sort of 'content' perhaps. I wondered if this was just him or whether this was the way most folk spoke in the Upper Eden area.

The gardens still had daffodils blooming, just. The spring, as it moves northwards is not a defined line but an irregularly shaped block. I have been using ash trees as a marker of the onset of the warmer season. I know they usually come out later than the oak - splashes and soaks and all that - and probably later than most other trees as well. The ash trees I saw today are still totally bare and wintry, no different from those I saw in the far south west.

I kept along the lanes and the verges were smothered in water avens. I crossed the railway line and went down a track. Here I found a strange-looking plant which I thought I had never knowingly seen before. It wasn't fully grown, I guessed, which made it a bit harder to identify. When I got home my researches with the Blamey and the Keble Martin etc led me to believe it was probably a marsh valerian. The farm-drive track gave way to a rather more overgrown section which was rather boggy in places, but it didn't continue for long and I joined a lane at Grassgill Rigg. Rigg - now that's a good north-country word which I would normally associate with Northumberland rather than further west. I trundled along a more main-ish road for a mile or so, before turning right up a lane which took me over Little Ormside Moor. I was reminded of my experience with a blackcap as I approached Wem a couple of weeks ago, as the same thing happened with the chattering little bird keeping me company along the lane, me on the track and the blackcap in the hedge. It felt as though it was high time for lunch but the lane didn't really present a cosy enough little nook to sag down into. I kept on rejecting *almost* suitable places and eventually reached Ormside Mill. Here there was a cluster of buildings which was an outdoor centre, but not in use at the moment. I sat on a damp seat in the yard and ate my lunch.

Much of the morning's walk has been punctuated by crumps and thumps from the Warcop firing range a few miles away. It was still tending to drizzle so I decided not to use the rather wonky-looking stepping-stones just outside the Mill and found a (private) footbridge nearby. After Great Ormside village I went uphill and under the railway and then joined the River Eden which flowed along on my right to Appleby. This was very pleasant walking in woodland, apart from the ground being what I call 'sticky-to-wet'. I have had it dry underfoot so often that I wasn't complaining!

I arrived in Appleby by about a quarter to four and found a good little café to sit in and warm myself up a bit. There were two well-laden bikes outside and inside were two lovely ladies, Janice and Heather. Their presence was a great delight and comfort to me. They were cycling from John O'Groats to Land's End and they were the first people I had met on the whole of my walk so far who were doing anything like my trek. I didn't care that they were doing it 'the wrong way round'. I didn't care that they were cycling not walking. I cared very much that I had two people with whom to share the enthusiasm, the joy, the triumphs and the trials. We talked eagerly and the café proprietor joined in. He seemed pleased to have been witness to this serendipitous happening.

Dragging myself away, I crossed the river and made my way up to Bongate House, a fairly busy Guest House, where I was looked after well. I walked back down the hill a little later, in the company of a 14 year-old boy who was going to his last 'cadet evening'. He was signing up to be an RAF pilot - for ten years. I wondered whether it was right for him to make such a momentous decision at such a tender age, but he seemed a sensible lad and came across as being quite sure of himself. I didn't quite follow the arrangements that would allow him to continue his education, seemingly now away from home. Such matters are somewhat alien to me as a Quaker and a pacifist, but I kept my opinions to myself and within only a few minutes we were at the river and we parted. I went into the previously reconnoitred Jade Apple Chinese Restaurant and had a good meal. At the end of the meal I was given a 'Fortune Cookie'. The message on the slip of paper inside said, "You will be successful in your work". They really must learn how to spell 'walk'. I suppose I could have crossed out the letter 'r' and left it with them.

Saturday 16th May
Appleby to Langwathby. - 14.0 miles

Bongate House was also accommodating a group of young men who were up for a golfing weekend. I can't remember whether all or some of the following was communicated to some of the party. Having told them what I was doing I may have told them I was on COURSE for John O'Groats and that I had already come a FAIRWAY. Each day LINKS with the next. I am trying to do the WHOLE IN ONE go. When I get to John O'Groats I may have a BALL. I must have been desperate if I also told them that I always look forward to my TEA.

In planning the day's route I had had some doubt as to the presence and/or reliability of the footbridge over the Eden at Skygarth. In order to try and settle the matter I went into the Tourist Information Centre where a very helpful lady sorted it out for me. Neither she nor her colleague knew definitely the status of the footbridge, but she rang up the woman who runs the B and B at Skygarth Farm, adjacent to the bridge, who confirmed that the bridge was certainly still there and perfectly usable. I felt that this was kindness beyond the call of duty and thanked her accordingly.

Some of the streets of Appleby have interesting names: Boroughgate sounds alright but what were the origins of Scattergate and Doomgate? The civic daffodils were still blooming, halfway through May, although they were beginning to look a bit tired. This was another reminder of the northerliness of my progress and the lateness of the spring. Daffodils in Cornwall were starting to be over about two months ago.

I found a path that climbed up and I was able to look down on the broad curving sweep of the River Eden with woods on one side and flat meadows on the other. I was delighted to observe a brown mare suckling her very new-born looking foal. Across the river in a northerly direction I was able to see Cross Fell and Great and Little Dun Fells. These are old friends from several excursions along the Pennine Way and I almost felt a longing to be up there, rather than down in the unadventurous flatlands. However, it wasn't long before the clouds came down and obscured them so I felt quite content sticking to my plan. As I walked along I imagined the following question and answer. I don't think this question was asked of me and therefore I couldn't have replied, it was all just in my head. Question: "Why do it?" Answer: "I've always been quite good at being stupid".

I followed a pleasant path along the top of the woodland as I left the skirts of the town and then cut across a dampish field to a lane. I followed this lane through Colby and on to Bolton. About a mile before Bolton I saw the top of a building peeping up over a low rise a few fields away to my left. It had a domed top and was reminiscent of an observatory which often has a similarly shaped top which, I believe, swivels round. I started speculating. Is it preferable for observatories to be located in places where there is very little light pollution? Are there not places in the UK which have been referred to as being quite dark places? I can remember seeing a satellite picture which showed the whole of the UK at night and showing all the dark spots, usually in uninhabited areas and the light spots where the big conurbations were. The speculation continued. Is the sort of triangle between Appleby-Penrith-Alston a 'dark area'? The land is reasonably flat west of the Pennines, and although there are a few villages perhaps it is a light-pollution-free zone. This kept me happy for a good quarter of a mile. Then I passed a side turning on my left and I could see a farm and its buildings roughly where I had seen the top of my 'observatory'. It was a tall silo. Collapse of stout party!

I came to the cross roads at Bolton and looked about for mid-morning refreshment. I wandered down the street away from my intended line and found a pub which provided me with a hot drink on a coolish morning. Retracing my steps I kept westwards along the road and soon after Mansgrove I cut off down a lane to Peatgate and then through meadows to reach the bank of the Eden. I was just thinking that this was just the sort of place that I might see a deer, when, blow me, I did. It whisked away quickly leaving me startled but pleased. A minute or so later I was able to take my time over photographing an orange-tip butterfly feeding on query marsh/bog stitchwort or even very grand cuckoo flower. I suppose knowing what orange-tips feed on would have helped me identify the flower. Anyway, it was all very lush along beside the river for a little way. Reaching Ousenstand Bridge I kept on beside the river bank to reach Skygarth Bridge. I had my lunch sitting in a dinky little wooden shelter near the river. It seemed newly built and had a fence around it and a bench inside. It was an ideal spot in which to eat my picnic. It was bit like a very small bus shelter, but more homely. While I sat there munching away there was a short sharp shower of rain, lasting barely ten minutes, luckily coming from behind the shelter. This was the first rain of the day, and I was glad to have found such a delectable spot so fortuitously timed. Skygarth Bridge is a footbridge, but solidly built and well maintained. It was a good place to be.

Passing the aforementioned Skygarth Farm, I went through a couple of fields and then had to contend with the newly constructed Temple Sowerby bypass. New pathways had been laid and it was all a bit pristine and clinical, but the saving grace was finding a meadow saxifrage, the first of the walk. I normally associate this flower with limestone meadows and this one seemed quite out of place. Perhaps it came out of a packet. On this Saturday afternoon, Temple Sowerby village was probably enjoying some new-found quietness, but possibly also some loss of trade. It was indeed very quiet there, with a gentle village green dozing happily, surrounded by stately horse chestnut trees showing off their upright candles.

I tip-toed away down the lane then entered a field and managed not to attract the attention of a herd of cows with a bull in attendance. At Millrigg Bridge I kept along the lanes to Culgaith. Here the rain came on again, more like April showers than proper rain. I spent some minutes sheltering under a conveniently thick hedge, then as the shower slackened I went up the hill to the village, but on the way another shower started and I spent another ten minutes in the dry under trees alongside the road. A mile or so after leaving the village it did come onto to rain rather more vigorously, so I dug out my over-trousers. The rather boring road was made more interesting, despite the rain, by views of the Lakeland hills. I could see Skiddaw and Blencathra etc. I eventually reached Langwathby, by which time the rain had stopped and I easily found my way to the home of Bob and Dinah. Dinah was in the form above me at Sidcot and she and Bob made me truly welcome.

Sunday 17th May
Langwathby to Armathwaite - 12.2 miles

I was to stay two nights with Dinah and Bob so I left some of my gear behind and walked with a light pack. The morning was fine with altocumulus cloud not obscuring warmish sunshine. The light breeze was behind me and I felt pretty good. I was away by about

At Staffield Hall

Orange - tip butterfly feeding

0915 and enjoyed the lane to Little Salkeld. A strung out party of cyclists passed me and they looked as though they were on some long trek. I can't remember whether they were doing an 'End-to-End', more likely to have been one of the coast-to-coast routes. They seemed to recognise a fellow intrepidiste, as I them, and friendly greetings were exchanged in passing. At Little Salkeld I went along a lane that led to a track beside the railway with the meandering Eden just beyond it. This led into woods which were calm and beautiful. After a while I reached Lacy's Caves. These are rooms carved out of the natural sandstone, immediately above the river. A notice warned that there was a 'dangerous path with sheer drops' and that I was to 'proceed at my own risk'. I considered doing the daring thing, which meant climbing out of one 'window' and stretching along to a further shelf which would have led me back to the path. The water was gurgling happily about 20 feet below me and I decided that being daring wasn't for me today. Of course, there was a perfectly sensible alternative around the back which took me on through more lovely woodland. A long riverside meadow led on to Daleraven Bridge where I touched the road briefly before returning to more flat meadows and along to the rather splendid Eden Bridge. I kept along the road into Kirkoswald village and sat in the square on a seat and ate my lunch. There were two pubs in close proximity, but I entered neither of them. It was Sunday lunchtime, but it all seemed very quiet.

After leaving the village in a northerly direction I took a left onto a footpath which led through fields for a mile. It was almost like parkland, indeed the map referred to Staffield Park and I could see on my left a large building in its own grounds, which I took to be Staffield Hall. I passed an oak tree with fresh young leaves, almost yellow in their light-green newness. I also saw a lady out with her dog. Reaching the road I turned left and paused to read a small sign by the roadside which said that refreshments were available down the drive. This was the drive leading down to Staffield Hall. I felt as though a little liquid refreshment might be in order and started off down the drive. I hadn't gone far when I came to a bend and I thought, "I wonder how many more bends there will be before I find the refreshments, and if it is going to be a long way, perhaps I won't bother". As I stood there dithering, the lady who had been walking her dog, came up behind me, with her dog, and she could see that I was undecided. She told me that the 'shop' wasn't far, and that if it wasn't open, she would give me a coffee herself. So I walked on down the drive with her and very soon the 'shop' appeared and it was welcomingly open. I thanked this kind lady warmly for her assistance and her offer, but turned aside to the 'shop' and went inside. It seems that Staffield Hall has been divided up into a number of separate flats or dwellings and one of the tenants had started up a small shop in her front room and also sold light refreshments. I was greeted by Pam, the owner, and she bade me sit on one of the chairs while she made me a drink. There were various items for sale around the shelves and the room was cheerful and homely. The setting was full of character, as was Pam herself. She was dressed in a long multi-coloured skirt which barely concealed a pair of well-worn walking boots. She was kindness itself and was interested to hear of my journey. Before I left I took a picture of her standing in the doorway and she took one of me. I might never have found such a cosy little nook if the lady and her dog had not come along just when they did. I might have dithered and turned away coffee-less. I have a photo of Pam with her lopsided cardigan. Her heart was in the right place, even if her buttons weren't.

There were occasional signs saying 'Beware - Red Squirrels' and although I paused in what I thought were likely places, I never saw one. I tramped along the lane crossing Croglin Water and, as usual, paused and looked over the parapet to see if I might see a kingfisher. No luck upstream, no luck downstream. Just before Coombshead I turned left into Coombs Wood. This was splendid open mixed woodland and a joy to walk through. I had occasional glimpses of the wooded gorge of the Eden which looked pretty stunning. I was unprepared for such a treat. The track led gently downhill and on the way there were some excellent examples of bugle, growing very tall. I also thought to myself, this is just the sort of place that one might see yellow pimpernel and then "blimmin 'eck", five minutes later, there was a great mass of them. Towards the bottom of the wood I had a similar experience. I said to myself this might be the sort of place where I might see a snake. I can't imagine why I should have thought that, but who am I to argue with my subconscious? I turned onto a smaller path and within three minutes of my 'snake-thought' I was confronted with a sign, the likes of which I have never seen before, which was triangular in shape and bright yellow with a picture of a snake in black drawn upon it. What's going on? I proceeded carefully and trod on no snakes and saw none. It's not really a red squirrel-kingfisher-snake day today. I did see 53 wild flowers, all of which I had seen somewhere or other on previous days. This was the third highest daily total so far. The daily count had reached 60 two days earlier and 56 yesterday. There has been a kind of two up one down kind of progress with the number of flowers seen, but there has been a steady increase as the spring gradually moves towards summer.

I soon found myself in Armathwaite village and made my way up to the station, where I waited not too long for the train to take me back, so conveniently, to Langwathby. Upon recounting to Bob and Dinah my tale of finding refreshments at Staffield Hall, served by the lovely Pam, they knew at once to whom I was referring. They know her quite well as she is known to them through some Quaker connection, possibly attending the same Meeting as Dinah. What a grand day!

Monday 18th May
Armathwaite to Brampton - 12.6 miles

Bob kindly drove me back to Armathwaite and I immediately put on my over-trousers to fend off some steady rain. It rained for a couple of hours then cleared up to a nice afternoon. I was mostly on lanes and by the time I reached fields and woods the going underfoot was not too damp. I took the pleasantly undulating lane that led me past Holmwrangle. In the hedge along the way I found a large shrub that looked like laburnum but with a slightly different shape to the flower. The jizz didn't feel right for the familiar laburnum. I guessed it must be a northern variety I had not met before. I also saw a white version of ivy-leaved toadflax - again not ever seen before.

I joined a larger road, passing Hornsby Gate and Carlatton Mill. On this wet morning I had my first definite glimpse of Scotland - away ahead of me to the left, roughly north-west. I thought it was probably hills behind Annan. The Pennines were dying quietly fairly near to hand on my right side. There were long straight stretches of road and the countryside was pretty devoid of villages. No coffee shops this morning! My map is littered with Ws and Ys that I had written in to indicate where I had heard or seen a willow warbler or a yellowhammer. I made my way into Castle Carrock and sat and ate my picnic on a seat on the village green.

I had virtually zero knowledge about this area from a walking point of view and I had quite a strenuous debate with myself about which route to take in the afternoon. The road into Brampton would be yet more road and navigationally 'safe' and dry underfoot. The alternative was to make my way towards Gelt Woods and take a chance that the footpath on the map really did exist on the ground. I should have paid more attention to the P for Parking symbol, just over the fold in the map at the northern end of the woods, which might have suggested to me a more popular area than I was expecting. So...half a mile out of Castle Carrock I bravely took a left turn and followed an uppy-downy track-cum-lane which took me to Middle Gelt Bridge. I was in for a pleasant surprise, because the path through the woods was well engineered and well maintained and was a joy to walk upon. The river rushed along below me to my left, but the trees prevented me from seeing the water more than just occasionally. At times there were cascades and falls and narrow bits, reminiscent of The Strid in Wharfedale.

I met a lovely gentle couple who were visiting the area from Northallerton, accompanied by their four black dogs. They told me that they came here quite often and they informed me that there were several of these Strid-like stretches. I could well believe it. I shall certainly make a point of returning here sometime and giving the river a closer inspection. After the rather damp and wide-open-spaces sort of morning it was great to discover such a delightful place so unexpectedly.

I left the woods at the 'P' at Low Gelt Bridge and made my way towards Brampton, now quite close. I had a much better view of Scotland now and Skiddaw and Blencathra et al were fast disappearing astern. I crossed the very busy A69 and carried on through fields to the west end of the town, then up to the square with its octagonal building with a clock tower on the top. I arrived here at about a quarter past four and had time to kill before finding my accommodation.

I had long ago asked Dinah and Bob if they knew of anywhere I could stay in Brampton and they had asked around and come up with an offer from a young couple, Emily and Matt, who Dinah knew through, yet again, a Quaker connection. I wasn't going to be able to arrive before 6 o'clock as Emily and Matt both worked. It was very good of these two to put up a complete stranger, albeit the friend of a friend, but I was made welcome and had a comfy bed and some good chat.

In the meantime, with time on my hands I decided to buy a pair of socks. One would have assumed that one would have been able to buy a pair of men's socks in a town the size of Brampton. Flippin' assumptions again! I must have tried half a dozen shops searching for a pair of socks - not a whisper, not a hint, not a murmur anywhere. I wasn't *desperately* in need of a pair of socks, I just thought it might be useful. Apparently there was a large out-of-town supermarket thing somewhere just … out-of-town … but I wasn't going all the way to wherever it was, just for a pair of socks. I really couldn't believe that it was so difficult! I would have stood a better chance in a small village boasting one store that sold everything. I thought: Go not hoseless to Brampton, thou wilt be disappointed. A hose! A hose! My Kingdom for a Hose!

Tuesday 19th May
Brampton to Stapleton - 11.0 miles

I had to leave my overnight stop with Matt and Emily fairly early as they had to go to work, so I dawdled down into the town and tried, almost half-heartedly to complete my sock-finding mission, but had no luck. Instead I lazed into a café and took my time over some very early elevenses. I eventually started my proper walking at about five to ten. I found a path through fields that led me onto Old Church Lane from which I turned right through more fields over a charming little hillock to reach the drive to Crooked Holme. I kept up the drive to the main road and crossed the River Irthing. I stayed on the rather busy main road up the hill to Newtown. The road sign saying 'Newtown' also said 'Please Drive carefully' except that some wag had obliterated the r and the v, so that it said 'Please D i e Carefully'. Perhaps such alterations are commonplace to you, dear reader, but I had not seen it before.

Newtown seemed to be a fairly small place, one claim to fame being that it sits astride Hadrian's Wall Path. Some years previously I had walked with my cousin Mike and my cousin-in-law Greg and my brother-in-law John from the North Sea at Tynemouth to Housesteads. The necessity of returning to work meant I had to leave the party, but the others carried on to the Solway. I would like to finish off the rest of the path sometime, certainly from Greenhead westwards. As I came into the village, such as it was, I

saw two women in the garden of a Bed and Breakfast establishment, and I cheekily remarked to them, "What, no pub? no shop? no café?" and immediately felt embarrassed at my pushy jocularity when I was invited into the garden by the younger of the two women, who said something like, "Oh, alright, then, I'll make you a coffee". This kindly woman was Susan Grice and she ran the
B and B, so she was used to Long Distance Walkers. She certainly has to be my 'Number One Person of the Day'. She sat me down at a little table on the lawn and brought me coffee and some excellent flapjack and would accept no payment for it, but I put a donation in a charity box, I think it was for the Air Ambulance. Best to keep them on-side, I've a way to go yet. I dragged myself away leaving Susan to carry on her explanations about the garden to her mother-in-law.

I stayed on the main road for another half mile or so and then turned right along a minor road towards Howford Bridge. The day had started rather cloudy but by now had become much brighter and sunnier. A very nice softish breeze coming from behind helped me along. The road wasn't too busy and I wandered along with nothing very much wrong with the world, except the silly knee, that is ever with us. At Hethersgill I was struck by the architecture of the single-storey cottages, which, although I was still in England, was what I consider to be typical Scottish vernacular. I am still a whole day's walking away from crossing into Scotland. The border, for the uninitiated, runs roughly south-west/north-east, not west/east and there is a heck of a lot of sparsely inhabited Cumbria tucked in here, north of The Wall. Anyway, I guess the houses can look Scottish if they want to - but it was another sign that a significant marker along my walk was gradually approaching.

I sat on a convenient bench at the crossroads in Hethersgill and spread my lunch out around me. The splendid signpost just beside me not only told me I was 5½ miles from Brampton and 10 miles from Carlisle and 8¾ from Bewcastle but also indicated that it 'belonged' to Cumberland County Council. If it ain't broke, don't fix it! While I sat there I took the opportunity to ring my sister, Juliet, as it was our Mum's birthday, and I would no doubt have rung *her*, had she still been alive. She died when she was 70 and today she would have been 98. A car pulled up and parked and a woman got out and she stopped to chat. She was the District Nurse and she seemed to be in no hurry. I think she was called Yvonne. She works in Scotland and England. I asked her about the accents of the local people. I wondered whether there was a clear cut divide between a Scottish accent and a Cumbrian accent. I find it mildly intriguing in the presence of borders, be it Wales/England or Scotland/England, to wonder how much overlap there is in the architecture, place names and accents etc. If you have ever climbed Pen-y-Ghent, up the steep end, you may have noticed the dry-stone wall which starts off as white limestone but higher up it is composed of the darker, overlying gritstone. However, in the middle, for a short distance, the wall is built of a mixture of light and dark stones. This assumes that the wall was built from stones lying around nearby, rather than having been imported. If you were driving up the M6 and the M74 you might well notice English accents from the locals at the last service station in England; then the next time you stop twenty or thirty miles further north at a Scottish service station you would definitely hear a Scottish accent. But what about the band in between?

'Political' or civil boundaries have often followed ridges or watersheds or rivers, which are purely physical features, and one might expect such lines to cut through established cultural areas so that the same accents, or whatever, would be on both sides of the boundary. But, I speculate, maybe the same physical boundaries, from ancient times, separated the cultural areas quite naturally, and so when the boundary makers came along, they drew their lines between the different areas along the same natural dividers. I daresay some professor in a university somewhere knows all about this.

I got started again and at Boltonfellend I was delighted to see clumps of Star of Bethlehem growing by the roadside. As far as I was concerned this was a rare find. They are a beautiful flower with six pointed white petals, looking clean and fresh. At Crowsikehead - in Northumberland would sike be a stream or ditch? - I stopped to talk to a friendly lady in her garden. There seemed to be no other houses for at least a quarter of a mile in either direction so I asked her, "Wasn't it a bit lonely here with no neighbours?" She seemed surprised and said, "Oh no, it's fine here. Where we were before was much more out of the way - a farm up on Spadeadam". Now my memory tells me that Spadeadam is/was the place that the military uses/used for testing rockets and other beastly things. I had always assumed that the ground must have been pretty useless, agriculturally speaking, and so the army/RAF? had taken it over without anybody really minding very much. I had always thought that such a place was just about the most God-forsaken spot in Britain. And here was this dear soul saying they had run a farm up there. No wonder she liked the gentle lowlandy bit at Crowsikehead, with neighbours only a few minutes up or down the road. I walked on, suitably humbled in my mind with the thought of the hardship they, and other hill farmers must have endured, and may still be enduring, for all I know.

Somewhere in the next mile I just went through an open gate into a field and lay down in the sunshine and did nothing except daydream for a while. Thinking about this whole venture I wondered if there was a sense of timelessness? I had escaped from the realities of home routines, but each day I had to keep to the reality of the target of *place,* but not always an obligation of *time*. There were moments when I let the world drift by or allowed my legs the privilege of doing the walk themselves without my brain interfering, and letting my imagination wander where it would. I couldn't escape, except momentarily, from the realities of the world - I wanted to *enjoy* the realities of whatever presented itself to my eyes, ears, nose. Also the fact of having no strict deadlines each day meant that in respect of 'time', life was pretty well stress free.

I spent the night at The Drove Inn, north of the village of Stapleton. I had had some difficulty finding accommodation in this area - I had wanted to find a half-way point between Brampton and Newcastleton and this turned out to be a very useful resting place. The couple running it, so I heard, should have retired some while ago, and maybe they will do so soon, so I cannot guess whether the Inn will still be there in the days to come, in such an empty corner of Cumbria. For a long time I had toyed with a route that would take me through Bewcastle, but I couldn't find any accommodation there. Anyway, The Drove Inn did me proud.

I am still having worries about finding places to stay further north. An entry in my notebook says, "Ann - can she find me a B and B at Chapelhall?" That is a place east of Glasgow about ten days ahead.

Wednesday 20th May
The Drove Inn, Stapleton to Newcastleton - 12.7 miles

My target today was Newcastleton, in Scotland! I suppose I must have felt slightly excited at the thought. I have crossed the Border plenty of times in a car or a train or a bus, not to mention on foot, nearing the end of The Alternative Pennine Way (once) and The Pennine Way (twice), but never having walked all the way from Land's End.

I left The Drove Inn at ten past nine and was soon enjoying a dinky little lane that took me down to Whitelyne Bridge. Up again a little to reach a wide bit of unfenced land, like a common, which I dare to call Dappleymoor, although this is not marked on the map as such, but I passed two farms, one called Low Dappleymoor and then High Dappleymoor, so I may have guessed correctly. Up a slope and along to reach a lane which took me past Nether Hill and then down a stony byway, which became rather damp at the bottom, to reach Oakshaw Ford. Here it started spotting with rain, but not really enough to bother about. It cleared up later. I crossed the River Blacklyne at Oakshawford Bridge - looked over both sides, just in case. Plenty of willow warblers today, though. Another narrow lane took me along past Sorbies and as I neared the junction with a rather more main road, a young lady with a dog came out of a nearby house. She was delivering some eggs to a neighbour. I did my, "I thought you'd come to put out 'The Coffee Shop is Now Open' sign" spiel, and immediately regretted being so forward. She did offer me a coffee, most willingly, but it would have meant her turning back and then later having to start her errand all over again, so I declined and said I was only joking.

On this more mainish sort of road, that is one vehicle every ten minutes rather than one every hour, a timber wagon came lumbering past (Oh no! did I really write that?) and I became aware that I was on the fringes of some very large forests. My notebook records "the soft smell of sawn timber". After dropping back down to the Blacklyne again I kept along the river bank for a little way, thinking to continue to Bailey Mill. At a footbridge the riverside path seemed to be less appealing, for various reasons, than a detour up the hill to Kiln Knowe, so detour it was. As I came down the lane towards Bailey Mill the postman in his van was coming up. When I reached Bailey Mill the postman had come back down again. There is quite a complex of buildings here with various activities on offer: pony-trekking? and a café/restaurant? and at first it looked promising for a late mid-morning break. However the postman was having difficulty delivering his parcels as there was no-one around. Between us we tried several doors and entrances but the whole place seemed deserted. He said he sometimes does have difficulty with his deliveries here. Dreams of coffee receded quickly. I gave him four postcards that I had been waiting to post and we made our separate ways onward.

Back on the 'main' road again I carried on, passing farms and the odd cottage. Just after Langley Burn Bridge I found a very pleasant grassy bank against which to rest my back while I ate my lunch. Whilst lazing here I heard a cuckoo, one of several heard so far. Was this to be the last English cuckoo? I speculated. I moved on steadily with Kershope Forest starting to close in around me. After a mile or so I reached a road junction at Roansgreen where I paused. I had stopped here because another adventurer had paused also. He was a young cyclist who had been following the Reivers Route but seemed to have lost his support party. The Reivers Route apparently runs from Whitehaven to Tynemouth.

The road started to descend, but what views there might have been northwards into Scotland were blocked by the trees. At the bottom of the hill, at 1425, I crossed Kershope Bridge into Scotland. There was no flurry of trumpets, but there was a fairly large sign saying 'Welcome to Scottish Borders'. Looking back across the bridge into England there was a complete absence of any indication that you were now entering England, let alone welcoming you. My scrapbook of the walk has a picture of the Scottish Borders sign and the caption I have put beneath it says, "Well - I've got this far anyway"! While I paused there for some minutes, looking up and down the Kershope Burn, I think I felt that, although I had got this far, there still might be problems about getting to John O'Groats. It was two months ago to the day, that I left Sennen Cove and Land's End and I did feel that I had begun to discover by now that I wasn't going to conk out, as long as I kept on nice and easy. On balance the uncertainties ahead of me, gave me pleasure rather than panic.

I still had about three miles to go to reach The Grapes Hotel, so I set off again just a wee bit exhilarated, perhaps. More so as I came up out of the valley and out of the forest and could see Scottish hills ahead of me. I knew I wasn't going to be tramping over the tops but they looked inviting. The road descended gradually to Newcastleton and I was relieved to find that the Heritage Centre was still open.

The kindly and helpful lady there was able to give me information about buses which I was pretty sure I would want to use the next day. Newcastleton has the main road running straight through the middle and the streets are laid out in a grid-like pattern. This was a planned village laid out over two hundred years ago by one of the Dukes of Buccleuch. I found The Grapes Hotel to be pleasantly informal and friendly and I enjoyed my two night stay there. Tomorrow I will have a lighter pack on a long trek towards Hawick.

Thursday 21st May
Newcastleton to 'South Berryfell' - 14.7 miles

In the planning phase of this grand jaunt there were always masses of ideas to pursue, alternative routes to consider, overnight accommodation to find and so on. Some of these tasks were completed successfully before setting off and Ann was a great help in tidying up behind me, as it were, and at times, doing the job for me. There just didn't seem to be enough time to do everything. I knew I could have been looking on the internet to find details of buses between Newcastleton and Hawick, but somehow it never got done. I already knew that it was virtually impossible to find B and Bs along today's stretch, and how to cope with this section of the route had been a nagging worry at the back of my mind. There had been several such unresolved worries, especially as related to Scotland, and this was one of the bigger ones. I had booked myself into The Grapes Hotel for two nights and I knew that I would proceed towards Hawick for as long as I felt I could and then worry about how to get back to Newcastleton later on. I had visions of summoning a taxi or thumbing a lift. However - there were buses! Not many, but enough to serve my purpose.

So on a bright morning I set off, knowing that it was to be tarmac all the way, but mightily relieved that my ill-founded worries were behind me. The main road - I call it main road, but it is the B6357 - was busy enough, not least with big timber wagons thundering by, battering their way down the valley from the forests of Kielder. After a couple of miles, at Hermitage Bridge, I turned off onto the B6399, a rather quieter road. The countryside was green and pleasant and Hermitage Water was never far away, sometimes on the left and then on the right. The gradients were virtually non-existent. The map indicated a Craft Centre at Hermitage and when I reached it there didn't seem to be anyone about. But the door was open and I found myself in a small shop with craft items on display, but not really a place where, I surmised, one would find enough trade to open a café. A young man appeared. He seemed to be somewhat hesitant about what he should be doing because he was half expecting a school party to arrive any time and couldn't settle to his duties until something definite happened. Nonetheless he obligingly made me a mug of coffee, for which I was grateful. By the time I was ready to move on the school party had still not appeared.

There started to be a rather more uplandy feel about the terrain and the water to my right was now the Whitrope Burn. After a while the road began to rise more steeply and at Whitropefoot the forest closed in on both sides. At Whitrope summit, at over 1000 feet, I was surprised that I was surprised to see a bridge across the road with a railway wagon perched on top. This, of course, was the old railway line from London to Scotland. I have a much loved old LP of 'Trains in the Night' with recordings of steam trains at Steele Road and Riccarton Junction. I had temporarily forgotten that this line would cross my path, the previous few miles of its course having been in the adjacent valley.

The Whitrope Summit indicated a Heritage Centre. There were signs that some activity had been going on, presumably with the intention, in the long run, of establishing a centre with steam-train rides etc. There was nobody to be seen working there and I didn't go and explore the yards and buildings. But what a lonely and unfrequented spot to attempt such a venture.

I had been unable to obtain the 2½" map of this area and made do with the Landranger instead. This didn't matter a great deal because I was sticking to the road today and tomorrow, but on the following day I would have a few miles north from Hawick to contend with before getting onto the Selkirk map which I already had. Heck, why am I worrying? Although I much prefer the 2½" map, I have walked with the Landranger before now and survived.

My brother Geoffrey had lent me a booklet about Scottish Hill Tracks and the only one I came anywhere near considering using was the one that led over the hills to the west of where I was. To take to these lonely hills would have meant a fairly big shift in my mental approach - like being braver and more adventurous. The somewhat meagre information I had didn't seem to be replicated very obviously on either the maps or the ground. Perhaps the clincher was that I would have had to have gone further than I intended before returning to Newcastleton. The road takes the easiest route through the hills and I was still minded of my determination to achieve my ultimate goal, and ignore enticing side routes, which in this case didn't seem very enticing at all. Thanks anyway, Geoff.

I carried on for a mile or so and decided it was time for lunch. As I cast about for a suitable spot, some unsuitable spots arrived in the form of rain. I was in an area of forest that had been felled recently and there were huge stacks of cut logs waiting to be carted away. I struggled my way across a rutted, muddy track to reach a solitary, small, unfelled fir tree and sat myself down on long grass under its meagre shelter to eat my bits and pieces. The shower didn't last long and I was soon back on the road. As the road started to descend more views opened up to the north and my mental horizon broadened, giving me just a few moments of reflection on the enormity of my walk, whilst not in any way detracting from the enjoyment of the moment. The showers came and went as I passed Langburnshiels and at Shankend Farm I crouched half under a small structure at the drive end where bins and such were standing, to escape the worst of a momentary heavy squall.

I was now having to decide how far I dared to continue before stopping and taking the bus back. I didn't want to ask it to stop in an unsuitable place, but I did want to get as many miles under my belt today as I could, thus reducing tomorrow's effort. I did stop eventually at a road junction just north of South Berryfell. I had found out that there was a 1550 bus from Hawick and I stopped walking just before four o'clock. I waited for a little while and sure enough, along came the bus. I stuck my hand out and the bus pulled up. I climbed aboard, thinking the bus was perhaps just a little early, and it turned out I was on the school bus, but the driver wasn't bothered. The scheduled service was some minutes behind. On such an infrequently served route it seemed strange to have two buses so close together. I realised that the driver must know the route to an inch as we sped, almost too fast for (my) comfort, down the valley after Whitrope Summit, with an unguarded drop on one side and a steep bank up on the other. The parapet walls of the little bridge above Whitropefoot, where the road switches to having the stream on its right, must have breathed a sigh of relief as we hurtled across, with only a whisker to spare on either side. I was soon back in the cosy friendliness of the hotel.

Friday 22nd May
South Berryfell to Hawick - 6.0 miles

In the morning I took the non-school scheduled bus service back up over the hill and got off at the spot where I got on yesterday. The day was fine and fairly warm. It became warmer as I descended into the valley of the unappetisingly named Slitrig Water. This was pleasant walking along a not too busy road, with occasional cottages and gardens to peer at. At one point I noticed a line of ash trees which were still quite determinedly not yet open. They stand out quite bare compared with the other trees. As I entered the outskirts of Hawick a few spots of rain began then came to nothing. I found my way to a café, Brydon's café, and received my lunch order just seconds before the place was inundated with schoolchildren coming in for their carry-out snacks.

This was a very short walking day and Hawick, pronounced Hoick, was the biggest place I had been in since Chorley a fortnight before. I had posted maps ahead to my B and B but I needed one or two more. It was a time for re-grouping and re-stocking. One of my worries had been getting to grips with the fact of Scotland not having its rights of way marked on the maps. I don't think it actually has 'Rights of Way' because you can walk anywhere you like that isn't obviously private. My point is that I need to be able to *see* rights of way marked on the map, as in England, so that I can plan a route through fields and woods and be reasonably sure that I will come out the other end. One can see where a track or path is marked on a Scottish map and could plan to walk along that route, but there might come a point where the path becomes private land or someone's back garden and one might have to turn back. Similarly, on the ground one might find an enticing path that seems to lead off in the right direction, but again one might be thwarted and have to waste time turning round and coming back. It's a nice idea to feel that one can roam where one wants to, but I found it a little frustrating not being able to do the forward planning.

I pottered about the town and did most of my little jobs. I rather liked Hawick. The architecture seemed solid and elegant. One curving street in particular reminded me of Edinburgh. The dominant feature is the big clock-towery building halfway along the main street. At one end of this main street is a statue of a man, mounted on a horse and triumphantly carrying a flag. I liked the artistic element of the work, which I thought was well done, but I thought the reason for it seemed a little over the top. My knowledge of Scottish history is almost non-existent, so I am not well placed to judge the idea behind the statue. The inscription said, *'Erected to Commemorate the Return of Hawick Gallants from Hornshole in 1514 when after the Battle of Flodden they routed the English marauders and captured their flag'.* My interpretation of that was that some brave people fought at the battle of Flodden and when it was over some guys on horses came out from Hawick, chased after some English stragglers and did them in and brought home the flag. It sounded rather a tame affair and hardly worthy of such a well-wrought statue. I think I subsequently noticed, over the next few weeks, a few other examples of statues or plaques that seemed to have been erected for the slightest reason. Perhaps the Scots feel a need to sing their own praises. And why not.

Some years previously, having completed my walk along The Alternative Pennine Way, I was making my way home from Jedburgh, and I had to change buses in Hawick before going on to Carlisle. I picked up the local paper and it was full of the controversy about what I think are called the Riding Outs. There seemed to be two rival camps, basically the forward thinking group and the diehard traditionalists. I think the diehards were against the idea of women having a particular role in the tradition. From what I gathered it all seemed a bit old-fashioned and unnecessarily combative. Some days later, on my way to Innerleithen, and here I get a little ahead of myself, I was sitting in the Ballantyne Memorial Club at Walkerburn and mentioned Hawick and a kind gentleman told me more about the ritual. It seems that each year an unmarried man is chosen to be the 'Cornet' who leads the Ride-Out. He has to choose his 'Lass' to accompany him. There was/is a particular man who has been putting himself in the position of not getting married in case he is chosen to be the Cornet. I think the previous argument had been because they wouldn't allow a woman to be the Cornet. I may be quite wrong about all this, so don't take my word for it. He went on to tell me that he thought Hawick was a terrible place because it is so insular. He quoted to me what I have read since elsewhere, "A man from Hawick might be heard to say that, 'A day out of Hawick is a day wasted'".

I found my way to the B and B and later sauntered back into town to eat a Chinese meal at 'The Laughing Buddha'. How cosmopolitan is that? I toyed with the idea of going to the cinema but there wasn't anything I especially wanted to see and it seemed a shame to waste a lovely evening by sitting indoors. Having had good relations with all the folk I met today, this 'English Marauder' eventually returned to a comfy bed for a good night's sleep.

Saturday 23rd May
Hawick to Selkirk - 13.1 miles

I got away from the B and B by 0915 and almost immediately started climbing out of the town. The road was steep and it went on and on. This was probably the stiffest climb of any size since leaving the Severn Valley at Buildwas to climb to Little Wenlock, and that was weeks ago. I was following the Borders Abbeys Way and for several miles I was using the Landranger map. After Sunnybank the path took to the fields and I hoped I was going the right way. I *do* prefer the 2½" map because micro-navigation becomes much easier. I *imagine* sometimes that I feel almost helpless without one. However, things worked out alright and the path became more obvious over Drinkstone Hill. Then I was into the forest on a grassy, and in places slightly soggy, path and somewhere along that stretch I was back onto the Explorer. "What a relief!" he said with mock thankfulness.

The Way descended a little to cross Ale Water and after passing a paddock with a mare and foal I found myself on a golf course. It was Saturday morning and there were plenty of people about with whom to bandy puns. I think you heard them all the other day at Appleby. Climbing again I came out onto a lane at Wollrig. Just a short way up the lane, as I gradually climbed to over 1000 feet, the views broadened out and I had a good view back at The Cheviots.

My notebook records, "The Cheviot itself looks bloody big compared with the rest, but then it *is* big"!

The day had been pretty overcast with plenty of cloud and it was cold, but now it started to spit with rain and at the top of the hill I found a delectably dry and cosy spot under a fir tree - my second lunch under a Christmas tree in three days. It overhung beautifully and I felt myself wrapped in a nestlike shelter. This was indeed the best bad weather lunch spot so far on the walk. The rain increased in intensity and became a heavy shower, which conveniently lasted no longer than it took me to eat my lunch.

Emerging from my cocoon I went to have a look at the nearby Bishops Stone which stood unassumingly not far from the road. I don't recall why it was there, or even whether there was an information board beside it. I soon turned off the road and the Borders Abbeys Way seemed to have gained an additional name which was the Buccleuch County Ride. I waltzed gaily down the broad track and after a while started looking for the turning I knew I should take to the left. After a careful and somewhat bemused study of, yes - you guessed it - my 2½" map, I realised I had happily missed the turning about a quarter of a mile back. I trudged back up the slope and got back onto the correct route again. As I have said before, reading the map is one thing and reading the ground is another. On occasions, never the twain shall meet!

The Way took me gently downhill to Middlestead where I joined a lane and a couple of miles later I was on the main A7 south of Selkirk. On the way I had passed a portion of forest that had been newly felled. A promontory of un-felled trees remained in a curving crescent, their tall, straight, orangey-brown trunks, uncluttered by side branches, giving a sense of clean verticality. The whole effect was distinctly sculptural and I wondered whether the guys who worked there ever stood back and admired their artistic handiwork. It wasn't long before I was in Selkirk and found my B and B on the main road. I had an evening meal at a restaurant in the town. My notebook reminded me that I needed to ring Bridge of Orchy Hotel to sort out my accommodation for a fortnight hence.

It was good to have gotten some softer soggy bits under my feet today instead of miles of tarmac. A couple of times in the last two days I have referred to being over a thousand feet high. Compared with much of the low level walking in England, to comment on the fact of being so high up seems rather daring. Almost nonsense, really, because where we live in Buxton we are about 1010 feet above sea level.

Sunday 24th May
Selkirk to Innerleithen - 13.6 miles

I didn't really get going until about 1000 on this quiet Sunday morning. I found a zigzaggy way from the town centre down to the river and then went over a bridge to reach the A707. It was bright and sunny and despite some traffic it was a joy to be out in the fresh air. After about three miles I came across a handsome beech tree leaning over the road. Even from some way up the road it seemed to be a beech tree and yet not a beech tree. Upon closer inspection it was clear that the leaves were definitely different - more angular and pointed - but in all other respects the tree *was* a beech tree. Upon my return home I consulted my friend Leonora, an expert tree-person, and she said that there is a hybrid that one finds occasionally. I had never seen one before, but what I found intriguing was that from 100 yards away the jizz was different, even though the overall shape was typical beech and it was only the leaf shape that made the difference.

Soon after this fascinating encounter I found myself at Yair Bridge which spans the River Tweed. I had been wondering whether I might find a pub, or even a café, in the near vicinity, but from what I saw there did not seem to be much on offer. However, I was aware that the river was in use as a canoe slalom course and that a nearby field was full of tents and that there were lots of folk milling about. It didn't take me long to discover that I had come across a National Canoe Slalom event and that the participants were being fed their lunch from a nearby building. I got into conversation with some of the people and I was invited to join the queue, which I did, and received, gratis, a coffee and a bun. These were outdoory, friendly folk and whilst I know little or nothing about canoeing, four or five of them were eager to hear all about my adventure while I sipped my drink. I tend to respect the comments of people who spend their time out of doors in active pursuits, as I feel they have a better understanding, compared with the casual 'man in the street', about what I was doing and why. As I progressed northwards I was aware of different reactions to my telling folk where I was going. Some thought it was quite commonplace - lots of people do it, but other folk were amazed. I guess the further north you go, as the possible routes narrow down a bit, then it is much more likely that folk take less notice of one's 'wonderful achievement'.

Crossing back over the bridge I saw some large flowers on the river bank which I was unable at the time to identify, but which I later discovered to be Pyrenean valerian. It was a good day for flowers overall, with 73 different flowers seen, easily the biggest daily total so far. I walked along the Southern Upland Way for all of a third of a mile and saw some excellent rhododendrons in the garden of a large house. It is nearly two months since I was admiring rhododendrons in bloom in Cornwall. The little lane became a track which led me pleasantly to Peel. I was glad not to be on the main road across the valley. It was here that I was reminded of Cornwall again, because I came across, outside someone's garden, what I thought I definitely recognized as a three-cornered leek, a lovely white flower with a three-sided stalk which I thought was almost exclusively confined to Cornwall. In fact, my notebook records the words I said to myself at the time: "Well I'm b---ered"! It was the first flower I recorded, within minutes of leaving my B and B at

Goosanders on the River Tweed

Sculptured trees near Selkirk

Sennen Cove, and I saw it on eight of the next nine days, all in Cornwall, and never saw it again until now. I assumed it had to be a garden escape, but that is not to belittle the floral abundance that I enjoyed in the Tweed Valley. Almost immediately after, I heard another cuckoo.

By now the track had become a lane again, but it was quite excellently quiet and peaceful and I felt really happy and calm, being in such beautiful surroundings. It was high time to stop for my picnic and as I came up a slight rise I could see a man sitting on a grassy tump just over the wall from the lane. He was finishing his lunch and by the time I came level he was climbing back over the low wall to get to his bicycle. He had come out from Edinburgh and this was his first proper ride this year. He told me that some years ago he had cycled from Land's End to John O'Groats in 10 days, averaging 103 miles a day. We had a good little chat, but after he had gone on I climbed the wall and went and sat on his grassy tump and ate my very late lunch. Sitting here afforded me a magnificent view down the valley. The weather was warm with the gentlest of breezes and I think I have to rate this as one of the best lunch spots of the whole walk.

Reluctantly moving on I noticed, down into and across the valley, the contrast between trees in full leaf beside the river and only a little higher up the hillside the ash trees still looking grey and bare. The delightful back lane I had been following eventually led me down to a bridge over the Tweed and I found myself in the village of Walkerburn. There were plenty of people clutching drinks, milling around happily outside the Ballantyne Memorial Club and I edged my way into the interior in search of a cold drink. The place was full of community jollity as it seemed that Rangers had just beaten Dundee 3-0. I didn't quite establish whether Rangers had won the cup or whether it was just a semi-final. I sat in a quieter back room where a kind gentleman told me of the riverside path that I could follow to Innerleithen. (It was whilst talking to him that

I mentioned Hawick and he told me what I wrote about a couple of days ago).

Notwithstanding the interest in football on the telly in the club, and despite the fact that this was only a smallish village, I noticed that there were *two* rugby pitches. As I walked along beside the river, with hawthorn trees heaving with may blossom, I was delighted to watch a parent goosander shepherding nine pretty, tiny goosanderlings, with their brown heads and zebra-striped sides, as they bobbed about on the water. This long riverbank mile was absolutely idyllic in the late afternoon sunshine and contributed wonderfully to the many blessings of the day. I found my way to the Guest House on the main road, without difficulty and had an evening meal in a noisy pub in the town. 700 miles now done!

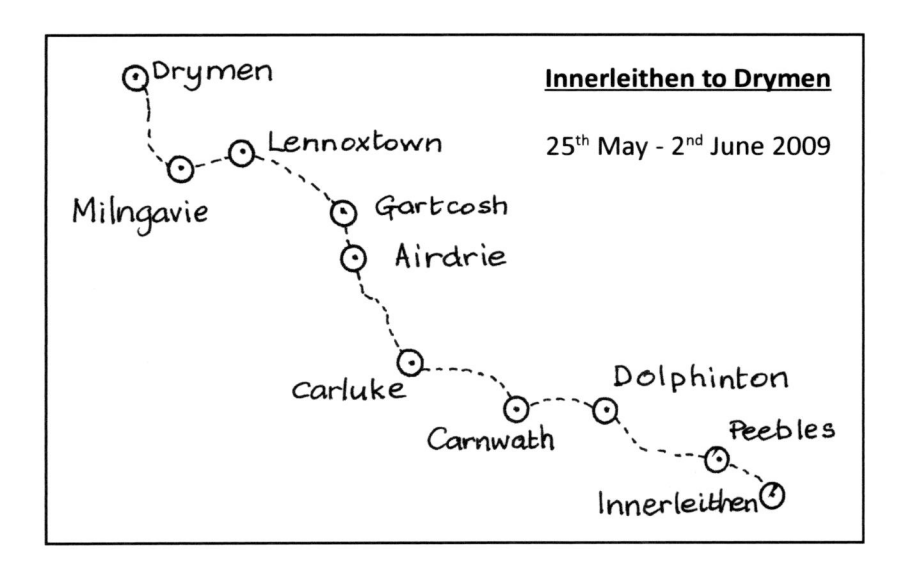

Innerleithen to Drymen

25th May - 2nd June 2009

Innerleithen to Drymen.

Monday 25th May
Innerleithen to Peebles - 9.3 miles

I wasn't really very chuffed with the Guest House I stayed in. I had a tiny room for which I paid rather more than I thought it was worth. The guy running the place was pleasant enough but too talkative and breakfast was served very slowly and lackadaisically. The saving grace was having interesting talks with a couple from Brussels who walked 1000 miles in 66 days to the south of France, albeit in fortnightly stages over several years.

I decided to keep off the main road on the north side of the river so went along by quieter lanes which took me past Traquair House. This is Scotland's oldest inhabited house and has been visited by twenty-seven kings. I went up a drive leading to the house and as I crossed a bridge over a stretch of water I found myself being accompanied by a hedgehog travelling in the same direction. It didn't seem to be too bothered by my presence and obligingly let me take a picture of it. At the house it was too early in the day for the hustle and bustle of visitors and a lassie I spoke to said that the coffee shop wasn't open yet. I didn't mind. I poddled on along the lane, at one stage passing close to the river for about half a mile. I had an early lunch sitting on a log in a field near White Bridge. Soon after that I was at the outskirts of Peebles and eventually arrived in the town proper by about half-past two.

A very helpful man in the bookshop gave me good advice about the route out of Peebles, which I did subsequently find most useful. My notebook seems to have several organisational notes concerning what Ann needed to send to the B and B at Carluke, a few days away yet. Ann had met me on four occasions so far, bringing welcome changes of clothes and fresh batches of maps etc, and

I was to meet her only once more, at Drymen, at the end of the first day of the West Highland Way. Before I left home I had prepared bundles of maps, all labelled, which Ann either had to bring or post ahead.

I don't think I have said much so far about my clothing and gear. I tried to travel as light as possible, by my standards, and not to carry unnecessary stuff. Around my loins I wore very light underwear which gave me all the support I wanted and was easy to wash each night and was dry in the morning. This was a stretchy light nylon fabric which I found really comfortable and never had any chafing. Such a garment was not easily found amongst any range of clothing designed for males. I clad my upper body in a long-sleeved Icebreaker 200 weight shirt. This was made of merino wool and was very warm and breathable. Two slight drawbacks - they were only available in black and the rather stiff bit of fabric that housed the zip would sometimes rub my chest, just slightly annoyingly. I wore one and carried another. The idea was to keep one 'dry' for evenings and wear the other, but the swop didn't always take place because I had such dry weather most of the time. I had four altogether and Ann would bring or post me the other two at intervals. On top of that I wore a North Face fleece jacket with good pockets and a full-length zip down the front. This was a really comfortable and warm garment and kept very light showers and speckles of rain at bay very well. I had a second identical jacket, except for the colour which Ann brought to swop. I also carried a very lightweight Montane Pertex top. This was yellow and excellently windproof. I wore Regatta trousers which were splendidly quick-drying and also had about seven useful pockets. On my feet I mostly wore Marks and Spencer sports socks and Asics trainers. I carried a spare pair of trainers for 'posh'. If I could have found something other than trainers for evening use my pack might have been a little lighter.

To keep the rain at bay I had Berghaus over-trousers and a rather old anorak jacket which had served me well for many years. It was pretty well on its last legs and I ditched it at Fort William and treated myself to a Mountain Equipment jacket which has been excellent. I had a white sunhat with a white hanky pinned to the back to cover my neck. I rarely really exposed my skin to elements. I wanted to avoid too much sunburn and to minimise the intrusion of ticks. In retrospect I probably was a bit too over-fussy about this as I do like to feel the air around my legs. I did carry a pair of black lycra shorts which I wore on a few occasions when it was very sticky and hot.

I had soap powder in 35mm film canisters, suncream for my hands and face, a fairly minimal first-aid kit, compass, whistle, torch, mobile phone charger, camera battery charger, penknife with a marlin spike (hardly ever used it) and a special device for removing sheep ticks (never used it). I also had a very convenient 'bum-bag' around my waist which did nothing to improve my already un-sylphlike profile. But look ……. No Sat Nav. No pedometer.

I had an evening meal in a Chinese restaurant - duck and pineapple - rather nice. I liked Peebles and hope to return sometime.

Tuesday 26th May
Peebles to Dolphinton - 12.5 miles

I got away from the B and B by half-past eight and after a quick dip into a shop for provisions was on my way through a park and then along a riverside path. I enjoyed good scenery and I had a few joggers and dog walkers for company. After a mile or so I came to an old railway track, now used as a bridleway, and this I followed for a couple of miles to Lynesmill Bridge. This was the way recommended by the friendly guy in the bookshop and was very easy and pleasant.

I was now obliged to walk along the A72 for the rest of the morning. The traffic wasn't overly excruciating and I was able to make steady progress without too many leaps onto the grass verge. Some stretches were very straight and this could have been disheartening, but I dipped into some of my fortitude and made the best of it. I was walking against a blustery breeze which was scouring down the strath, but it was bright enough with a hint of showers. After a while, sure enough along came the shower. I had time to cross to the 'wrong' side of the road where there was a steepish bit of bank and sat down among the grass and pulled my knees up to my chin and hunched there, virtually untouched by the short-lived downpour. As I think I mentioned in Cornwall, there's nothing like a little bit of adversity to put one on one's mettle and make you cheerful.

Lyne Water, which had been on my right, gave way to its tributary, Tarth Water, and the surrounding hills made a lovely backdrop. I stopped for my lunch where a track came in from the left and sat under some hazel trees on a grassy bank. Whilst eating along came another sudden burst of rain. Again I did my hunching up trick, with my anorak round my shoulders and stayed dry inside my little cocoon.

I carried on until I finally reached the junction with the A701 near Blyth Bridge. I turned away from the village and then shortly after onto a lesser road leading to Dolphinton. This was much quieter. I paused as I passed along the edge of a wood and, lo and behold, along came another shower. Again I was well sheltered by the overhanging trees and the squall soon passed. Near Newmill there was a most excellent display of bistort and a sign informed me that I was entering South Lanarkshire.

At the A702 I turned left to drag all the way through the village and some way beyond to reach my B and B. This is a much busier road which provides a main link from the M74 to Edinburgh. Ann and I have used it on visits to Caroline in Edinburgh - it did seem slightly familiar. Luckily there was a pavement most of the way. I arrived at about 1615 and my B and B host, Ian, invited me to make use of the hot tub round at the back of the building. I sat there for half an hour looking out over the fields to distant woods and listening to the birds singing. I had a playmate in the tub, a little plastic duck. It did tricks - swimming backwards, going round in circles and hiding in the foam. After a bit it got tired of me and so I retreated indoors and was given an evening meal by Carole. They were both interested to hear of my adventure and Ian, who was, I think, a retired farmer, told me about *his* adventure, which he had undertaken some time previously, which involved travelling around, as near as he could manage, the 'coast' of Scotland, on a quad-bike with a covered cab. I am glad to find other daft people occasionally.

This has been a cool day with a lot of unremitting tarmac but I seem to have survived without hitting any lows.

Wednesday 27th May
Dolphinton to Carnwath - 9.8 miles

Carole told me the best way to go was "up between the two hills, there'll be a nice view". I followed her directions from the B and B and found my way up a track, through a wood and onto open hillside. After a short climb I came through the pass between 'the two hills' and there was the view. I was looking mainly north-west and the country ahead was rather flat and it looked pretty empty. This viewpoint, between Windlestraw Top and White Hill, is called Charlie's Bower. I can only assume that Charlie refers to the Bonny Prince and that this was somewhere that he camped on some excursion or other. Good look-out point to the north-west anyway.

The day was rather grey and overcast and threatening rain, but the few drizzly spots that came never lasted long. Going down the hillside I found a beautiful patch of yellow mountain pansies. They were arranged in a rough ring, like a fairy ring of toadstools. I've seen mountain pansies lots of times but never in a ring. It may have been a coincidence or there may have been some specific reason why they were arranged thus. I have seen mountain pansies which are yellow and some which are purple and some a mixture. I always associate the purple ones with the northern Pennines - I have seen lots around the Alston area, for example. I have seen the yellow ones in the Peak District, although I have found one field, not far from home, where there are yellow ones and purple ones and two colours on the same flower. I have assumed, in a rather over-simplistic way, that the further north you go the more likely you are to find the purple ones. They were very beautiful just the same. A mile further on I came across several of the 'northern' laburnum trees that I had previously seen a mile or so out of Armathwaite a week or so earlier. Leonora, or the faithful Blamey, will tell me when I get home.

I passed through Dunsyre and there didn't seem to be a soul about - very quiet. Having flirted, visually and ambulatorily with the Pentland Hills, after Dunsyre I felt I was leaving them behind. A little further on I stopped to watch some forestry operations. I was intrigued by a giant machine that seemed to swallow - horizontally - a whole tree trunk and strip it of its side branches and spit it out clean the other end. I think it did several other clever things as well but I was too far away to see properly how it managed to do it. As I plodded on, the gradients were easy and the lane extremely quiet. I stopped and ate my picnic near Weston, sitting on a grassy bank beside the road. Another couple of miles took me to the village of Newbigging. I felt a little in need of warming up so I went into the Nestlers Hotel and had a coffee and a scone with jam. The folk there were very solicitous and friendly and were interested to hear about my journey.

I have often made reference to having elevenses and lunches. These were not always just moments for eating, but for pondering over the rest of the day's navigation. Whilst eating an evening meal in a pub or restaurant I would often be reading a book or doing a crossword, before returning to the B and B or wherever, to deal with the rather time-consuming tasks of the evening.

I had now joined the A721 a rather busier main road, but it was an easy enough couple of miles into Carnwath. I stayed at a B and B called the Carnwath Vineyard run by a lovely couple called George and Beth. They were very welcoming and I immediately felt at home. I don't know whether to refer to Carnwath as a small town or a large village. It was, perhaps, momentarily disconcerting to see graffiti that said 'F--- the polis'. At least I recognised that I was definitely in Scotland as far as spelling was concerned. 'The Wee Bush Inn', a charming old inn on the main street, was a cosy place to enjoy a good meal. They were short-staffed that evening and the young lassie who served me was rushed off her feet with lots of customers, but she bravely kept her head and her temper and was a credit to the establishment.

Thursday 28th May
Carnwath to Carluke - 9.6 miles

In the morning I was invited to sign the Guest Book, which I did. The entry from the day before said, 'Lovely people. Good B and B. Only stayed because I lost my motorhome!' George and Beth were able to fill me in with what this meant. A man had turned up on his motorbike at 1130pm and asked Beth if there was a room available. It so happened that there was, so he booked it. In the morning he explained what his entry in the Guest Book meant. It seems he lives in Tunbridge Wells with his mother and he had arranged to buy a motorhome from a place in Scotland called Inch. He had driven up to Scotland on his motorbike and been to Inch and bought his motorhome. He shoved his motorbike in the back and started driving south. On his way through the countryside he was very taken with the scenery and as it was a nice afternoon he pulled into a lay-by, got out his motorbike, and his camera and started taking pictures. He drove around on his bike for some time, enjoying the scenery. After a while he thought he would return to the lay-by but couldn't figure out where it was. He drove around for 3½ hours in the gathering gloom and still couldn't find his motorhome. He ended up ringing the bell at Carnwath Vineyard B and B. Having listened to this tale, George said to him, "Let me see your pictures". The first picture was of the motorhome in the lay-by. George was able to identify the location quite easily and eventually, with fresh instructions, this chap went off on his motorbike to find his motorhome. George and Beth presumed he found it and that he then drove it back to Tunbridge Wells - where he works as a taxi-driver! I loved this story, although, strictly speaking, it is not 'my' story, but I couldn't resist including it in this account.

Having recounted to numerous folk several of the amusing tales I had collected along the way, I was told by someone, before I had even got halfway, that when I got home I 'would be able to work the WI circuit'. I enjoyed listening to snippets of other people's tales as I went along. I didn't *always* disclose to folk I met that I was walking from Land's End to John O'Groats.

I popped into the Co-op in the village to buy provisions and to top-up my mobile. As I left the friendly assistant said, "See you again!" I said that I was walking from Land's End to John O'Groats and that it would be unlikely that I would be in again, so she said, "See you on the way back, then!" Cheeky, but very cheering. I carried on along the main road for half a mile or so and reached the bridge over the main railway line to Edinburgh from Carlisle, which at this point is not far from Carstairs Junction. I turned northwards on a minor road and then left along Whiteloch Road, which shortly passed beside White Loch. I was intrigued to discover a flower I didn't immediately identify. The marshy margins of the loch lapped almost against the road and there was a yellow flower which I reckoned I had never seen before. When I got home I identified it as a celery-leaved buttercup.

The area hereabout was pretty flat and I passed a works where machines were removing what was left of Ryeflat Moss. This is a peat bog and various machines were moving up and down extracting the peat. The surface that was being worked seemed to be about six feet below the surrounding ground level. I wondered how much deeper the excavation might go. The road surface was uneven and affected by subsidence, no doubt due to the soggy, boggy nature of the ground across which it was laid. I carried on over Westshield Bridge and then left to pass Muirhouse and to reach the A706 near Westertown. After a while I stopped and ate my lunch, sitting under some trees beside the road near Easterseat. The countryside was very empty and quiet with only very occasional passing vehicles. The Southern Uplands are definitely starting to disappear behind me.

I dawdled on gently and at Yieldshields a gentleman was happy to spare time from tending his garden to come and have a chat. We must have got on to the 'Hazards of the Highlands' and I have to admit that I had some unresolved anxieties about ticks and midges. I knew I wanted to lay my hands on Avon Skin So Soft but hadn't managed to find any yet. This man said he swore by Avon Skin So Soft for keeping midges at bay. When I said, "Where can I find the nearest Avon lady?" he didn't rise to the bait and rush indoors and decant some of his bottle for me. A little later on I sat on the grass in the middle of the village but couldn't really settle to relaxing. It wasn't really hot enough to lie back and bask.

Soon enough I was down at the main road - the A721. I had chosen the quiet route through the back lanes in order to avoid this busy road and am glad I did. I did have to endure the pavementless perils of the main road for a quarter of a mile to Burnhead Farm where I received a very warm welcome. I had my evening meal at a Chinese restaurant just a little way back down the road again.

I see from my notebook that I was undecided about my route the next day. I was to spend two nights with friends in central Glasgow and I spent some time this evening pondering over which railway station to aim at to take a train into the city. I had my eye on the station at Holytown, but... that's tomorrow. A gentleman who was also staying at the B and B told me that he was at Eton with Ranulph Fiennes, who was recently in the news, having climbed Everest at the age of 76.

Friday 29th May
Carluke to Airdrie - 15.7 miles

I set off at 0825 to walk the 1½ miles into Carluke town centre. The road was streaming with children on their way to school. I waited a short while for the Post Office to open, made a few purchases and was soon on my way out of town northwards along the pavement beside the A73. I knew I was going to walk through a lot of urban areas today. I knew it would almost certainly be pavements and roads. I knew I wouldn't mind. After a long couple of miles I turned left and came to Waterloo. A friendly lady in a corner shop provided me with a coffee and an iced fruit slice. I sat on a seat near the War Memorial and enjoyed the warm sunshine. Having had several cool days recently this was a welcome change.

Carrying on I cut across the corner of a park - a welcome few minutes on grass instead of tarmac. Unfortunately, my route did not take me through nearby Gowkthrapple - what an intriguing name! The route I *did* take was through the eastern side of Wishaw then along and down a nice wooded bit to cross Coltness Bridge. On the way I popped into a garage to see if they had any drinks for sale, and the old man there, hearing of my long trek said, "Just take your time". He was definitely on my wavelength. It felt like lunchtime when I reached Cleland. I tried the butty bar but the queue was far too long. Kelly's Bar 'didn't do food today', so I went into the fish and chip shop and had two fish cakes and a coffee, which I consumed outside on a convenient seat. The man in the chip shop informed me that 'Ben Nevis is *that* way'.

I had a bit of fun amusing myself a little way out of Cleland. I came across one of those road signs that light up when a vehicle approaches. This one lit up with a left hand bend picture inside a red triangle and then changed to 'SLOW DOWN'. I waited for a car to come along - the thing doesn't work with pedestrians, even rucksack laden ones - and when the 'Bend' sign appeared I took a photo of it. Then when another car came along I took a picture of the 'Slow Down' sign. These two pictures are now stuck side by side in my scrapbook with the wording altered slightly to read "Ben - Slow Down". But of course I am going pretty slowly already. Like the old man said, "Take your time".

I came on through Newarthill and along Legbrannock Road to reach the A775. I was confronted with a large industrial estate which blocked my direct line, so had to do two sides of a triangle to get round it. Some days or weeks earlier I had tried to book a B and B in Chapelhall, but was unsuccessful. I had by now arranged to stay in central Glasgow and the question was which railway station to aim for to take me there. I had thought that Holytown might fit the bill, but I found I had made better progress than expected, so I pressed on. Every mile today is a mile less tomorrow. The afternoon was becoming very hot and my sun hat with its pinned on white hanky to protect my neck provoked occasional honks and hoots from passing motorists. It was long straight trudge into Chapelhall. The pavements were crowded and I went into the Post Office to enquire about the mechanics of Poste Restante, with a view to the possibility of using this service. In the end I never did use it, and relied on Ann sending stuff to me at B and Bs.

I have been amazed at how little rain I have had. With hindsight I know that today was the fifth day into a three week spell with no rain at all. My rough calculations a day or two before had led me to believe that 93% of my 'walking time' so far had been in the dry. I amused myself by thinking that I would try and get that up to 100% by the time I reached the end of my walk! In fact it was 94%. I wondered at the time, and have asked people since, what would be a reasonable percentage of time spent walking in the rain on a long distance walk, in the spring and early summer, where you are obliged to be out day after day regardless. Answers received have varied from 50% of the time to 5%. I reckoned the more knowledgeable the person was about walking, the lower was the percentage. 50% seemed to me to be much too high. 20% rain seemed more reasonable and others were fairly insistent that it wouldn't ever be more than 10%. A friend in Bristol told me that he cycles to work every day and he thought it was only 5% at the most. My feeling was that I was experiencing well below an average and that I was being incredibly lucky. However, later on this very hot day, I spoke to a postman about this matter and he said he thought it would be raining about 40% of the time when he was working. If true, I guess he must be one unlucky postman.

After another two or three miles I reached Airdrie and finished my walking at about 1615. I pottered about and then went to the station and caught a train into Glasgow. I spent the night, and the next night, as guest of my friend Barbara, who lives with Max in the flat above the big Quaker Meeting House in central Glasgow. I was well looked after and had an interested audience for my stories.

It was today that I had the idea for the title of this account, taking precedence over "The Long Spring" and "The Long Spring Walk".

Saturday 30th May
Airdrie to Gartcosh - 7.2 miles

This was to be a day, like yesterday, with an open-ended destination. The only requirement would be that it was at a railway station. I was carrying a light pack and the mileage was likely to be small so it looked like it would be quite an easy day. The bonus was that I was to be walking with Caroline, the youngest of our three daughters. She lives and works in Edinburgh and as this was a Saturday it was fortuitous for us both that she was able to join me. I met Caroline off the Edinburgh train at Queen Street and we took the train out to Airdrie. We spent an enjoyable time in a baker's shop choosing our lunch. The highlight was a couple of individual rhubarb tarts which disappeared into a rucksack and reappeared at lunchtime in a crumbly, sticky mess. However, they tasted good.

We didn't really start walking proper until about eleven-thirty. We worked our way through streets and down through a housing estate. We came across a man leaning on his garden gate. He had been watching us coming down the street and asked me why I was limping. I told him a little about my condition and my adventure, but he soon took over the conversation and told us about his 39 years down the pit. "Where ye fae?" he asked me. Caroline translated this. I told him where I was from. "I like your twang", he continued. Caroline translated again. He rattled on and I understood about one word in ten. I have always thought that the Glaswegian accent is, by and large, thicker and stronger than the rather genteel and lighter tones to be found in Edinburgh. I guess an Airdrie accent might count as similar to that of Glasgow. It was great fun listening to him talking and we had a job to tear ourselves away. We found our way into quiet lanes that upped and downed through pretty countryside. The weather was bright, sunny and very hot. We found a shady spot near a field entrance and sat down to enjoy our lunch, sticky crumbs and all.

Wandering on, we found some clumps of Star of Bethlehem growing by the roadside, not seen since north Cumbria. At Glenboig we came across a little café, I think it called itself a milk bar. We retreated inside out of the heat and consumed various thirst-quenching liquids before making our way over the M73 and into Gartcosh and found our way to the station. A train arrived a short while later and we were soon back at Queen Street. This had been a lazy, sauntering sort of day, made very special with Caroline's excellent company.

In total I had specific companions for about 36 miles, not including various folk along the West Highland Way.

I returned to the Meeting House and spent the evening there. I had not yet booked myself a place for the night at Milngavie for Monday night. I thought that there would be plenty of places to choose from, even at the last minute. However, this very Saturday evening the dear folk of the Glasgow Quaker Meeting and, no doubt, the surrounding area, were having a party right there under my nose. I felt a bit of an outsider and hovered round the fringes for a while. Word got around about my presence and it wasn't long before I was introduced to Jim and Liz, who live in Milngavie. They were delighted to offer me accommodation for Monday night and I immediately accepted. I also met Janey at the party who was, by previous arrangement, to put me up on the Sunday night. I was also trying to book up at the Kings House Hotel at the head of Glencoe for 8th June, but there was no room. There were these continuing little worries about future overnight stops, and I had to set aside time to sort them out.

Sunday 31st May
Gartcosh to Lennoxtown - 10.5 miles

After bidding farewell to Barbara and Max I made my way to Queen Street station and took a train out to Gartcosh and started walking at about 1045. This village is situated on the north-eastern fringes of Glasgow so I reckoned in north-south terms I was more than halfway past the big city. The weather was fine and sunny and became very hot. I passed by Johnston Loch and soon took a sharp right turn along Drumcavel Road. I joined the Strathkelvin Railway Path which made very pleasant walking. This old railway track was rich with may blossom - a grand treat.

I followed this track for several miles, passing Moodiesburn and Lenzie. For some distance the path was lined with temporary fencing as there was a considerable amount of civil engineering work going on, but not today, it being Sunday. Near Millersneuk I must have missed a notice informing me that the path was diverted. I could see another path, which had people walking on it, across the little valley, but the trackway ahead seemed unobstructed so I carried on. In a few hundred yards I came to an impasse with a contractor's yard or depot and diggers and huts filling up the space. The way ahead was definitely blocked off here and I contemplated going back several hundred yards and following the diversion. But I thought, "What the heck!" and clambered my way round all the excavations and muck and machinery, which involved a slight descent down a loose soil bank, then up again to rejoin the line of the old railway again on the far side of the 'works'. I was half expecting to be challenged but there was no-one around so I carried on my carefree way. The track went through a wooded area behind the backs of people's houses and this gave welcome coolth. As I came into Kirkintilloch I left the old railway and entered a corner shop in search of extra liquid refreshment. I then went and sat in the park to eat my lunch.

I meandered through the centre of the town, then through a bit more park, beside Luggie Water and eventually left the town along an old railway track, which, like the one I followed in the morning, is also used as a cycle track. There were lots of bushes and trees alongside the track and it wasn't very easy to see the surrounding scenery. I crossed the Forth-Clyde Canal and found I had another stretch of water alongside, but such was the amount of foliage I only glimpsed it occasionally. The path was a paradise of flowers and today's new sightings were yellow flag, yellow rattle, ragged robin and foxglove. The daily count was 68, second largest total since Land's End and just behind the 73 the day I walked along the Tweed valley.

At Milton of Campsie, again barely seen, the track took me more westerly for another couple of miles to Lennoxtown. At one point there was a mass of wild strawberry plants with huge flowers, the largest I have ever seen. I had little trouble finding my way to the home of Janey and Colin and their two sons.

Very early in the planning phase of this walk I had written to my old Quaker friends, John and Gisela Creed, who I knew from the time before I was married. In fact John, being a goldsmith, made our wedding rings. John is an extremely talented sculptor/artist/smith, whether it be gold, silver or black and has produced many fine works ranging from cutlery to cathedral gates. Their home in Lenzie was to have been one of my main staging posts and I had been looking forward to it. However, before I left home John emailed me to say that they had to be in Japan on the date we had booked and they wouldn't be able to entertain me after all. He went on to say that he would ask around various other Quaker folk and he would try and find me someone within a four mile radius of Lenzie. I was happy to go along with this plan and his ploy was successful - finding me Janey and Colin.

The family greeted me warmly and we got on very well with each other right from the word go. They were extremely interested to hear all about my adventure and Colin told me about some of his. He sometimes rides a motorbike and, as I remember, he has visited the four cardinal points of Great Britain. Lowestoft - east; the Lizard

- south; Ardnamurchan Point - west and Dunnet Head - North. It was good to swop yarns about our various exploits.

Monday 1st June
Lennoxtown to Milngavie - 6.3 miles

After an early breakfast I skedaddled away before half past eight, as school and work beckoned the family. The weather was fine and sunny and it was blazing hot at eight thirty on this first day of June. At the end of this short day I actually ended up further south than my starting point. Had I stayed at Lenzie with John and Gisela this might not have been the case. I particularly wanted to start the West Highland Way at Milngavie and do it all.

I climbed up a track going west, and as I gained height the Campsie Fells stood out prominently behind Lennoxtown. I had hardly seen them yesterday because of the dense foliage surrounding my path, although I knew they must be there. I joined a lane which petered out within a mile and became a rough track through forestry plantations. A man had parked his car at the end of the tarmac and was some hundred yards or so further on with a wheel barrow. At this point there was a previously felled area on the left. I stopped to talk to this man who was loading lumps of wood into his barrow and carting them back to his car. He said that he has a licence from the Forestry Commission to clear 'brush' and logs, to take away as firewood, from a designated area; and that other people have similar licences. It seemed a bit like emptying the ocean with a handful of teaspoons. I have often wondered, particularly since entering Scotland this time, what happens to felled areas of forest. The huge stumps are left lying about and the surface is stony and uneven. If the intention is to replant trees at some point in the future, what action is taken to clear the ground in readiness? How long does it 'lie fallow'? I can't remember ever having seen stumps being cleared and carted away. I seem to want to kick myself mentally for not having been observant enough in the past in my various wanderings.

I emerged from the forestry onto Blairskaith Muir, an elevated spot about 600 feet high, but giving a good view in several directions. Leaving this pleasant bit of moorland I came southwards down a path to join a track which joined a lane which took me to Baldernock. The lanes were blessed with lovely flowers, a new find today being dog rose. I also found some wild strawberries, but they were still green. Summer is obviously on its way.

The hamlet of Baldernock was bathed in sunshine and I sat down on a triangle of grass near the little kirk, with my back against the War Memorial, and did nothing for a little while. Part of me was saying, "This is no way to march towards John O'Groats," and another part of me was saying, "No, but this is the life, sitting in the sun without a care in the world". I tore myself away and carried on down a lane which led me to a delectable spot with a ford. A little further on I came to a triangular road sign which had no official wording, but a picture of a man-figure holding the hand of a female child-figure. This was a 'Beware of pedestrians' sign, but some wag had written across the bottom of the sign, 'DO YOU KNOW HIM?'

I descended into Milngavie, pronounced, I believe something like Mullgigh, soon after midday and took my time acquainting myself with the town. This started with the railway station, and I imagined that this was where many West Highland Way walkers would emerge from further afield. I followed signs into the town centre and enjoyed reading the various notices and illustrated sign boards which explained the WHW. Milngavie clearly wants to be remembered for its devotion to seeing people off properly. I had gleaned from somewhere that there was a baggage carrying service for WHW walkers and it wasn't long before I found my way to the ironmongers-cum-general store which was the nerve centre for the efficient 'Travel-Lite' run by Gilbert. I instantly made arrangements for my pack to be carried for the next nine days to Fort William, at what I thought was the very reasonable cost of £35. He gave me a small backpack to use as a day sack, but after squeezing all I wanted to carry every day into it, it seemed inadequate and not very comfy, so after a day or so I swopped it, so that I carried on with my rucksack and used his pack as the one to be transported.

I found somewhere to have lunch and then treated myself to a haircut, the first since Crediton, in Devon. I made several purchases of necessary items and my worries about the non-availability of Avon Skin So Soft to keep the midges at bay were finally and most satisfactorily allayed, because I found some in Gilbert's excellent emporium. Apparently the forestry guys buy it in five-gallon drums. Gilbert told me that about 50% of his business of baggage-carrying this spring/summer has already happened. Those who are in the know walk the West Highland Way in May before the midges get going in earnest. In fact, due to the daubing of Skin So Soft upon my person on appropriate occasions, I only had two midge bites, both on the inside of one wrist. The instant application of some Savlon cream prevented further irritation and that was all the trouble I had with them.

After a time I found my way to the very conveniently situated home of Jim and Liz who were extremely hospitable. I think they are used to putting up visitors on a fairly regular basis and I wanted for nothing. I booked up my B and B at Kinlochleven, just eight days ahead.

Tuesday 2nd June
Milngavie to Croftamie - 11.7 miles

Wanting to include the West Highland Way in my route almost went without saying in the early planning phase, because I had for many years thought to do it on its own sometime.

Well - I felt pretty good. I had done all my bits and pieces of shopping. I was in good nick. I had a lighter pack, I felt I was starting afresh on a new leg of the adventure. The absolute bonus was - the other walkers. I was on a popular, recognised route and I was no longer alone. For the first time since 20th March I was in the company of fellow walkers, with their own hopes and doubts. Folk with attitudes and aspirations similar to mine - a desire to achieve, to enjoy, to be out in the open air with wonderful scenery and a sense of satisfaction at the day's end. I was to walk the ninety-five miles of the West Highland Way in nine days. Others were to do it quicker. (Quite some years ago I walked ninety-five miles in 36 hours. But speed was not the object, neither then nor now.) Over the next nine days I was to realise how lonely I had been during the previous 73. As I walked along during those ten weeks or so, I had had no-one with whom to share what I will invent, as a convenient word, 'walk-talk'. Now I was alongside people who, if they discovered my mission, would understand why I was doing what I was doing and actually ask meaningful questions. I didn't just want a trip from one end of the country to the other, I suppose I wanted an ego-trip. I didn't want to lord it over the others who were only walking to Fort William and then going home again. I didn't mind secretly enjoying a (hopefully) well-concealed sense of smug superiority. I wanted to be carefully unassuming. I had no achievement to boast of, except for distance, but I did want to share the excitement I felt and above all to tell them of my enjoyment.

I left Milngavie town centre at 0925 and walked steadily through municipal parkland. About a third of a mile into the walk I came to an open space with what looked like a stretch of newly constructed path. Upon closer inspection I found I was looking at a thistle design made of light-coloured bricks, set into the ground at a place where several paths met. The thistle is the emblem of Scottish Long Distance paths. A council worker was putting the finishing touches to this imaginative piece of work, so I asked him if he would mind if

I took a photo of him standing beside his handiwork. He very kindly obliged, leaning on his broom.

The way gradually escaped from the park and climbed the side of a little hill and proceeded through lovely woods, where one had to beware of tree roots. After crossing the road at Craigallian Bridge the view widened slightly and then Craigallian Loch appeared on my right. I had already been passed by and had passed several groups of walkers, but near the loch I got into conversation with a chap who was stopping to look at birds. He told me a bit about birds and I told him a bit about flowers. For the next mile or so we leapfrogged each other while we stopped to study our respective interests. He was going to follow the Rob Roy Way which branches off a little further north. The vista became even wider after Easter Carbeth as the path swooped gracefully down and round some grassy knolls. The Campsie Fells now presented a rather more end-on view than the day before.

At Dumgoyach Bridge I joined the old railway line which the Way follows for several miles. It was a good day for new flowers, one being a pick-a-back plant which I spotted when looking over the parapet of the bridge. Other flowers seen for the first time today were common spotted orchid, rest-harrow, bramble, cut-leaved cranesbill, monkey musk and heath bedstraw. After nearly two miles of very pleasant old railway track I came to the Beech Tree Inn. I bought a drink and sat outside at a picnic table to eat my own fodder. If you bought food in the inn you were allowed to sit in the garden. It was just as hot wherever you sat. There were plenty of fellow walkers and a smattering of cyclists. Heard a cuckoo. After lunch I continued along the Way and then crossed what I took to be Endrick Water at Gartness.

Less than a mile later, I abandoned the West Highland Way - you did *what* I hear you cry - and continued along the railway track to Croftamie. The high level view down onto Endrick Water, here re-crossed, was delightfully pastoral. I had hoped to have found a B and B in Drymen but I was unable to book anywhere and instead was very pleased to have found 'Croftburn', which was some way out of the village along a rather too busy road. Here I was made very welcome.

Ann was to join me today for the fifth and final time. She had been holidaying for a few days with Beth and Andy in Ambleside and today she was to drive from there and round/through Glasgow to Croftamie. She was very apprehensive about the long distance and the navigation, but she is made of sterner stuff than she lets on, and she arrived safely at the B and B in good time. We drove into the village and enjoyed a meal at the pub before returning to sort out clean clothes, dirty clothes, old maps, new maps and various other little organisational tasks before retiring. This has been a very satisfying day in all sorts of respects, not least venturing onto yet another new phase of my journey.

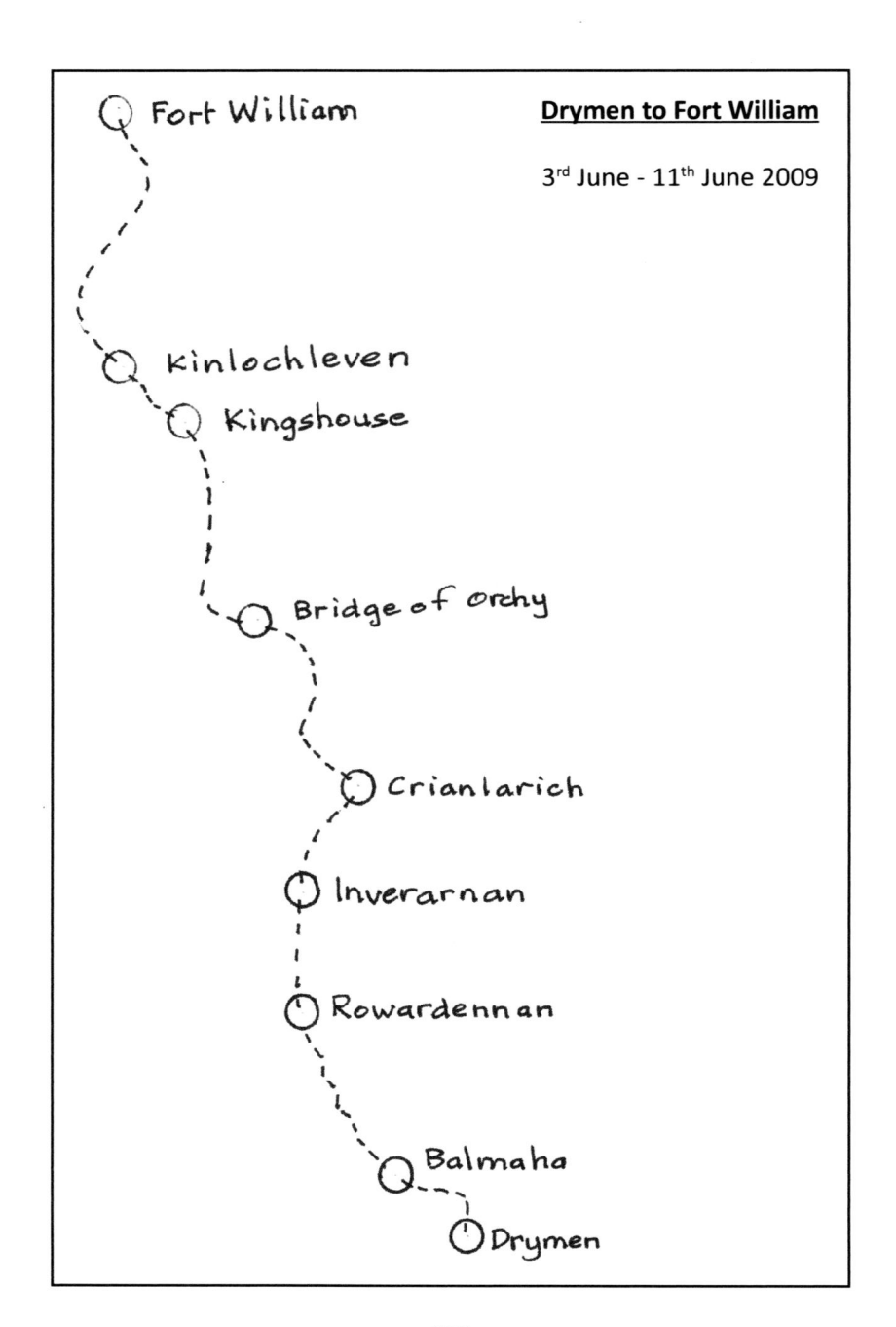

Drymen to Fort William

3rd June - 11th June 2009

- Fort William
- Kinlochleven
- Kingshouse
- Bridge of Orchy
- Crianlarich
- Inverarnan
- Rowardennan
- Balmaha
- Drymen

Drymen to Fort William

Wednesday 3ⁿᵈ June
Croftamie to Balmaha - 9.2 miles

With the benefit of the car, we drove back to the point where I left the West Highland Way yesterday and spent a minute or two in fond farewells. Ann was bravely driving back to Buxton and I was battling on to the far north. No I wasn't. I was smoothly strolling, or whatever gentle alliterative phrase springs to mind. If all goes well I won't be seeing Ann for another four weeks. That is to say, if it is going to take me another four weeks it means I will have finished my walk. I must admit to feeling rather less apprehensive about 'Scotland' than I was some weeks ago. The remainder of the WHW is still a bit of an unknown, but the actual quantity of remaining, niggling little organisational worries is diminishing day by day, thank goodness. Ann drove off with her navigational instinct intact and I, freshly attired in clean clothes, went along a leafy lane where I found, to my delight, honeysuckle growing in the hedge. My notebook records, "Honeysuckle smell - that is *so* gorgeous!!" I eventually found myself in Drymen.

I did some shopping and had some elevenses and then set off along what is labelled on my map as the Rob Roy Way. An almost parallel set of green diamonds a mile further east is also labelled Rob Roy Way, but meets the former in Queen Elizabeth Forest Park. I think there is the option for the WHW to visit Drymen, but the map labelling is ambiguous. Be that as it may, I did not retrace my steps but took the direct route up a very pleasant lane to the forest park. The broad track through the forest made easy walking and was cool enough. The cloudyish start to the day was gradually being superseded by sunshine and it was grand walking weather. Out in the open again I met a retired couple who were having their lunch. They were just out for the day and were interested to hear of my long walk. I must have mentioned that I was on day 76 from Land's End. A little further on I stopped to eat my lunch on a very convenient bit of low wall and quite soon along came this couple. The woman said, "After you had gone on I said to my husband, 'Seventy-six days he said, but look how clean his trousers are!'" I told them that they were clean on this morning! To tell the truth, my trouser bottoms stayed remarkably clean the whole way, with only minute bits of 'splat'. I cannot believe how incredibly lucky I am continuing to be with the weather.

I had picked up snippets of conversation about Conic Hill and the effort that would be involved in climbing it. I could see it ahead of me and it looked like a very interesting little climb, neither absurdly steep nor high. I approached it with equanimity and climbed it with pleasure. The delights of this mild ascent included a cuckoo, and the first marsh thistle and butterwort of the walk. Arriving at the highest point on the path the view that opened up was absolutely tremendous. There was Loch Lomond ahead and beyond that loads of mountains, the only distant one that I thought I knew being The Cobbler. Away to my right the bulk of Ben Lomond rose loftily to a summery sky. The camera was busy. My notebook records, "That is a feast for the eyes to behold!" This was probably one of the best views of the walk so far and I was certainly very pleased with my first proper taste of 'The Highlands'. Having said that the ascent of Conic Hill was an easy enough gradient, the descent to Balmaha was much steeper, but straightforward enough.

At Balmaha there was an information centre, which I hoped might provide me with a map of my route further on, to assist my B and B planning. The place was closed and I would have to return in the morning. I found my way to the B and B where I was treated to a relaxing sit in the warm garden with a pot of tea. A short evening stroll took me to the very cosy pub, the 'Oak Tree Inn', where I enjoyed my evening meal. On the way back I had my first proper encounter with midges. The loch is only a few yards away.

Thursday 4th June
Balmaha to Rowardennan - 8.1 miles

I returned to the visitor centre in the morning and was unable to find the particular map I wanted. I was trying to fix up B and B accommodation in Fort William and for the next day after that. I eventually got going just before 11am and carried on along the West Highland Way, which immediately climbed up and then immediately down again, a small hill. From then on the rest of the day was either along a loch-shore path or a little road or over the occasional shallow rise. The way was *almost* always very pretty with glimpses of water to my left, glimpses of Ben Lomond massively ahead on my right and glimpses of The Cobbler and its neighbours ahead on my left, but way beyond the loch. I say *almost* because the east side of Loch Lomond is accessible by road, at least in these southern parts. The beaches and the shore are accessible to the road; disposable barbecue sets are accessible from numerous outlets and the throwaway mentality is easily accessible through genes, upbringing and peer pressure. The shoreline in these first few miles is littered with unsightly rubbish and thrown-away disposable barbecues. These devices may not be the 21st century's best idea.

I had almost stopped fretting about the non-purchase of a map when I came across a small building, seemingly a sort of base for the Park Rangers/Wardens. Three of these gentlemen were standing outside the building so I asked them, not being quite sure what sort of an establishment it was, "Do you sell coffee?" The reply came, "No." "Do you sell maps?" says I. "No," was the answer. "Do you sell flower books?" "No," was the response, but the man continued, "we're saving you a lot of money here!" However I was advised I could try the campsite a little further on.

Passing Cashell Farm I heard yet another cuckoo. Reaching the campsite I found the shop and was just starting negotiations with the kind lady there when my mobile rang. I left the shop to answer the phone and it was the lady in Fort William that I had tried to get hold of earlier. By the time I had sorted that matter out, the shop had closed. Somewhat disconcerted by this sudden reversal of fortune I scouted round the back regions and found the kind lady who opened up the shop again so that I could - hurrah! - buy a map. My notebook indicates that I was wondering how to escape from Gairlochy at the end of my first day out from Fort William, as I would probably have to return to Fort William to find accommodation which was unobtainable at Gairlochy. Would I find a bus? A taxi? Hitch hike? These little worries all needed resolving - and of course they did eventually. More of that anon.

I ate my picnic lunch sitting by the shore in a comparatively clean little bit. The weather was slightly cloudy and the temperature varied between cool and warm. I carried on and the going was good. It was always dry underfoot, as it had been for days and days. Flowers were abundant with cow wheat - a very deep yellow version, meadow vetchling and heather to be added to the list. At Rowardennan I paused briefly and examined the interesting circular sculpture/memorial, a large ring set upright on a plinth. I carried on to Rowardennan Youth Hostel where I was to spend the night. Evening meals were not provided so I walked back to 'The Clansman' hotel, which I had passed previously. Both here and in the Youth Hostel I started to chat with fellow walkers. Some were doing the Way in seven and eight days as against my nine, so some folk were not seen again. However there was a good handful of people with whom I related all the way to Fort William. From here on a fair amount of 'comradeship' developed.

It had always been my intention to make use of Youth Hostels where I could, but hadn't deliberately varied my route significantly to include them. I was mildly disappointed that I hadn't stayed in any in England at all, and this was the first since Land's End. I take a certain amount of pride in the fact that there has only been one year in the last 57 years, that is, since I was eleven years of age, when I have not spent at least one night in a Youth Hostel somewhere. I also take some satisfaction from the fact that Jack Catchpool, one of the founders of the YHA, and its first General Secretary from 1930 onwards, was a fellow Sidcot scholar. His daughter, Carol, was in my year at school and she, with her husband Tim, are very close friends.

I had also been reflecting on the route I have taken so far. Apart from one or two short stretches of road here and there, and places where I may have crossed my route at right angles, as it were, and not counting a few miles in the Quantocks, a few miles around Sidcot, Keynsham, and along the River Severn north of Bewdley, about a daysworth of miles along the Sandstone Trail, and some very short bits around Casterton and Sedbergh, the way I went was completely new to me. The rest of my route northwards would also be new territory. This is a very satisfying feeling and added to the excitement of the walk, because I never quite knew what was coming next.

The Youth Hostel was, perhaps, a little stuffy in the dormitory, possibly because of the fine-mesh screens on the windows which kept the midges at bay. On balance I was happy to be stuffy rather than bitten.

Friday 5th June
Rowardennan to Inverarnan - 13.7 miles

I managed to get away in very good time at about 0820, before most of my companions of the Way. It was only later in the day that I discovered that I was carrying a Youth Hostel room key. I used, fortuitously, the baggage carrying service to get it back to Rowardennan. The weather was cool but became sunny later. The guide book I was using said that soon after Ptarmigan Lodge, a house a good mile along the Way, there was an alternative route that one could follow. The map clearly indicated the two routes, both labelled. The slightly more 'inland' route climbs higher along the wide forest track and the other way hugs the loch shoreline more closely. I had decided on balance that I would prefer not to tramp along a boring forest track, probably stony underfoot, and climbing up just to come down again. So I chose the shoreline path.

At the appointed place where the shore path led down and away from the wide track I turned left and my first impression was that it didn't look very well frequented. It was much less clearly trodden than I had expected. Nevertheless I pressed on and it didn't widen or improve. It kept climbing up and down, it was muddy and slippery in more places than I would wish, it had more tree roots to contend with than usual, it was rather overgrown in places, it had big 'steps' (ie natural ones) both up and down and the loch wasn't as visible as I had hoped. I discovered that midges were quite happy to try and discover if they liked the taste of me. I doused my exposed parts liberally with Avon Skin So Soft and they were never a big problem. These midges like the shady bits. They like the damp days. They don't like hot sunshine or windy places. I might have been better off on the wide, stony forest track, higher up in a windy place. Someone else has said before me that if you kill one midge, a million come to the funeral! I also discovered that you are more of a target if you stop than if you keep moving. I stop all the time. I stopped earlier this morning to do three things, like, for example, check the map, have a swig from my water bottle, or adjust a rucksack strap. It would normally be sensible to do all these at one stop, but before you have had time to do the first thing, say within about thirty seconds, Mr. Midge has arrived and started shouting for his mates, "Over here, boys. Feast over here". So for a while it is 'do one thing per stop' then get moving again.

There was a fearful lot of clambering up and clambering down, slipping and slithering, swearing and steaming as I made very slow progress. I probably climbed more along this path than if I had taken the upland route. But it was all very pretty in the woods, although somehow I wasn't in the mood to appreciate it. I knew that this path would rejoin the main route at some point but because of the winding to and fro and the upping and downing I had lost track of how far I had really come. So it went on, for what must have been a couple of miles. Then in the vicinity of Rowchoish the woodland opened out a bit and the path became more definite and I felt a bit more encouraged. There was a lovely bluebell wood and I heard a cuckoo. It isn't all bad, then.

Eventually I regained the main path after probably the most difficult couple of miles of the whole walk so far. I had, of course, seen no-one on my self-inflicted diversion but now there was a smattering of folk in view, mostly ahead of me. The next 2½ miles were very good indeed and my spirits rose considerably. The sunshine was warmer and the scenery was excellent. There were bits of fields and more woods and one high bit with a stream rushing down between two rocks where you had to leap across, which was actually quite easy, but made it a bit more fun. It was near here that a party of cyclists came along on mountain bikes. I think there may have been six of them. They would have had to have stopped and carried their bikes over the gap I had just jumped. It would have been too daring altogether to have tried to 'jump' it on a bike. They were attempting to do the whole of the West Highland Way - 95 miles - in twenty-four hours. They looked pretty fit and fanatical. At last I came to Inversnaid Hotel. There is a road that leads to it from the Trossachs, coming in from the east, but there is also a ferry-boat link across the Loch from near Inveruglas. There were some splendid waterfalls and footbridges just here.

Inversnaid Hotel is a very decent place for the passing walker. Once you have bought a drink at the bar you can sit outside at the tables on the forecourt and eat your own food. You can pop in and use the loo. Quite apart from anything else - the view is superb. I discovered what the form was from the assembled company of a dozen or so fellow trampers who had all overtaken me on their walk along the wide forest track I had so scornfully shunned. There was a very good sense of comradeship and sharing of experiences between the walkers. Some were loners, like myself, but mostly they were couples. I ate my lunch here, but most of the others cleared off before I had finished, so far was I behind my schedule. Not that I had one.

The path continued to be excellent with great views over to the west, where there were numerous mountains that I have not attempted either to identify let alone pronounce the name of out loud. I can usually manage Ben, a name with which I am fairly familiar. After a while I caught up with some of the other walkers and chatting with them was really good. Near the delightfully picturesque cottages at Doune I sheltered under some trees for five minutes while a light shower of rain passed by. No need to get anoraks out etc. The way continued to be quite charming. I sensed that I was gradually nearing the north end of the Loch and at one point where there was a little knoll, one could look back down the length of the loch. In fact it wasn't the whole way, as it is a very long stretch of water indeed. After another couple of miles I arrived at Beinglas Farm, Inverarnan, where I was booked in for a B and B. This turned out to be in a chalet, and very comfortable it was. I had booked in at the main building and then walked across the green to the chalet. As soon as I closed the door behind me the rain absolutely tipped down in torrents for quite a little while. It was a Friday evening and the place was swarming with people using the adjacent campsite. I pitied those who were trying to pitch tents in the pouring rain. The midges were having a field day and I could see folk having quite some difficulty with them. A couple of girls were wearing midge-proof headgear, somewhat such as beekeepers use; rather ungainly looking but no doubt effective. I took my evening meal and my breakfast in the bar in the main building. What with rain and midges I did not attempt an evening stroll anywhere but enjoyed the comforts of the chalet. I reckoned that this was probably the hardest day so far for my arthritic knee.

Saturday 6th June
Inverarnan to Crianlarich - 6.7 miles

What with one thing and another, I didn't get away until 1000. I wasn't in a hurry as I had a very short day ahead of me. A broad grassy track led me up the glen with the River Falloch tumbling noisily not far away. The Falls of Falloch, half hidden in the trees, were vaguely impressive. The Way then steered uphill away from the river, and my casual map-reading hadn't anticipated, what my notebook records as an 'unexpected rise'. My mind was content to follow the well-trodden way and I hadn't really been thinking much about the navigation, except to assume that it would keep pace with the river and only be a gentle gradient. The path ahead seemed to go up and up and I said to myself, "I'm not going up there!" This was not because I don't like climbing hills, because I do; but because my placid contentment was jolted out of its complacency by the unexpectednessness. I found myself saying to myself, "Discipline, boy, discipline!" which was less to do with the imagined strenuosity needed ahead, than with adjusting my mental mindset. Of course, the slope was nothing, as I knew perfectly well it would be. When I am walking alone, I find myself talking to cows and other creatures as the need arises, or mostly when there is no need; or sometimes having a conversation with myself or even an argument. I've lost arguments with myself before now.

I crossed the river near Derrydarroch and sheltered in a handy tree-lined dell for five minutes while a sharp shower of rain started boldly then dwindled to nothing. A little further on I ducked under the railway line through a Sheep Creep, as the map calls it. There isn't much headroom and in order to remind potential users of the tunnel some well-meaning English-speaking person had scratched on the lintel, 'MIND YOUR HEAD'. However, as this is Scotland, someone else had over-written the letter A with an I, so that it read, 'MIND YOUR HEID'. There's no harm in the Sassenachs being put gently in their place. Quite a few of the folk I met along the Way were from countries other than the UK. I don't know what they made of it.

The terrain now opened up considerably and there was much more of an upland feel about the walk. You could see the track rising ahead and the views eastwards were excellent. The Way follows the line of an old military road and it was good walking with occasional streams running across the path and there was a good scattering of tormentil and milkwort. Since my encounter with midges I had been trying to remember the words of an old Guy Carawan song. He was an American or Canadian folk singer and we used to have an LP of his songs. The song was 'The Little Black Flies' and it has brilliant tongue-twisting words and a rollicking tune. I came to a signpost which said Tyndrum to the left and Crianlarich to the right. I knew I would have to go for the best part of a mile downhill to the Youth Hostel in Crianlarich and I knew I would have to climb the best part of a mile uphill to get back to this point the next morning. I didn't mind. Just near this signpost I met an American or Canadian man and we stopped for a chat. Amongst other things I asked him about the midges and told him about the song 'The Little Black Flies', which is about a surveying team out in the wilds of Ontario and being plagued by the terrible creatures. He wasn't acquainted with the song so couldn't help me with the lines I was striving to remember, but he did say that the midges here were as nothing compared with the black flies in North America. I got the impression that these flies were much worse than our clegs and horseflies and you really, really don't want to be around at the same time as they are. They wouldn't just bite and cause itching, but bruising as well. I'll probably not go there, then.

The path to the village was delightful. It wound its way down through pinewoods and before you knew it you were there. I went to the railway station which has a café on the island platform and had a late lunch. I had been here years ago, when we were driving to a holiday further west, and I liked the café, and the thought of visiting it again had sustained me through many of the days gone by. I spent some of the afternoon trying to fix up accommodation in a couple of places along the Great Glen Way for a week or so ahead. I had a clutch of phone numbers to try and I wasn't always successful in finding somewhere straightaway. Gradually it sorted. I also visited the village shop to stock up and then went to the Youth Hostel. Later I went to the 'Rod and Reel' pub in the village. A couple sitting at an adjacent table were obviously not British. The man had a heavy moustache and they both looked very serious. I thought he looked exactly like what I thought a stereotypical Dutchman would look like. He very carefully, and without as much as a flicker of a smile, took a photograph of his plate of food before he started eating it.

Of the several groups and individuals I enjoyed travelling with over these days, one group needs singling out for special mention. This was a party of three Australians who have walked fairly widely in the UK and Europe. They were husband and wife Neville and Ivy and their friend Robert. I walked with them on and off for a goodly number of miles. That evening in the hostel, I 'entertained' the three of them - and sundry others who were obliged to be within earshot - with a full blown performance of 'The Little Black Flies', the words for which I had managed to get together. This was politely, but not perhaps enthusiastically received. However, Neville and I worked our way through 'Frozen Logger' and he told me of an extra verse, hitherto unknown to me.

We carried on chatting in the common room and sitting just nearby were a group of three young men who were talking loudly about their Alpine adventures. I said to them that we were mere West

Highland Way walkers and that if they wanted to play the one-upmanship game, then something much more modest than 'Alpine Adventures' would be more than enough. (Thinking of Munros and the like). I continued in bantering vein, saying loudly, and inventively to Neville, "Do you remember when we were at Everest Base Camp?" Before Neville could say anything, the reply came back across the room, "Oh, we've been there as well!" I bet they had, too. I didn't dare drag out my Land's End to John O'Groats tale. They'll have probably done it backwards in a wheel barrow or something. Twice.

Sunday 7th June
Crianlarich to Bridge of Orchy - 13.3 miles

I was away before half past eight and I enjoyed the climb up the zigzaggy path through the woods to the signpost where I had left the West Highland Way the day before. I saw a little bird which I thought might have been a siskin. I am not used to seeing them. The next couple of miles were lovely. The air was cool, I felt fresh, the path wound to and fro, with few straight bits. It climbed little banks and then went down again. It was all in the forest and there was never a boring moment. Walking on the softness of pine needles is pretty special, too. I suppose I could say, that for these two miles at least, I 'swung along' like any old-fashioned tramper on the Road to the Isles. The 'Far Cuillins are pullin' me away' is not strictly true because I have a different direction to take, but the sentiment is just the same. The track descends to the railway line and then immediately crosses the A82. This is one of the few main arteries to the north and is pretty busy.

Having survived that, a dinky little path led down to cross the River Fillan. A few yards down this path I found a most unusual - to me anyway - fungus cum lichen. It was grey and beautifully formed, like sticky up ears all among dead leaves. There wasn't more than a square yard of it, I suppose, but it was fascinating. I took photos.

Researches since lead me to believe that it may have been Field Dog Lichen or possibly Felt Lichen. I could not remember ever having seen it before but have seen it twice since in different locations. I am told that this lichen goes grey when it is very dry and turns brown in the wet. I may have passed other specimens before on a wet day and not noticed it.

I was now in the wide vale of Strath Fillan which was rather more agricultural than the countryside I had experienced over the last few days. There were fields and cows and sheep and horses. A sign fixed to a farm gate said, 'Horses - Please shut the gate'. I didn't actually see one doing it, but I suppose they are clever enough not to let on, and do it when humans aren't watching. Crossing the strath to St.Fillan's Church (remains of), I looked back and had my first sighting of snow high up on what I took to be Ben More. Nobody shouted 'Ben, More!' when I was singing last night. Most of the snow I saw in the next few days was in small patches, in gullies where it would have drifted deep and where the sun wasn't catching it.

The walking was pretty easy past Auchtertyre and on through forest tracks and old industrial workings to Tyndrum. This was a Sunday and there were plenty of people about. Tyndrum is a useful stopping point for walkers and is also a 'tourist attraction' in that it has a large café complex called the 'Green Welly'. I mingled with the throng and had lunch in the main café. I was on the lookout for Ivy and Neville and Robert but didn't see them. It turned out they had paid a quick visit to the small snack bar café and then gone on. I left the Green Welly and went into the very useful village store. Just before I entered I could see three figures up the lane. It looked like the three Australians but I had to do my shopping first. I made several purchases very quickly and then hared up the lane with the other three just in view. Within about half a mile I had caught them up. The next five or six miles were absolutely splendid. The weather had changed from being rather cloudy to nice and sunny, the way ahead was visible, gradients were very gentle, the views were stunning and the companionship fine. *This* was how I had expected the West Highland Way to be - very satisfying. There were countless small streamlets running down the mountainside which gave me ample opportunity to hunt among the beautiful tiny rock pools and damp ditches in search of whatever I could find. I was hoping for starry saxifrage, but was unlucky today, but I did find what I later identified as yellow saxifrage. Two other new flowers were alpine lady's mantle and thyme. The railway kept us company most of the way, leaving us at one point to swoop away to the right to cross a viaduct over a side valley and then swoop back to join us again. The A82 was, thankfully, across the other side of the strath. The Way would have felt even more authentic had it not been there.

Eventually this wonderful stretch brought us down to Bridge of Orchy, where we arrived before three o'clock. I had booked into the bunkhouse which is part of the Bridge of Orchy Hotel. I had paid a bit extra to have single occupancy of a twin room. I had hoped to book in at Kingshouse Hotel the following night, but they had no vacancies. So, being aware of the bus service along the - ah, it does have its uses - A82, I had arranged to stay a second night in the bunkhouse at Bridge of Orchy. The hotel is very friendly and bunkhouse folk may make full use of the lounge and the dining room. I enjoyed my two nights there. This has been another great day with plenty of interest and still no rain. I had heard tales of the bleakness and the distance across Rannoch Moor, which I was hoping would be one of the high spots for me. Can't wait for tomorrow.

Monday 8th June
Bridge of Orchy to Kingshouse - 12.6 miles

This was a day that I had been looking forward to for a long time. This was to be the 'best' bit of the West Highland Way. Rannoch Moor seemed to have developed a certain mystique from the various bits I had read. Following an old military road didn't sound too difficult to me. There was to be no tramping over trackless wastes and falling into bogs, or having to use a compass in the mist. The worst that could happen, as far as I could make out, would be being out in cloud and rain and cold and being bored with the length of the journey. Strictly speaking, the Way runs across Black Mount, which I suppose is the western edge of Rannoch Moor. I think the true wilderness of the Moor is to be found east of the A82, and is perhaps more easily viewed from the railway than from the road. Guesswork here. Whatever the facts of the matter, and for whatever reason, I was definitely looking forward to it. I was not to be disappointed.

I left the hotel at eight o'clock and paused on the bridge over the river. The water sparkled and shone a reflective blue in the cool early morning sunshine and the backdrop of a couple of Beinns made the view just magical; and I had only been going three minutes. This augured well. I climbed the gentle slope into the forestry and then came out onto the open moor. Here the path wound teasingly ahead of me and I soon found myself on a little summit. This was barely a thousand feet in height but the view was absolutely tremendous. The clarity of the air was brilliant and the mountains round about stood out clearly. I couldn't attempt to identify them, but they looked exceedingly inviting and just itching to be climbed. Loch Tulla made a perfect foreground to the picture. In many years of walking I have often stood on a mountain top and stared into the cloud, knowing there would be a great view if it cleared. I had a brief moment of sorrowful thought on behalf of those other people who must have passed this way in cloud and rain and missed the lot. I felt supremely lucky and privileged to be here on such a lovely day.

I descended to the Inveroran Hotel. A sign indicated that it served morning coffee and such like, so somewhat hesitantly I went in and sat in a little room and ordered some coffee, elevenses as it were.

Various members of staff were bustling about looking mildly harassed and there were several guests finishing their breakfast. I was served, but received a funny look or two because it was only 0915. I felt a little guilty about dropping in at such a busy time. However, I escaped in due course and followed the tarmac lane round to Forest Lodge. Now there was a long steady ascent and as I climbed I looked back every so often to see who was coming up behind me. After a mile or more of ascent the view spread out again and I was continually stopping to take photographs. I had been, as far as I could tell, 'leading the field' of today's other Way walkers, but in twos and threes they gradually overtook me. Some I had seen before and other faces were unfamiliar, but everyone had a cheerful wave or a friendly greeting. The gradients were easy and you could see the path a long way ahead. This old military road had been built, I think, by Mr. Telford. He did a darn good job, because the surface of the track was well packed and firm and pretty even; and although there were gravelly bits it didn't seem to be seriously broken up by wind and weather. Despite this accolade, I must have caught my foot on a little sticky out bit and just managed to avoid a full-scale stumble into the ditch. I was probably looking at the view. My notebook records a reminder of a maxim I have long tried to remember to adhere to, "If you want to look at the bloody view - bloody stop!"

Occasional burns and damp patches gave me plenty of places to examine in my quest for the elusive starry saxifrage. Today's new flowers - only two - were yarrow and Grass of Parnassus. Yarrow is common enough in mid or late summer so I was a little surprised to see it out so early. The Grass of Parnassus is a beautiful white flower, and although I can see it in Buxton in season, it was a great delight to find it today. The mountains were nearer at hand and some had snow patches on them. One couple who passed me asked me if I had seen the red deer. I hadn't, although I had glanced into the middle distance quite often, between looking where I was putting my feet and delving into ditches. Lochans added interest to the near views. The view opened out to the east and one had a sense of the extent of Rannoch Moor stretching away, but the wildness factor didn't quite ring true because one knew that just over there, just out of sight, would be the main road. I came to Ba Bridge and this was a delightful spot. The River Ba, albeit without much water flowing down it, comes tumbling down from the mountains and flows through a tiny vee-shaped gorge before gurgling under the bridge and dashing on, only to spread itself out on a flat expanse a little further down. Had I been in need of urgent cooling, a deepish pool just upstream from the bridge would have made a good wallow. I stopped for my lunch by another stream a bit further on, and there Neville, Ivy and Robert caught up with me.

The altocumulus of the morning was gradually thickening and the weather stayed cool. In company with the others I climbed another mile or so to a low summit and then descended towards Black Rock Cottage and the main road. A different view had opened up, and several more unpronounceable mountains dominated the scene. I *did* know that I was looking at Buchaille Etive Mor, which I have understood to translate as 'The Big Shepherd'. Strictly speaking it may be that the bit you see prominently from the A82, before descending into Glen Coe, is Stob Dearg. Anyway it was all quite magnificent and awe-inspiring. We crossed the main road and continued down the 'old road' to Kingshouse Hotel, arriving just after two o'clock. This seemed quite awfully early but I found my way to the bar/café round the back and sat there with a drink for a while. In a bit I dared to go into the hotel proper and found one or two people I had been walking with, so I sat in the lounge with them, and for the second time that day felt a bit guilty about being there. When sufficient time had passed I made my way up to the main road and waited for the bus to take me back to Bridge of Orchy. There is a decently frequent service along the A82 and the buses mostly start in Edinburgh or Glasgow and thunder their way northwards with various destinations in their sights. Some just go to Fort William and some, I think, to Inverness. These buses are emblazoned along the side with the name of the service - CITYLINK. I was amused to see one bus battling its way northwards and the destination board said 'Uig'. I happen to know that Uig is a small, nay tiny, village at the northwest end of the Isle of Skye. It is from here that ferries travel to the Outer Hebrides. Long live the City of Uig, say I. The evening was spent quietly in the hotel again - good food, good service. A happy place to be. Well, that has been a really grand day.

Tuesday 9th June
Kingshouse to Kinlochleven - 9.0 miles

I took a little stroll near the hotel before breakfast and it was a brilliant morning after rain. There was an almost cloudless sky with only one or two tiny bits of fractus. After a good stoking up I bade farewell to the friendly folk at Bridge of Orchy Hotel and took the 0851 bus to Kingshouse. After alighting I spent some time taking more pictures of the wonderful surrounding scenery and walked down the three-quarters of a mile old road to the Kingshouse Hotel. I've done that bit twice now. I barely paused at the hotel and kept on along the lane and then took the path off to the right which led gently upwards. For two miles the path keeps along the lower flanks of Beinn a' Chrulaiste. There were numerous wee burns running down the hillside and crossing the path. These little streamlets are immensely attractive and each one has its own distinctive charm - a mix of rock, water, flora, moss and splashing sunlight. These are the places I linger over, scanning the damp water margins for yet another new find. Today I was in luck - yes, at last, starry saxifrage. Ben is happy.

As well as keeping my eyes in the ditch I also had time to look away southwards. The mountains around the 'entrance' to Glen Etive were stunningly beautiful in the morning sunshine. There were plenty of walkers around and there was a joyful sense of companionship between us all. We were approaching the head of

Loch Lomond - looking south

Starry saxifrage

Glen Coe but the Way never gets quite near enough to get a decent glimpse down its rugged length. At Altnafeadh the Way leaves the main road and starts to ascend the Devil's Staircase. I had heard about the Devil's Staircase from fellow walkers ever since leaving Milngavie. It seemed to strike fear (I daresay I exaggerate) into most of those who mentioned it. I am afraid to say that I took these comments with a pinch of salt. Surely, I said to myself, it can't be that bad. The path ascends fairly steeply for a reasonable distance and actually reaches, at 1798', the highest point on the West Highland Way, and also the highest point, in terms of altitude, of my whole walk. It is a climb from the road of about 850' and may well be the longest steepest climb on the Way, but it is certainly not Devilish and its supposed fearsome reputation, in my opinion, is much overrated. I climbed the rather stony path steadily and overtook several groups on the way up. To be fair, have you noticed how on a steep climb there are always more views to stop and look at, more flowers at which to stop and study?

I had been wondering what new vista might be opening up at the top of the climb. The climb up was not especially awesome but the view that was presented to me as I breasted the rise, was, indeed, spectacular. There were numerous peaks spread out in the background and nearer, the Way wound intriguingly away below me. I think I knew that I was looking at the Mamores and I had little hesitation in identifying the distinctive massive shape of Ben Nevis. Everything I had experienced over the last eleven weeks or so, dissolved into obscurity behind me as my mind focussed on this new promise laid out before me. I will be over there, albeit not on the tops. I will be over there and beyond 'over there'. The romance of the whole adventure ran through my being. It took me some minutes to still the thrill and return to the mere business of watching where I put my feet.

The path led attractively down to cross a burn and then rose again to round a shoulder of hill, giving the 'new' view all over again. I stopped near here to have my lunch and could see Blackwater Reservoir away to my right. It was now downhill virtually all the way to Kinlochleven. Six great pipes run steeply down the hillside, fed from the Reservoir and leading down to the valley, to provide hydroelectric power. I think I should use the past tense here, because I am not sure about the present status of this venture. Little holes in the pipes occur in places and a fountain of water leaps a few feet into the air. The path became a rough stony track and went down very steeply. For a few hundred yards this was probably the most uncomfortable section of the 850 miles so far, with gravel and small stones continually sliding away from under my feet. I arrived in Kinlochmore, just across the river from Kinlochleven some minutes before half-past two and wondered whether it was too soon to go to the B and B. No worries. Mrs Maclean welcomed me in and my notebook says, 'blessed bath'. Later on I sauntered down into Kinlochleven, observing on the way, the outlet of the big water pipes where it stormingly joined the River Leven. I found a few other Way Walkers when I went for an evening meal in the 'Tail Race' pub, presumably named after this turbulent feature.

Yet another day has gone by, full of excitement and wonder. Each day has had its own points of interest and I am never bored.

Wednesday 10th June
Kinlochleven to Fort William - 14.8 miles

Another early start - away by 0815. The weather was cloudy bright and the temperature changed from cool to warm as the day progressed. Throughout this longish day of nearly fifteen miles the going underfoot was varied, with quite a lot of stony track but also some lovely soft pine needles in the forest in the early afternoon. This was, for me, the longest section of the West Highland Way and I was geared up mentally for this final push before having a rest day in Fort William. Physically I was fine too. I continued, as always, to have discomfort from the arthritic knee but in all other respects I was in very good nick. Walking day after day was doing me good. My trainers are very comfortable and there is never any sign of blisters.

Having left the village I easily found the path which led uphill through woodland. This was fairly steep but was utterly delightful. It was a *path* for a mile or so, rather than the broad track of the last day or two, which made it more intimate as it twisted and turned as it climbed. I have often said to myself that I will be able to climb a steep hill better if I have been walking for, say, half an hour beforehand, to get my lungs into training. I started this climb after perhaps only a quarter of an hour but I emerged onto the broad, stony track west of Mamore Lodge Hotel, without any breathlessness. As I left the woodland behind the track lifted gently away ahead of me and I felt as though the day was full of promise. The views around were magnificent. Loch Leven lay far below and the scurrying clouds cast moving shadows on the surrounding mountainsides. It was during a moment when I had paused to take a photo that I had a phone call on my mobile and it was Peggy. Peggy was in my year at Sidcot and she was going to put me up in Thurso after the finish of my walk. She wanted to know how I was getting on and we made arrangements regarding future communications. It was heartwarming to look ahead like that and realise that the chances of me actually finishing this great trek were looking more solid by the hour.

There were several of my companions of the Way in view and particularly I spoke with Clemence and Marcus, who had spent the night at the Mamore Lodge Hotel. Clemence is from Germany and his son Marcus is only six years old. I had first noticed them at Balmaha and on and off most days since. Marcus seemed very tiny to be undertaking the rigours of the West Highland Way and I was led to believe that they had done it all on foot so far. Young Marcus seemed to be enjoying it whenever I had seen them, sometimes darting ahead and sometimes lagging behind on some private exploration.

As at times on the previous three days the Way followed a line along the slope of a mountain so there were numerous streamlets trickling down the hillside and giving me continued opportunities for flower spotting. In the June sunshine these little streams look captivatingly attractive, and I found a northern marsh orchid and several more starry saxifrages. The track rose steadily in open countryside in a pass between the hills. It is called Lairigmor and my knowledge of Gaelic, tiny as it is, leads me to believe that Lairig means a pass between the hills and Mor means big. Away down to my left a burn ran the opposite way to my line of travel. After a couple of miles or so of enjoying the gently undulating but ever-rising track, I must have, imperceptibly, reached the highest point and gone past it without realising. There seemed to be plenty of scope for optical illusions, as the mountains were high on both sides. As I went on along, with more gentle downs and ups, I had to force myself to realise that the water, way down on my left, was now moving in the same direction as I was. The overall effect was as if one was still walking uphill into a corrie. This effect was enhanced because the gap between the hills and the track and presumably the stream, took a sharp turn to the right. So as I moved along I seemed to approaching ever closer the dead end of a glen. Intellectually I knew that the map indicated the right turn, the track to Fort William couldn't just stop in the middle of nowhere. The stream at which I peered to try and establish which way it was flowing, gave me inconclusive results. One has to assume, I suppose, that the broken whiteness of water would occur just below a little rocky-tumbly waterfall, but it was too far away to verify this. To clinch this, the line of electricity poles which had accompanied the water all the way, marched steadily on; and the poles, like the track, would not be stopping in the middle of nowhere, either. All this I knew. My mind knew it but my senses rebelled. I took several pictures of the view ahead as I approached 'the bend' to try and prove to myself that this really was a pretty good optical trick. It was only at the last minute, as it were, that the view round the corner eventually presented itself and my 'mental turmoil' ceased. Alfred Wainwright, in describing the ascent of Catstycam by the north-west ridge, says that you only realise you are at the top when you are just three strides from the summit. I have done it and he is quite correct. The approach to this bend, with the mountains closing in on all sides, was rather like that.

I met a couple of walkers with their dog and I was impressed by the originality of the route of the long walk that they were undertaking, which was from Poole to Cape Wrath, until they added that they were taking seven years over it. Within a mile, on a descending track, I came to what the map showed as a forest. In fact it had been felled comparatively recently and the area was rather ugly and untidy with stumps jutting out at all angles. After a mile or so of this I came to a significant point at Blàr a' Chaorainn, where there was an information board, signposts and a road nearby. There was quite a cluster of folk here, I think mainly cyclists, and although I glanced at the information I didn't feel like stopping and pressed on and shortly came out of the felled area and onto open grassland. I stopped on a low rise and perched on a grassy bank beside the path and ate my lunch. I was right beside the path and loads of people, most of whom I recognised, came past. One of them, Jenny, saw me and said briefly, "We are going to meet at 'The Grog and Gruel' at seven o'clock." Obviously one or two of the Wayfarers had conspired to come up with the idea of a celebratory meal in Fort William this evening and this message was being passed up and down 'the line' as best it could. I thought this was a great idea and looked forward to being there. By now superb views of Ben Nevis were stridently presenting themselves. Short-lived, however, were they, as the path led into more forest (unfelled) and the going underfoot became soft and the resinous smell of the trees was sharp upon the nose. This was glorious, cool walking and I made good speed for a couple of miles. At one point the path descended steeply to cross a deep little ravine and down here in a damp recess in the rocks I saw a tiny display of four primroses. They seemed very lonely after the vast patches I had seen in Devon and Cornwall two months earlier. I was to see primroses on only one more day between now and the end of the walk.

I joined a wide forest road which took me steadily downhill for a couple of miles. I found some more yellow saxifrage, which I had seen for the first time only a day or two earlier and there were several vibrant clumps, conveniently placed on a wet rock face at a sensible camera level, so I took a few pictures without having to bend down with my bum in the air.

I eventually reached Fort William and without any difficulty found my B and B by about half past four. Having spruced myself up a little I found 'The Grog and Gruel' in the main street of the town. About ten of us gathered in the upstairs restaurant for our celebratory meal and it was good to reminisce about the achievement of concluding the walk. For some less experienced walkers it was, indeed, a great achievement and they were duly congratulated. However, it was a somewhat poignant and sad moment, having to say goodbye to one's companions of the last week or so, particularly Neville, Ivy and Robert, who had been so interested in my longer walk and had been supportive and understanding.

Well, here I am at a major staging post on my journey, still with little worries to resolve and arrangements to make on the morrow, my first rest day since Sidcot at Easter.

Thursday 11th June
Fort William to Fort William - Rest Day - 0 miles

Although the above says zero miles I probably walked a couple in my wandering around the town. I have not included them in my overall mileage count. When I arrived at my pre-booked B and B yesterday I found a note on the door explaining that my hostess, Mrs McCleod, had had to go to a funeral and wouldn't be back before whenever. The note told me where to find the key and how to brew tea. I felt very welcome before I had even got through the door. I was staying here for two nights. My room looked out over the town and across Loch Linnhe to hills beyond. Beautiful.

In the days previously I had been trying to find accommodation at Gairlochy with a distinct lack of success. I discovered almost all too late that there was an event taking place on the Saturday called 'The Caledonian Challenge' and just about every B and B was full to bursting. My lovely Mrs McCleod couldn't put me up on the Friday night but she found a kind neighbour along the same street who took people in when demand was high. Phew!

Anyway, back to Thursday. I felt I had a lot to do, particularly with trying to obtain maps of places further north and making arrangements for my accommodation. I worked out that I would walk to Gairlochy the next day and come back on a bus from Spean Bridge to Fort William. I sounded out one or two taxi drivers on the rank in the town and found that someone would be able to take me to Gairlochy on the Saturday morning. Another phew!

I went into the large outdoor shop and bought myself a new waterproof jacket. My old charcoal grey jacket was getting very tatty and feeling its age; and despite having been little used in the last couple of months I felt it was time it retired. I had had it for at least seven years and it had served me faithfully and well on many a walk, but I dumped it unceremoniously into the hands of the somewhat surprised assistant in the shop, asking him to dispose of it for me please.

The day didn't start out as being particularly restful, but as the jobs gradually sorted themselves I felt a little bit more at peace with the world. I am not adventurous enough to bash on at things regardless and hope that things will turn out alright. I like to have at least some sort of reasonably secure back-up plan so that my walking hours are worryfree. Most of the afternoon was spent in pottering mode. I went to an Indian restaurant and spent rather more than I would have liked for what my notebook records as 'a very ordinary' meal.

As I have probably said already, I didn't feel that my body needed a rest, I just needed time to deal with my arrangements. Fort William was to be the last major staging post on my journey and tomorrow I will be on the Great Glen Way.

I cannot let this narrative continue any further without mentioning Sally Thomas's wonderful book 'A Walk for Jim'. (ISBN 978-0-9558206-0-1) This book was published in 2001 and narrates how Sally walked from Land's End to John O'Groats in 1999, as a walk in memory of her son Jim, who died of leukaemia at the tragically early age of 28. This book moved me deeply and also inspired me to get on and do the walk myself. Her effort was a much more heroic achievement than mine and I admire her tremendously, not only for her courage but for the delightfully honest way she tells her tale. I recommend the reading of this book most strongly.

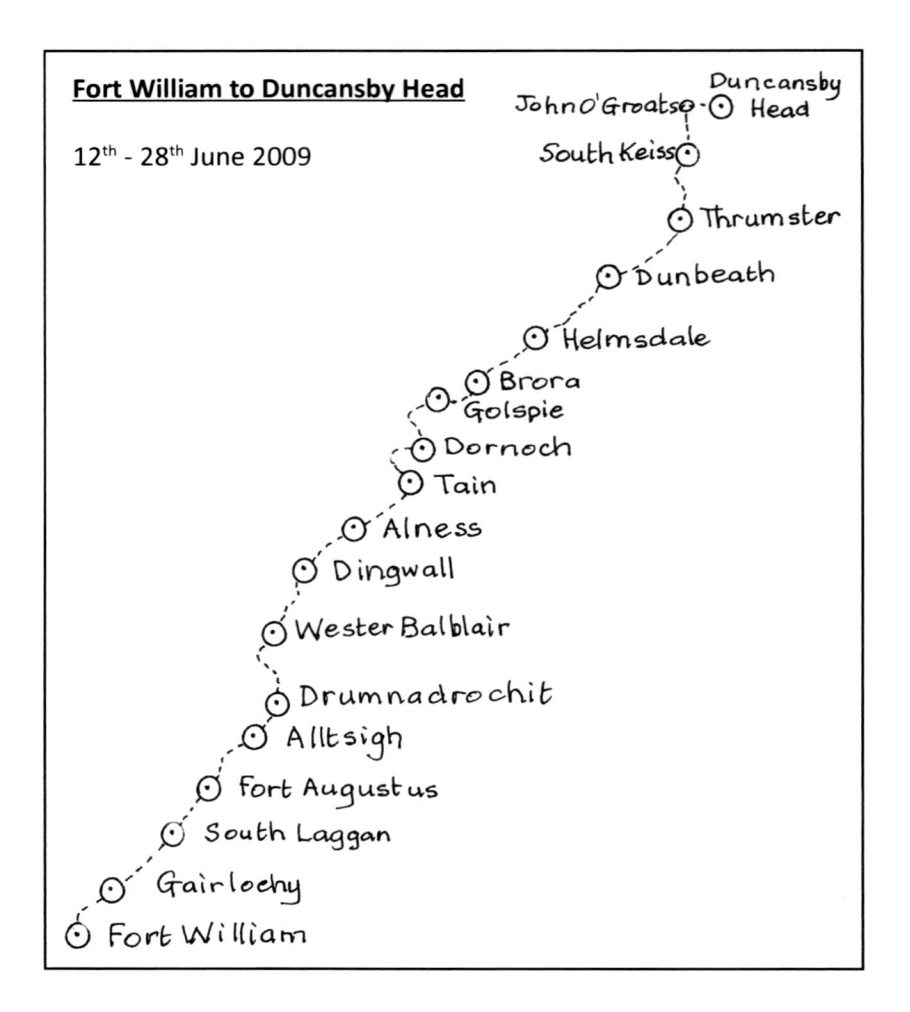

Fort William to Duncansby Head

12th - 28th June 2009

- Duncansby Head
- John O'Groats
- South Keiss
- Thrumster
- Dunbeath
- Helmsdale
- Brora
- Golspie
- Dornoch
- Tain
- Alness
- Dingwall
- Wester Balblair
- Drumnadrochit
- Alltsigh
- Fort Augustus
- South Laggan
- Gairlochy
- Fort William

Fort William to Duncansby Head

Friday 12th June
Fort William to Gairlochy - 14.1 miles

The day was bright and warm as I set off to start the Great Glen Way. I stopped to look at a large vertical flat slab of stone with a notice board attached to it indicating the start of the Way. I crossed over the River Nevis just where it joins the River Lochy just a few yards above where it runs into Loch Linnhe. I looked back across the still waters of the Loch to see the buildings of the town and the blue sky reflected in it. Everything was calm and peaceful with only a little cloudlet or two wafting gently by.

I continued through flat meadows beside the Lochy and was then impressed by the rushing, crashing outflow into the Lochy from the works upstream. This was similar to the one seen at Kinlochleven. I watched a fisherman with his line almost in the midst of this white water. I assumed that the fish would find good feeding on stuff disturbed by the raging flow. Within a few yards I had joined a path onto a bridge beside the railway which here crossed over the River Lochy. As I looked back towards the town I could see smoke and steam and a few minutes later along came the steam train, the same or similar to 'The Hogwarts Express', as seen in the Harry Potter films. Photos were taken.

I carried on along a suburban road into Caol where I found not only a handy little café but also two people who were walking from Land's End to John O'Groats. These two folk, a brother and sister, had started 11 days after me and were averaging 15 miles a day and were also camping. I guess they were in their fifties and looked very fit and experienced. We swopped stories for a few minutes before they moved steadily on. I didn't meet them again. They were

Looking across Loch Leven

Loch Linnhe at Fort William

the first people I had met since leaving Land's End, who were actually doing what I was doing - on foot and in the same direction.

I kept along the shore of Loch Linnhe to reach Corpach. I could have cut the corner here but it seemed good to go the long way round. I joined the path alongside the Caledonian Canal and then on to Neptune's Staircase, an impressive set of locks which takes the canal to a higher level. I noticed two men who were obviously on some sort of long distance trek. These two were called David and Anthony, and I was to meet them intermittently over the next few days. They were interesting company.

I found the towpath rather disappointing because it was wider than I had expected and harder underfoot, mainly because it was to accommodate cycles, and, I suspect, permitted works vehicles. However, I made reasonable speed along it and then soon after hearing yet another cuckoo, found a convenient seat where I stopped to eat my lunch. The hot weather in which I had been walking was in stark contrast to the top of Ben Nevis capped with snow, which I glimpsed occasionally, a few miles away. Not to mention being about 4000 feet higher!

I plodded on through the heat and eventually found myself at Gairlochy. Now 'off route' I walked a little way with David and Antony and we passed the large field, complete with flags and a row of portable loos etc, which was to be the start, the following day, of the 'Caledonian Challenge'. David and Antony turned off into a B and B which I had tried to book some time previously, but to no avail. They had booked in February and this was June.

I walked on a short distance and came across a car parked at the side of the road and the driver taking his ease for a few minutes. I asked him if he was moving on soon. He responded positively and gave me a lift for the next couple of miles to the Commando Memorial, on the A82. The driver was a photocopier salesman on his way back to Inverness having just driven back from, I think he said, Ullapool. I took a look at the Memorial statue but my eyes were drawn to the mountains in the distance which I took to be the Monadhliath group. They looked very good, but it wasn't the direction I was taking on the morrow. I plodded on down to Spean Bridge and before too long caught a bus back to Fort William. I had a meal in a Chinese restaurant which provided me with very poor service. I found my way to my B and B, along the road from where I had been the night before. My notebook records that my arthritic knee was quite painful today. I could have done with a softer towpath.

Saturday 13th June
Gairlochy to South Laggan - 12.6 miles

I left the B and B as soon as I could and found a taxi in the town centre. I was driven to Gairlochy along the 'back' road, rather than via Spean Bridge. Along this road there was a great amount of traffic coming the other way, and we surmised that these were folk who were supporting the participants on the Caledonian Challenge. The walkers must have started quite early because we saw plenty of them on the outskirts of Fort William, I think making their way to a checkpoint nearby.

Having paid the friendly taxi driver I stayed a few moments at Gairlochy watching the swing bridge being opened and closed to let through some water traffic. I started the walking proper at about 1020 and set off along the lane on the west side of the loch. The map showed a way through woodland near the water's edge but for some reason I can't remember, I stayed on the road. The willow warblers were quite busy along this stretch . The day was overcast with low cloud and threatening rain, but this never really arrived. The morning was brightened by the sight of a large red rhododendron bush in a wayside garden. I was reminded of the huge rhododendron bush/tree that I had seen in Cornwall on 29th

March. It also highlighted the gradual arrival of early summer in Scotland compared with Cornwall two and half months earlier.

At Clunes the lane turned strictly westwards leaving me to follow the Great Glen Way 'off-road'. I was somewhat disappointed with the next six miles along the way, which was rather hard underfoot. I quote from my notes written at the time, "I don't rate the Great Glen Way very highly. The path is too wide and straight. It is rather boring. OK - there are glimpses of loch and hill, but not much waterside walking today so far. It is not *intimate* enough. Thank goodness I have been able to make it interesting by looking for flowers on verges and in ditches. Without that saving grace it would have been dreadful. Few places to choose for lunch. The place I found was in the shade. Bloody midges!! Lunch with midges is no picnic!"

Looking back on the above comments, I realise that I was perhaps a little harsh. I could have taken the (not very long) waterside path earlier in the morning, but had chosen the lane instead. After this stretch the Way improved for the rest of the time I used it.

The weather had brightened quite a lot by the time I eventually arrived at the head of Loch Lochy and found some tarmac again. Feeling much more content with the world I strolled along the little lane with the loch on my right and some marshy land on my left. This was a change of floral habitat from the dry track I had just been on, so I was eagerly peering through gaps in the hedge at the reedy marshland. I had been longing to reach Scotland where I hoped there might be a better chance of seeing a marsh cinquefoil, and this habitat seemed an enticingly likely spot. At one point there was a good view over a fence and I must have exclaimed out loud, because my notes record, "To my utterable joy", as there in front of me was a mass of marsh cinquefoil flowers, with their feet in the water and their intricately patterned and coloured crimson heads nodding gently in the breeze. The camera was certainly in action.

A few yards further on I came to Laggan Locks where the Caledonian Canal becomes a canal again after its ten mile sojourn with Loch Lochy. Moored beside the canal bank there was an old boat called 'Eagle', which had been turned into a pub. I spoke to a man there, who I assumed was the proprietor, and told him I was aiming to reach the Forest Lodge Guest House, and he told me not to go along the main road. "You'll never get there, you'll be brown bread". I told him I was on my 86th day from Land's End and he said, "That's a bit slow". I didn't care and we both agreed about the enjoyment that such a sluggish pace allowed. He directed me to follow the canal-side path and then come back southwards along the dreaded A82 main road.

There were several travellers at the Guest House, some on foot and some on bikes. The proprietor gave some of us a lift to a restaurant further up the road and after a good meal and plenty of yarn swopping he gave us a lift back again. So this has been a mixed day of trudge, drudge and high elation.

Sunday 14th June
South Laggan to Fort Augustus - 10.2 miles

Leaving the Guest House at about 0930 I retraced my steps along the A82 but was then able to rejoin the canal-side path for half a mile. I crossed the main road and passing the restaurant of the previous evening joined an old railway track which ran along the east side of Loch Oich. This is the middle, and smallest of the three lochs that inhabit the vast cleft that is the Great Glen. The water was now on my left and was much more visible than Loch Lochy had been yesterday. The path remained level and was soft underfoot and shaded by trees. I felt much more charitable about the Way as the scenery was delightful and the going easy.

The overcast start to the day had now changed to warm and sunny and later on pretty hot. At Aberchalder, at the head of Loch Oich, there is a swing bridge which carries the A82 over the canal, now making its way to Loch Ness. There was a technical fault with the bridge mechanism and great queues of cars stretched in both directions. Just over the main road and alongside the towpath there was a small café, the Bridge House Tea Garden. It was very pleasant sitting in the sunshine having some mid-morning light refreshment. The weather was fine but I noticed some cumulus mediocris and possibly even some congestus looming over the hills to the northwest. I have occasionally made reference to clouds. Cumulus you probably know. As I remember there are four types. Humilis, where the cloud is longer than it is high; mediocris where the length and height are about the same; and congestus where the height is more than the length of the base. Congestus is on the way to being a thunder cloud. The fourth type is fractus which is very small wispy bits in an otherwise clear sky. Of course there are names for the other types of clouds but I haven't mastered the subdivisions.

A bridge took me back to the west side of the canal and I continued in hot weather for another four miles or so to Fort Augustus. I was to stay at a B and B, Tigh na Mairi, right alongside the towpath. I reached there at about 1420 and I felt it was too soon to call, so I went just a little further to the town. The locks here make a little staircase and there were several other attractions along with cafés and so on. One of the main points of interest to the Sunday sightseers was at a swing bridge where the A82 (again) crosses over. I don't know what it was about the swing bridges but this one had an electrical fault and a large pleasure cruiser was trying to pass under it. The bridge was 'locked' to allow car traffic to pass over so there were not great queues. I caught snippets of the instructions from the bridge man to the young folk on the boat. "I'm not opening the bridge". "You'll have to duck down". "You'll have to move away from there - the top deck". "You may have to reverse out again". "Go very slowly", etc. When it came to it there were a couple of feet to spare. In one of the locks there was pair of swans with several cygnets and one or even two of them were having a ride on a parent's back. That was something I had hardly ever seen before. Since my arrival at the locks it had been spotting with speckles of rain. I went back to the B and B and later returned to have an evening meal at The Bothy Inn. As I remember, it pelted down with rain while I was eating, but it didn't last long.

That has been a lovely easy day.

Monday 15th June
Fort Augustus to Alltsigh - 11.4 miles

I left the B and B at nine o'clock and came down through the village and took a looping back road away from the main road for half a mile and then joined the track into the forest. This stretch was more interesting than the plod from Clunes two days earlier. The trees gave more interest and the Way wound around a bit. It wasn't long before I had to put my over-trousers on, but the shower only lasted a quarter of an hour. I didn't see much of Loch Ness because of the trees.

After a few miles the Way curved away from the Loch as it approached Invermoriston. There was a rather zigzaggy descent to the main road and then I was able to view Telford's old bridge below me to my left. At 1145 the rain came back with a prolonged heavy shower and I took refuge in a bus shelter for a while. I had been told of a good café to go to but having discovered its location I found it was closed. Instead I retreated to the Glenmoriston Arms, where I enjoyed a lazy meal. This was to be my main meal of the day, the evening arrangements being somewhat uncertain. I spent a very pleasant two hours there in the company of several other Great Glen Way-farers, while the rain continued to pelt down outside.

Eventually I decided it was time to go and face the weather, which I did, fully kitted up. The rest of the afternoon was spent walking in heavy rain. I zigzagged my way up the hillside and chugged along happily. At one point I came across a little rock shelter beside the track which I entered for a few moments. I left the Way at Alltsigh and descended to the main road where I found the Loch Ness Youth Hostel. Today was probably the day when I experienced the longest period of rainfall, and was the only day on the whole of the walk when I was glad to make use of a drying room.

The hostel enjoyed views across the Loch and on the wall beside a window was a list of 'sightings' of the Loch Ness Monster, which included several in the previous month or so. I made myself a simple meal with stuff from the hostel store and then retired to my room to write up my notes etc.

When folk are on holiday, anchored in one place, but perhaps with a car available, they can say to the family, "What shall we do today?" and there is a sense of flexibility about the day's plans, perhaps depending on the weather. But one is not obliged to do any of those ideas. Walking from Land's End to John O'Groats, as on many other long distance trails, I knew where I was going and pressed on regardless of the weather conditions. At the day's start I knew that the destination was sorted, but the adventures had yet to be revealed.

As I progressed through Scotland there was an increasing sense of achievement of ground covered so far. Looking back over all those many miles from Land's End it seemed almost impossible to comprehend. I found myself saying, "Have I really done all that?" And the answer came, "Yes", and that led to a great feeling of deep satisfaction.

Tuesday 16th June
Alltsigh to Drumnadrochit - 10.0 miles

The day dawned grey with barely a hint of rain. I left the hostel at 0855 and retraced my steps for a short distance to rejoin the Way. This part of the Great Glen Way was by far the best section that I experienced and was quite delightful. It climbed through the forest to a higher point than any in the last few days. The forest thinned out and I was able to enjoy magnificent views of Loch Ness and the mountains beyond. The weather had become considerably warmer with a gentle breeze and was to become quite hot through the afternoon.

I revelled in the wild flowers I came across and recorded 80 different species, the best day's haul of the whole walk. There were several with which I was unfamiliar and I was busy with the camera and making notes in my little book. A special find was a wild strawberry plant with ripe red fruits. I'd seen the flowers in Cornwall but this was the first edible fruit. A photo showed two fruits on a stalk. Had I taken the picture a few minutes later it would have shown only one. Delicious!.

I also came across a very interesting Information board which explained how you could 'Make Your Very Own Loch Ness'. It was informative, imaginative and humorous and with coloured diagrams. I write the 'recipe' below.

Step 1.
Choose a site on a tear fault like the Great Glen fault (one about 380 million years old, lined with shattered rock would be ideal).
Step 2.
Add masses of ice - a layer around 1700 metres (5,577 feet) thick, if possible. Use the height of Ben Nevis as your guide, then add a bit more.

Step 3.
Grind the ice slowly along the fault - crunchy bits of shattered rock will get carried along as you go.
Step 4.
Leave the ice/rock mixture to scour out the bottom of the fault into an even surfaced u-shaped trench.
Step 5.
Leave the ice to melt. It will take quite a while!
Step 6.
Now, for that finishing touch, fill the u-shaped trench with water (and allow one end to reach the sea). You'll need around seven fair-sized rivers and 100 wee burns (streams).
Preparation time:
Around 20,000 years (steps 2 to 6).
Storage:
Set freezer to Ice Age.
Serving suggestion:
Best matured for around 10,000 years. Garnish with heather and forest before visiting.

The use of the word 'burns' in the above recipe reminded me of the different names for small bits of flowing water as I progressed up country. Down in the south streams or brooks would be common. In the north of England one would come across becks and into Scotland we have burns.

The Way turned away from the loch and descended a little from the forest and into pasture. Near Grotaig I found a pleasant spot with picnic tables and this was a good place for lunch. I was joined by David and Anthony, with whom I had walked on and off along the Way.

The Way now followed a quiet lane and after a mile or so reached a highish point, which allowed me a clear view northwards. I gazed interestedly at the terrain yet to come, but at the same time knowing I wouldn't be ascending great mountains, but following as lowland a route as possible. I had a slight sense of an ending drawing near. But then I thought, "Not yet, please".

Carrying on I eventually descended to Drumnadrochit and easily found my B and B at Glen Rowan House at West Lewiston just before four o'clock. I was warmly welcomed by Alistair and Vanessa and given a cup of tea. I followed this with a bath, having received a parcel of clean clothes from Ann. I found a pub later on and enjoyed a meal and then a stroll in the warm evening. Alistair was very helpful in advising me about the best route to follow on the morrow. I had been a bit worried about the next section, but it gradually became clearer as to what I should do. The Great Glen way continues to Inverness but I was leaving it now.

What an excellent day!

Wednesday 17th June
Drumnadrochit to Wester Balblair - 15.0 miles

At breakfast, Alistair appeared in a tartan waistcoat and tartan trews. I asked him if this was Scottish Serving Men's rig and he replied that it was for breakfast only and he wouldn't be seen dead in it outside the house. All along my route I had been having variations on the 'Full English' cooked breakfast and later the Scottish Breakfast. I often chose only selected items and this was fine in England. Coming into Scotland I found I had to cope with a battle between 'trying to reduce the cooked breakfast' and Scottish hospitality. I ask for, say, three items out of an offered six, and when it comes it *is* three items but double quantity! You can't win!

I left this very pleasant B and B and made my way into Drumnadrochit proper. I bought some lunch items in the convenience store and then turned west on the A831, finally abandoning the Great Glen Way which went eastwards. I passed

Marsh cinquefoil

Loch Ness - looking south-west

Milton and then turned northwards on the A833. This was to be a day of road walking, which I didn't really mind. Straightaway there was a gert, long, steep hill. I think I heard that this is part of the route that cyclists often take on their way to JOG from LE. It would certainly be a good test of stamina and strength.

The road levelled out and was not too busy with traffic. Rainclouds started gathering and after a while I had to stop and don my over-trousers. It was quite a long trudge but I was kept awake by the songs of willow warblers. Peering into ditches and roadside banks carried on as usual.

The rain became a little more insistent and I kept looking out for a place to nestle into beside the main road, where I could eat my picnic lunch in reasonable dryness, but nowhere seemed to be suitable. The map indicated a pub in the village of Kiltarlity, which was on my planned route. Glad to be off the main road I came into the village, but before I found the pub I was enticed into the Post Office which included a little café. This was a good find and I enjoyed a substantial late lunch. I was not expecting to find anywhere in Wester Balblair for an evening meal so this café was very much appreciated, not least because as well as good food it provided me with a Guardian to read.

By the time I was on my way again the rain had stopped but the roads were still wet. Almost immediately after leaving the village I was delighted to find a whole line of roadside bushes of dog roses in full bloom. I don't ever remember seeing such a profusion all in one stretch. Quite delightful. I wandered along the quiet lane through farmland. This was a change from the hilly area behind me and I felt I was entering a new phase of the walk. I came to a bridge over the River Beauly, which I guessed may have been tidal at this point, but it wasn't really 'the sea'.

I walked close to the sea for a couple of days in Cornwall, then only had glimpses from the Quantocks, the Mendips and the Mersey estuary near Frodsham. I caught sight of it again - Liverpool Bay - from Beacon Hill, but no more sightings until I reached Loch Leven. The sea was also seen at Loch Linnhe, the Cromarty Firth, the Dornoch Firth, Loch Fleet and then for the last few days the sea proper from Golspie onwards.

I joined a rather unpleasant stretch of main road which took me towards Wester Balblair. Nearing the village I came across an establishment called The Kirk House, a rather posh gallery cum craft centre cum coffee shop. I went in, thinking about my non-existent evening meal, and partook of further sustenance. There were quite a lot of mirrors for sale. I read a notice that announced '25% off all wooden mirrors'. I did find one with glass in and actually took a photo of myself in the mirror. Not a very rewarding sight.

Moving on I found my B and B - Cruachan - which offered me comfortable accommodation. During the course of the evening I may have eaten a little of the roadside lunch that I never had. I was in a top floor room and I kept being drawn to the skylight. I had been intrigued by the lengthening evenings the further north I came. Every so often I would get up from my evening tasks and look out of the skylight at the view outside. 8pm - very light. 9pm - still very light. 10pm - surprisingly still quite light. 11pm - sort of getting dusk. This has been one of my longer days and, despite the rain, still very enjoyable.

Thursday 18th June
Wester Balblair to Dingwall - 12.6 miles

Every morning before leaving my overnight accommodation I always packed my rucksack very carefully. This was a slight joy, knowing that everything went into a special place. When going on holiday by car, one tends, perhaps, to make free with the available space and just chuck everything in. For me, once the rucksack was packed and every pocket secured properly, that was it! Ready to go!

Today was to be road walking again, as, indeed, was to be much of the rest of the way. I soon joined the A862 and walked into Beauly. I didn't feel a great need to stop, but did wander through the Priory gardens, before marching on along the main road to Muir of Ord. By now it did feel a bit like elevenses time and I looked out for a likely place. Café - Closed. Shop - Closed. The whole place seemed rather run down. A lady I spoke to agreed that, "Muir is sad". I did find a small convenience store where I was able to obtain a mug of coffee out of a machine.

The day had started with a couple of very short-lived and gentle showers but by mid-morning had become brighter but still with a bit of a breeze. I took a road which I hoped would take me out of the town but I ended up going round three sides of an extended rectangle on suburban streets before finding the right route. I was trying to keep away from the main road so I zigzagged my way by pleasant lanes via Balvaird to Bishop Kinkell. On the way a rabbit very obligingly sat on the roadside verge allowing me to take several photographs of it from quite close up.

I found a grassy bank, out of the wind, against which I was able to rest my back. Here I ate my lunch in luxurious comfort. I was soon obliged to rejoin the main road and tramped into the village of Conon Bridge. Here there was, amongst a few other shops, an Aquarium. It had tanks of brightly coloured exotic fish and various accessories for sale, but it also included a small coffee shop in one corner. I wrote in my notebook - equatorial, piscatorial, caféterial (the Bristolian extra 'l'- see Truro).

Carrying on, I crossed the River Conon and then on until I came to a big roundabout. I was still following the line of the A862 but was able to walk along parallel with it on a path. I found my way into Dingwall, which I guessed was probably the biggest town I had been in since leaving Fort William. It seemed a busy and pleasant place, and I wandered up and down the main street doing bits and pieces of necessary shopping and re-stocking my larder.

My B and B was away from the town centre very close to the 'sea', down near the disused harbour. I walked back into town for an evening meal in a pub near the station. I was amused by a sign on the station door, which said, 'DINGWALL STATION   Hours of Business   MONDAY - SATURDAY 0730 - 1434'. I thought this was very precise and I imagined the station staff, no doubt all one of them, scampering away as soon as the afternoon train had departed.

Looking back over the whole of the walk so far, I realised that I had hardly ever enjoyed an evening stroll with the aim of spying out the country to be crossed the next day. Apart from being pretty busy in the evenings, there were not in fact many places where a little rise would have given me a glimpse of a view ahead anyway. I can only really think of Minions, on the fringe of Bodmin Moor, where I might have had a good look at the morrow.

Friday 19th June
Dingwall to Alness - 11.7 miles

Leaving the B and B at ten past nine I walked along beside the canal which let me bypass the town centre. I crossed the railway at a level crossing just short of the spot where the track divides. Left for Kyle of Lochalsh and right for Thurso and Wick. I climbed up a suburban street or two to reach a lane that ran roughly parallel with the A862, but higher up. As I walked along there were one or two tiny un-bothersome showers and after that the day warmed up to be nice and sunny. I glimpsed the Cromarty Bridge carrying the A9, the road with which I was to become all too familiar later.

The road was fairly level and quiet and the going was easy. I reached Evanton and soon found The Cornerstone Café, which I entered. The service seemed friendly and informal. While I sat and enjoyed my snack quite a few elderly people came in and made their way to a room further in. I found out from the waitress that this was a regular community lunch for old folks and that this café was run by volunteers. I felt a similarity between this enterprise and the projects I had met at two places in Devon - Northlew and Thorverton - where members of a community were working together. I had a strange feeling that I wanted to speak to the group, who by now were tucking into their lunch. I spoke to the lady in charge and at a suitable moment a few minutes later the lady called the group to order, and they listened to what I had to say.

I told them that I was walking all the way from Land's End and making for John O'Groats and that I had met some places where community projects were blossoming. I told them that this project of theirs was an excellent idea and exhorted them to keep it going. I don't think I sounded patronising. I had felt moved to do this by some force, either from deep within myself, or even from somewhere beyond me. It was all rather odd and it was over in a few minutes, but I felt glad, and somehow humbled, having done it.

I was not obliged to walk along the road all the way to Alness because a very convenient path kept alongside, veering off into lovely woodland occasionally. The path was soft underfoot, a welcome change from tarmac. I did have to walk the last stretch into Alness along a pavement, but then I found a grassy slope where I lay in the sunshine for a while, watching and listening to buzzards playing above.

In the town I spent a little while in a café having a drink and I spoke with a helpful couple, who lived in Dornoch. They took a great interest in my trek. They told me the best way to leave Dornoch was to go via Embo and Loch Fleet. Later, in the health food shop, one of the other customers was telling me about Golspie and people she knew there etc. Very friendly.

I found my way to the Tullochard Guest House where I had a comfortable night. One little incident took me aback. In the bathroom there was a device hanging on the wall. I thought it might have been some sort of air freshener and there was button on the front. I stupidly and somewhat daringly pressed the button and got a face full of spray of something or other, which I found unpleasant and annoying. I managed to get rid of the taste of it in an Indian restaurant where I enjoyed a biryani. Later that evening I received a text message from my dear friend Rose, in Frodsham. She said, "good 2 hear you r living experientially rather than missing joy in rush 2 meet targets. Keep walking cheerfully etc. xxx Rose". These words echo some well-known Quaker phrases. That was another interesting day. I slept well, as always.

Saturday 20th June
Alness to Tain - 12.6 miles

I left the Guest House at 0910 and soon found a way through an estate of newish houses and onto a quiet lane which led me to Bainaguisich (goodness knows how you pronounce it). Continuing, I passed Newmore Mains, Wester Stonyfield and eventually reached Scotsburn Bridge. There were some hills not far away to my left, mostly covered in forests. The dominant feature of this morning's walk was, indeed, trees. There were patches of pasture and occasional farms and cottages, but the name Stonyfield, Easter as well as Wester, didn't sound very agriculturally promising. I saw a deer, but no antlers. I spoke with a postman. What he said echoed scores of similar comments all along my route. "Going far?" *"John O'Groats."* " Where have you come from?" *"Land's End."* "Well done!" All these remarks have had a positive element of goodwill about them and this has cheered me as I went along.

The weather was excellent for walking with scudding clouds, sunshine, and both coolth and warmth. This minor road was very quiet with about one vehicle every 10 minutes. I had my lunch leaning against a grassy bank, similar to the one a couple of days earlier. I carried on past East Lamington and down to Quebec Bridge. The scenery was all very lovely. I continued until I found myself in Tain. This seemed a solid and reliable sort of town with plenty of character. I had a view across the Dornoch Firth, now more like the sea proper, to hills north of Dornoch, and I knew I would be over that way very soon.

I must have stopped at some point along the way to jot down in my notebook various thoughts that had been accumulating in my mind. I will quote them virtually verbatim.

"To walk LEJOG was a young man's notion. The young man knew he couldn't do it as a young man (no money, a family, job). By the time he was middle-aged he still remembered the notion of doing it, but overlooked the fact that it was a young man's notion, and that he was no longer young. This, notwithstanding the fact that as a young man the thought of doing it would, indeed, have to be deferred until middle-age. The urge to do it was not so much an urge as a thought that, 'I have always said I will do it one day'. A fulfilling of a subconscious obligation rather than a current desire to do it." That's what I wrote at the time, but it is rather muddled. But, I said to myself, here I am doing it at the age of 68! No wonder I feel chuffed. When does middle-age cease?

I was gentling along the main street and there was a bus, driverless, parked at a bus stop. It was bound for Dornoch. Somebody was knocking on a window of the bus from the inside. It was the nice couple I had met the day before in the Alness café. I climbed aboard the bus and chatted with them for a few minutes, until the driver returned. Window Knock? Door Knock? That's enough, Ben.

I found my way along Morangie Road to my B and B where I was greeted warmly by Mollie. She immediately ushered me into a room - was it a muniments room? - full of artefacts and antiques and told me at length about her collection. I stood there with my rucksack still on my back for what seemed like 10 minutes until Mollie's enthusiasm gave way to hospitality mode. The accommodation was very good and I had a splendid hot bath. I found an Indian restaurant in the town and then enjoyed the evening light as I wandered back to the B and B.

Sunday 21st June
Tain to Dornoch - 8.3 miles

The weather was fine with a cool breeze as I set out at ten to nine. The day became warm later. This was to be an easy day so, as most days, I felt no need to hurry. I walked along the grassy verges of the A9, passing the Glenmorangie Distillery and fields where haymaking was in progress. I was very close to the seashore with just the railway between me and the beach. There were views of distant hills and in the foreground the Dornoch Firth Bridge. I reached a roundabout, turned right, crossed over the railway and started on my way to the bridge. Just before I reached the bridge proper four northbound cyclists passed me, then stopped and circled back towards me. They were bound for John O'Groats having come from Land's End. They were doing the ride in 9 days at about 100 miles a day. Their bikes did not look at all heavily laden so I think they must have had a support vehicle somewhere in the offing. They had stopped because they wanted me to take a photo of them, which I willingly did. After mutual words of goodwill they sped on their way, leaving me to enjoy the delights of excellent scenery, water and sunshine. I took my time crossing the water, with none of the needless fears and anxieties of my crossing of the Mersey weeks before.

As I was leaving the bridge there was a large sign welcoming me to Sutherland. I had been noticing county boundaries in England but I couldn't really follow the Scottish regions/counties or whatever. I seemed to be still in 'Highland' and was leaving Ross and Cromarty, as was, and entering Sutherland. I reckoned that this was the last but one county. I soon left the main road and took to a quiet lane which led me towards Dornoch. This was level and delightful with plentiful flowers in the hedgerows - 64 seen today, including two new ones, sweet briar and wild pansy.

I arrived in the centre of Dornoch at about 1215. I wandered around the town being disappointed on two counts. ONE. I had somehow managed to imagine that Dornoch would be full of cosy little streets and with pretty little shoppes and tourists wandering in and out buying souvenirs and whatnot. This idea was quite erroneous and I can only think that I had read about somewhere else then got the two mixed up. Coping with that wasn't too difficult. However, TWO. I needed to purchase another map or two, which I had been unable to find on previous days. I found the Tourist Information Centre - Closed Sundays. Four other shops and cafés were Closed Sundays. I then went round again taking photos of the Closed signs in the windows in an attempt to deflect my dismay into a more humorous mode. I ate my bread and cheese lunch on the green in front of the cathedral.

I did eventually find a café that was open, which I had passed previously on my way in, but had thought was a bit 'posh'. I had a coffee and a bun, and then got into a friendly argument with the waitress and then the proprietor because the top quarter of my mug of coffee was all froth. I agreed to pay a reduced bill and came away not dissatisfied. "We want people to be happy", the proprietor said.   I have learnt since to ask for a Latte 'without froth'. There seems to be a confusing range of coffees nowadays, mostly incomprehensible to my feeble brain. Small, regular or grande is just about understandable but then you find somewhere where regular is the largest. Why is the whole country obsessed with 'froth'? I don't often get into arguments with folk, so perhaps I was still smarting from the fact of coming to terms with a Scottish Presbyterian Sunday, where the frivolity of actually wanting to buy something is definitely forbidden. Irreverent 'froth' might well be something the Scottish Presbyterians could get their teeth into.

Leaving the town centre I strolled down a road and found my B and B. It was far too early to 'arrive' so I continued on down to the beach, which wasn't 'Closed', and communed with the sand and the sea and the breeze, hoping that this would appease whatever Sunday Defiling Inspector Gods were out to get me.

I came back to the B and B and settled in and then went back into the town and found a good restaurant, in an upstairs room, above a pub, as I remember.

Monday 22nd June
Dornoch to Golspie - 11.8 miles

Today I passed the thousand mile mark. This day was somewhat overcast with bits of short-lived drizzle. Tarmac again all day, quiet lanes then the dratted A9.

The first thing I did after leaving the B and B was to visit the bookshop, which was, miracle of miracles, OPEN. *And* they had the at least one of the maps I needed. Whew! Then I took to the minor road that led me past Hilton and on to the shore of Loch Fleet, which is a National Nature Reserve. I paused near the car park and viewpoint to fiddle with my over-trousers and I was pleased to meet another End-to-Ender, going my way. This man was David who had left Land's End on the 19th April, virtually a month after I did. He was four years younger than me and he seemed pretty fit. He must have been doing significantly longer mileages per day to catch up a whole month. We chatted as we sauntered along together and the drizzle died away. David stopped to eat his lunch but I carried on. The road was right beside the water and level with it. The tide must have been in because there didn't seem to be much of a foreshore, although I managed to walk along a little of it. At one point I came across a clump of thrift which is normally found on shores and cliffs, but this clump had been swamped by the tide and a mass of petals was floating, clustered around the somewhat denuded clump of stems. I took a picture of this, to me, unusual sight. Further on I found in a ditch some more marsh cinquefoil flowers. Out came the camera again. I found a sticky-out bit of rock and sat perched above the water and ate my lunch. I thought this shoreline road to be a very attractive section of the walk, full of bird life and interesting views.

I soon joined the A9 and crossed the River Fleet on a causeway called The Mound, with near views into Strath Fleet. I had wondered about taking a looping route into Golspie via Balblair Wood. As well as hoping to see a marsh cinquefoil, I had wondered whether I might see the rare twinflower, which, I had discovered, might be found in northern pinewoods and this woodland was a likely spot. So having crossed the railway I looked for a possible entrance into the woodland. I think I may have turned up my nose at one conceivably viable way in, but then there were no more options. (A year later I visited these woods with Ann, on our way to Orkney, and found the twin flowers and several other flowers not seen before by either of us.)

So I stayed on the main road. A sign said 'John O'Groats 76'. From here on the road signs gave me countdowns of the distance yet to go to the top. The road was fairly busy with traffic and I kept stepping on to the grass verge to be safe. I had worked out that if I saw a vehicle coming towards me, I would glance over my left shoulder and if there was nothing coming up from behind, I kept on walking in the gutter. Nearly every time, the vehicle would move out to give me a wide berth and I would acknowledge this with a raising of my left hand. If a car was coming up from behind and nothing coming towards me I would carry on unperturbed. If traffic was coming in both directions at the same time I would stop and stand on the grass verge until, all was clear. One cannot expect oncoming drivers to pull out to pass me in the face of oncoming vehicles. Grass verges can conceal little holes and ditches, and can be pretty bumpy. I tended to stand on the verge rather than walk along it for fear of being jerked or thrown back onto the roadway because of some hidden hazard under my feet. At Culmally I waited, as did vehicular traffic, while a large flock of sheep crossed the road from south to north. The caption of a picture in my scrapbook says 'Ovine A9'.

I carried on and was soon in Golspie by about 4.15. I was very warmly welcomed at Granite Villa Guest House by Jane. This was an excellent establishment and in fact Ann and I stayed there for two nights a year later, on our previously mentioned journey to Orkney. I had my meal in a very good fish and chip restaurant, 'The Trawler', where I met David again and we continued our conversations.

Tuesday 23rd June
Golspie to Brora - 8.4 miles

This was to be another excellent day. There was beautiful sunshine and it was pretty warm, still and peaceful. I had various tasks to see to in the town including the successful purchase of the map for my last day of walking. As I have probably already mentioned, I needed to have maps of several days ahead so that I could see where particular locations were for possible B and Bs, as my forward booking was now down to only a day or two ahead. I eventually left the village about 1120 and abandoned the main road to walk the coastal path to Brora. As far as I could establish this was to be the only stretch of sensible path along the coast between Golspie and John O'Groats. It was delightful.

After about a mile I paused to admire Dunrobin Castle, although I couldn't think of anything kind to say about one of its owners, whose 100 foot high monument dominates Golspie from the hill, behind the town. The First Duke of Sutherland was, I understand, mainly irresponsible - I hesitate to omit the 'ir' - for the vastly unfair and devastating Highland Clearances in the 1800s. Some folk would have it that he could see the poor conditions under which crofters lived and sought to rehouse some of them along the 'more favourable' coastal strip. This was a nonsense because conditions there were little better. Many travelled abroad and made successful lives there.

Sometime during the previous two days I had spoken with the young lady warden at Helmsdale Youth Hostel and managed to book myself in for the following night. As I walked along the fields after Dunrobin, I met a young lady going the other way. We both stopped and she said to me, without further preamble, "You must be Ben". Of course it was the warden from the Youth Hostel, and she must have cleverly guessed who I was. The further north one goes the fewer possible routes there are for JOG-bound walkers. In England it was a rare event for folk to meet an End-to-Ender, but in Scotland it was much less noteworthy. We chatted for a few minutes then it was, "See you tomorrow".

As I walked along the view ahead became less well-defined and I realised that I was entering an area of haar, the Scottish sea mist. I passed through this patch and then through another later on. The path wound its way through coarse grass, similar to that found on sand-dunes, and I was intrigued to notice that the trodden path was densely packed with daisies. Beside the path there were barely any and I had to surmise that they thrived by being trampled on. I had never noticed this anywhere in all my walking life, but was to find similar patches further on.

I ate my lunch on a grassy hillock surrounded by wild flowers. After having passed a charming little cascade where the Sputie Burn ran into the sea I soon came across several seals basking in shallow water. They were quite close to the shore and didn't seem to be bothered by my presence. There was at least one baby seal and I took a few photos. They seemed rather ugly and ungainly almost out of the water, but sleek and efficient in the sea proper. This was probably the nearest I had been to seals outside of a zoo.

I carried on into Brora village with plenty of time to spare. I took money out of a cash machine and topped up my mobile in the Co-op shop. I wandered down to the bridge over the River Brora, here rushing through a narrow little gorge. There was a very steep grassy bank just outside the railway station. I climbed this and tried to lie down to do nothing for a while, but the slope was against me as I kept slipping down. I tried further down but I couldn't really get comfortable. In the end I gave up and came back to the bridge over the gorge. Here, several teenagers, I think mostly boys, but with lasses watching, were jumping from the bridge into the water below. It seemed to me to be a heckuva way down, but these lads were up for it. They had to aim their leap extremely carefully because of rocks above and below the surface protruding into the main flow. Their daring and skill was quite a sight. They would clamber out and come back for another go.

My B and B at Seaforth Croft was about a mile and a half out of the village on the way I wanted to go the next day. Therefore I had an early meal in a fish and chip shop/café before carrying on. Enjoying the early evening stillness, I wandered on to arrive at 1900 at the B and B situated at Achrimsdale just off the main road. What a great day full of surprises, interest and idleness, not to mention 70 different wild flowers.

At some point during the day I must have played about with an anagram of "LAND'S END TO JOHN O'GROATS". After several attempts I came up with "LOAD. GO NORTH SON AND JEST". When my dad was a young man he cycled 152 miles twice in a Whit Weekend (Bristol to Saffron Walden and back) and then again another year. At a similar age my longest cycle ride was 140 miles in a day, never repeated. I wanted to at least equal my dad's achievement but never managed it on a bike. Over time I became a member of the LDWA and on three occasions finished the annual 100 mile walk. I felt this made it honours even. I was able to afford this trek because of money left to me by my dad when he died. So, in a way, this walk is partly in memory of him. It has, perhaps, been a serious walk and I wonder if I have 'jested' enough. I have been told off many a time for my futile jokes, but perhaps my dad is saying, "Don't lose your sense of humour and sense of fun".
O come on, it's only a silly anagram!

Wednesday 24th June
Brora to Helmsdale - 10.3 miles

Today was overcast with low cloud and a headwind. It became brighter in the afternoon. I left Seaforth Croft at 0840 and soon came back to the A9. Walking along this road was not exactly a barrel of laughs with traffic passing at fairly high speeds. Occasionally a smooth stretch of verge was available to walk on but most of the time I was in the gutter. The railway was between me and the sea and I wasn't tempted to go in search of a coastal path. Hills shrouded in mist were crowding in on my left. They were not appealing and I felt no 'guilt' about staying on the road. Along the whole route I never had any need to navigate in fog, cloud, mist or darkness. I enjoy the challenge of being up high in cloud and testing my micro-navigational skills to the full, but this was never going to be an option on this walk.

Friends have said to me since I finished the walk that they admired my 'stickability' and commented on how starting each day, over and over again, must have been tedious. I have responded by telling them that each day I was fit and 'ready to go' and that I could face the coming adventure with eagerness and equanimity.

Although it was road walking I was still able to record 66 wild flowers. I was very pleased to note a seemingly wild fuchsia absolutely dripping with red flowers. I think this plant grows more readily in the wild in Scotland than in England. A young man on a bike stopped and we had a chat. He seemed glad to have someone with whom to swop experiences. He was wild camping as he went on his way from Essex to John O'Groats via Kent, Land's End, Wales and West Scotland. I don't know how long he was taking but he didn't seem to be rushing.

After a while the road descended towards sea level and for a mile or more the road and the sea were very close with the railway sandwiched in between. I soon found myself in Helmsdale in time for lunch. I visited the Post Office at five past one just after it had closed. I retreated to Gilbert's Restaurant for a reasonably substantial lunch and a very helpful young lady gave me two addresses for ongoing B and Bs in Dunbeath and beyond. Gilbert suggested that I try the TIC in the craft shop, which I did, but no additional information was forthcoming.

I wandered around the village, had a look at the harbour then made my way up the road to the youth hostel. I settled myself in there and as no meals were provided I drifted back down to the village to shop for breakfast food. I also went into the La Mirage café and had a smallish evening meal. I then did a further wander around the village and came across, behind The Wee Café on the main road, a most wonderful statue. This sculpture by Gerald Laing. unveiled in 2007 by Alex Salmond, was entitled 'The Emigrants' and showed, possibly a somewhat larger than life-sized man and his son, and the wife holding a baby. This work of art was a memorial to all those evicted from their homes during the Highland Clearances. The man is looking forward to the uncertainties that lay ahead, but with a kind of determination to make the best of virtually nil opportunities. The young lad is looking questioningly up to his father and wondering what is really going to happen and not quite understanding it all, but following him with dogged loyalty. The father has a thrusting forward stance which contrasts clearly with the wife and baby. There is a clear space between the two sets of figures, which intensifies the two different emotions. The wife is half turned around, holding the babe in her arms, looking sorrowfully and longingly back at the burning croft, and she isn't really ready yet to face the upward struggle of the future.

I was intensely moved by this sculpture and took several pictures of it. I felt Gerald Laing had captured most poignantly the essence of the sadness the Clearances caused. I would recommend anyone passing that way to take the opportunity to seek it out, because, for me, this was one of the most moving moments of my whole journey. I could have expanded this book into an essay on many of the places I passed through, but I have resisted the temptation to search the internet to find information with which to pad out my text, which is probably overlong already. However, as I write, I felt the need to make an exception and Googled 'Gerald Laing The Emigrants' and found that many of the critical comments about the statue echoed very much what I had already written. I did find one quote from Laing which I append below, as it seemed to relate to my trip northwards. Ann had sent me a text message just as I was about to leave Land's End, which I repeat here, "Congratulations! To have even started to realise a dream is special. Happy walking!" Laing says, "But life is what you make of it and when you have the confidence to go out and follow your dreams it can take you on an incredible journey".

I made my way back to bed in humble contemplation.

Thursday 25th June
Helmsdale to Dunbeath - 15.3 miles

I set off at a quarter to nine and kept on along the A9. The weather was sunny and bright with a cool breeze, but nevertheless lovely. The road kept up pretty high and proceeded in large sweeping curves and long straight stretches. At East Helmsdale a new road had been built and for about a mile it was wide and fast and with newly planted verges. The old road takes a winding route past Navidale which must have been unsatisfactory in some way, hence the new stretch. My map said that the road was due to open Mid 2009, so it was very new.

I have already mentioned the hazards of traffic, either from behind, oncoming or both, and what evasive action I would expect to take. As I trudged up the rising road I heard a vehicle coming up behind me, but as there was nothing coming towards me I felt no need to look behind. So I was somewhat discombobulated when a car flashed past me with only what seemed like inches to spare. This quieter vehicle had been coming up behind the one I had heard and chose that moment to overtake it, with no regard for the quiet unassuming pedestrian. Another variable learned. To compensate for this slightly unnerving incident I was able to enjoy the wonderful scent of white clover which had been newly planted on the verge and was there in great abundance and profusion for most of the way up the hill.

I paused at the Ord of Caithness to take in the view looking back across the sea to places I had been through days before. Almost immediately after gazing at this impressive view I took a photograph of the sign welcoming me to Caithness. This is the last county and the end is now only about 50 miles away. I carried on along this not really very busy road, mile after mile, stopping occasionally to examine a wayside flower - 77 different kinds today.

For much of the way to Berriedale there was a belt of trees or more substantial forest on my left. This prevented me having continuous views of the hills which rose gradually away into the distance. Looking at the map there is a huge area of wild country with no roads through it, making me think that there are few places in England to match such vast 'emptiness'.

I descended the long hill into Berriedale where I decided that it was time for lunch. I found no hostelry or place of refreshment so I sat on a wall capped with smooth coping stones to eat my lunch. For a siesta I stretched myself out along the wall which sloped gently upwards in a pillow-ish sort of way so I was very comfortable.
I eventually decided I had a few miles to go yet so I ascended the very steep hill, which must have been a true test for JOG-bound cyclists.

The road rose and fell gently with long curves. In the afternoon warmth and sunshine it was absolutely idyllic. On my left there were low hills and on my right, barely a field away, was the sea, which seemed to drift calmly away to the horizon. There were a few fluffy white clouds in a bright blue sky. As I strolled along some words of John Masefield came into my mind. These were from the poem 'Sea Fever', beautifully set to music by John Ireland. These thoughts must have been prompted by the clouds and the occasional boat seen out to sea. The opening words are, 'I must go down to the sea again, to the lonely sea and the sky'. Later, 'And all I ask is a windy day with the white clouds flying'. Then finally, 'And quiet sleep and a sweet dream when the long trick's over'. I have sung this song plenty of times in my life and it is great tune, the words are lovely and the sentiment exact. I tried singing snatches as I went along but my throat clagged up and my eyes welled up with tears and I found myself sobbing. Sobbing with the joy of such a beautiful afternoon, but also with the realisation that 'the long trick' was nearly over. I had been wondering how I would feel when

I reached the end of my journey, now only three days away, but the surroundings must have triggered a reaction to several weeks of pent-up emotion. This was a joyous, sad and memorable moment. After a little while the lump in my throat subsided and I was back in control of myself again.

The road stretched away ahead of me, but every step was glorious. Approaching Dunbeath I detoured to visit the Heritage centre but didn't stay long. I zigzagged down to, and crossed Dunbeath Water on the old Telford bridge. I pressed on out of the village and found my B and B at Toremore Farmhouse. I was given a most friendly welcome by Mary Macdonald. She kindly rang round several folk and found me a B and B in Lybster for the next night. After I had tidied myself up a little she ran me in the car the mile or so back to Dunbeath to the Bay Owl café. I enjoyed a macaroni cheese and pondered over how I got the impression that there were quite a lot of cafés offering macaroni cheese on the menu in Scotland, compared with a dearth of the same in England. I walked back up the road in the glorious evening light very satisfied with yet another outstanding day.

Friday 26th June
Dunbeath to Thrumster - 16.4 miles

This was another bright and sunny day and it was to be a long one. I left the delightful Toremore Farmhouse at half-past eight and carried on along the A9. As the road dropped down into a valley near Latheronwheel I came across some bushes growing by the side of the way with raspberry/loganberry type fruit. I could not identify the berries. I didn't try tasting the fruit because it was right beside the carriageway and on a hill and I suspected it might have been polluted by traffic fumes. A little further on I spoke to a man tending his front garden and asked him about this strange fruit. He said it was almost certainly salmonberry which was probably of

Canadian origin. He talked about how difficult he found living where he did. He was thinking of moving to the south of England.

At Latheron the A9 and I parted company and I was now on the A99. This probably halved the amount of traffic that passed me, not that there was very much anyway. The sign said 35 miles to John O'Groats.

The sea was not so much in evidence but there was still plenty of interest along the roadside. I found 70 flowers today including the fairly rare Jacob's Ladder. At one point I passed John Gunn's heavy machinery works and the focal point, on the forecourt, was an old crane cum excavator with a dummy man at the controls in the cab and an old lorry having stuff tipped into it. All in brightly painted colours.

It wasn't very long before I found myself at Quatre Bras where I turned right down the long main street into Lybster. On the way down this peacefully empty road I made use of a convenient 'Gents'. As I was leaving someone else was trying to come in, followed by several more chaps. I asked myself, "It was quiet just now, where have they all come from?" The answer was soon obvious as, neatly parked across the road, were ten mini-cars and on the door of each was a panel which announced:-

22nd June - 26th June
YEAH BABY!
Land's End to John O'Groats
"Hippy Mini Run 2009"
CELEBRATING 50 YEARS OF THE MINI IN AID OF THE DEMELZA HOUSE CHILDREN'S HOSPICE.
Flower Power
www.smallcarsbighearts.co.uk

All the participants were colourfully dressed up in hippy costumes and they were very friendly to chat to. It seems they do a 'run' every year but this was special because of the 50 years thing. They were going on down to the harbour for their pre-booked lunch.

I was to stay with Brenda Gunn at Bolton House, thanks to the kind efforts of Mary at Toremore. It was barely lunchtime when I knocked on Brenda's front door, but no reply was forthcoming. After another try I walked to the end of the terrace row and found my way, with careful counting, to Brenda's back garden, which I dared to enter. She spotted me from a skylight attic window and came down and gave me a very warm welcome. She allowed me to settle myself in and I unpacked some of my stuff so that I had a light rucksack for my afternoon walk. I had been able to find out that there was a bus service back to Lybster in the evening. I wanted to continue while the weather was fine and to make the next day's mileage a little less. I didn't have a particular target in mind but just to stop when I felt like it.

In need of some light lunch refreshment I went out into the main street and the only option immediately visible was 'The Cross Restaurant'. I went in only to discover that the family running it had only just moved in and the floor was covered in cardboard boxes and other stuff. They were trying to get organised so that they could open the next day. I was prepared to withdraw, but I was invited to stay and the mum said she would see what she could rustle up for me. At one point mum told little Jennifer to run across to the shop and get some sugar. Despite their obvious busyness they were kindness itself and I wished them well in their new venture.

The rest of the day's walk was very easy with a light rucksack. Instead of returning to the A99 by the way I had come in I went along lanes and rejoined the main road at Parkside. The gradients were insignificant, the larks were singing overhead and the weather

"The Emigrants" - Helmsdale

With Iain at Thrumster

continued to be warm and peaceful. I had long been interested to know a little more about the Flow Country, with its flatness and dampness and relative inaccessibility. As I looked around me the countryside did indeed start looking more like I had somehow expected it to be. Often I could see ruined cottages and crofts, some beside the road and some further afield. When I was at school a map in a geography textbook showed the British Isles with reference to crops grown in different areas. I have a strong image of the word 'OATS' printed in the far north east of Scotland. I had seen no sign of oats growing as I tramped along so I wondered if they are still a feature of local farming. What I did see, which caught my eye, was an abandoned garden full of red hot pokers in full bloom.

Over the last few days I had been in touch with our eldest daughter, Bryony. She was busy monitoring the progress of her friend Iain, who with seven other determined cyclists, was undertaking a sponsored ride from Land's End to John O'Groats in six days. This meant cycling about 150 miles a day. They were due to reach the end this very day and were on the same route as I was. They had a support party with at least two vehicles and meals and overnight accommodation had all been pre-arranged. The good cause was to 'Help Stop Aids in South Africa' and the event was called 'The Race Against Time', or 'TRAT' for short.

About a mile after passing Bridge of East Clyth I was passed by one of Iain's support vehicles. It stopped and Alan and Ashley, two of the supporting team, came back to meet me, guessing correctly that I must be Bryony's dad. Alan walked along beside me for a few minutes before returning to the minibus and carrying on. Bryony had been acting as a communications link between me and Iain and the support lot, so I was just about up to speed with the cyclists' progress.

I wanted to carry on as far as I dared so I continued walking. I passed Whaligoe and Ulbster and still the road led me on. At 1745, having reached Thrumster, I decided to call it a day. Five minutes later I received a phone call from Bryony saying that the team were just leaving Berriedale. I therefore had a bit of time in hand and easily found the Old Smiddy Inn where I enjoyed a relaxing evening meal. I then retraced my steps for a few hundred yards where an abandoned garage forecourt looked like a good place to meet Iain and co. I waited a little while, then in the distance I could see a small cluster of cyclists. At 1915 this group of five arrived, but they paused only momentarily to tell me that Iain was about 4 or 5 miles behind. The support van arrived at about 1935 and then at 1945 Iain and Liz and Phil pulled in for a few minutes rest. Someone took a couple of photos of me and Iain standing in front of the van, with its large display of what the venture was all about. They pushed on with about 1½ hours to go to John O'Groats, whilst had 1½ days to go. Well done them, say I. The end seems awfully close now.

I crossed the road to the bus stop and after a while the bus came to take me back to Lybster. On the way I had a phone call from Brenda to see if I was OK. I told her I was on the bus. What a lovely, feeling, thoughtful lady Brenda is.

What another glorious day this has been!

Saturday 27th June
Thrumster to South Keiss - 11.0 miles

I said fond farewells to Brenda and caught an early bus back to Thrumster. I started walking at 0835 in, yet again, sunny weather. I have had no rain since leaving Beauly, nine days ago. I am truly blessed. As I walked along I came across another clump of salmonberry, with some fruits on it. I picked a few and ate them, not unpleasant, but a bit sharp. A bit further on three cyclists stopped for a brief chat. They had come from Land's End in nine days.

It wasn't too long before I was on the outskirts of Wick, surely the biggest town since Fort William. Nearing the town centre I stopped to talk to two somewhat frustrated cyclists. They had one of the bikes upside down and there was a problem with a tyre valve. The two lads were on a Round Scotland tour.

Wick was 'Saturday morning' busy and I wandered around the town centre to try and get the feel of the place. I still hadn't fixed up my overnight stay for today. The Tourist Information Centre wasn't up to much, but somehow or other I did discover a place to stay, which was a great relief to me. I had been enjoying a fairly carefree few days, but always in the back of my mind was the need to secure a bed somewhere. I stocked up on food which I would need for, perhaps, two lunches. I went into Morag's Café for a panino and two mugs of milky coffee. I can be a bit of a pedant at times, but on this occasion I didn't draw attention to the fact that the word panini on their menu was plural. Paninis, with or without the apostrophe, is still wrong. I tried in several shops to buy a fine point black Bic biro and after several failures did manage to do so. They look at you blankly if you ask for a biro, you have to say ballpoint.

Having got myself sorted I strolled out of town, again on the A99. I was still enjoying discovering wild flowers - 70 again today. There were, indeed, several with which I was unfamiliar. One tiny flower growing in profusion along the gutter and verge for a stretch, I found intriguing, as it was so small. The identification of quite a few flowers throughout the walk had to wait until I returned home.

I came to a road junction at Reiss where the straight ahead road, taking most of the traffic, went on to Castletown and Thurso. I turned right onto what was now a much quieter road. The sign said 'John O'Groats - 13' Mmmm! That close! I found a grassy spot at Lower Reiss and for a dessert I tucked into a punnet of fresh raspberries, which I had bought from a market stall in Wick.

Carrying on I met a Japanese man on his bike. He was from London. I can't remember his route but he was doing 1000 miles in 25 days. The larks were singing as I tramped along. I stopped for a while at Bridge of Wester. The bridge crossed the outflow from the Loch of Wester nearby and also a 'railway line', which had been built, in a straight line, to assist the construction of a pipeline to convey gas?/oil? from a rig far out to sea. The pipe was constructed inland and was put together as one long tube. This was supported on bogies which ran along the rails for 7½ kilometres. At this point the track was about one kilometre from the sea.

After another lazy mile or so I arrived at the B and B near South Keiss, appropriately named 'Dunroamin'. Here I was welcomed by Mrs Elvira Harrold. She must have put up thousands of End-to-Enders as she has been running the B and B for, I think she said, 42 years. She kindly supplied me with a light evening meal. One day to go!

Sunday 28th June
South Keiss to Duncansby Head - 11.3 miles

The day started rather overcast but became sunny later. I left 'Dunroamin' at 0755, probably one of my earliest starts. I felt I wanted to get on, but not to hurry. I passed through Keiss and on and along. There were larks singing overhead yet again. Lovely. At intervals there were great patches of pink and white dame's violet and then a little later there was a field of purple wild pansies. It was odd to see them in one field only and not in adjoining areas. I have subsequently seen a similar hillside field on the outskirts of Kirkwall and I wondered if they had been cultivated as a crop, but for what reason I cannot think. The number of flowers seen today was 69, a goodly number in an increasingly open and windswept place.

I was just coming up a rise on some moorland when a car pulled up and out stepped Dave, whom I had met at Loch Fleet and Golspie. He was with his wife and they were spending a day or two in the area since Dave had finished. They had spotted me and had turned round and come back to greet me. It was good to chat with them for a few minutes. Dave had taken 61 days from Land's End, forty days quicker than me. He jokingly said, "I can give you a lift". We laughed happily. A little further on a cyclist was coming towards me. He stopped and we chatted. He was on his way to Land's End, hoping to do it in 13 days. He went on and soon after a young man on a bike came up behind me. Then his mate appeared. They stopped and we talked for a few minutes. I didn't quite remember the whole story, but one of them lost his bike on the second day out from Land's End. They were quite impressed with my 101 days, they had taken 12. One of them said, "I expect you'll be feeling elated".

At about 1045 I began to see water ahead, instead of to one side. I could see Orkney very faintly through the haze. A little later I was able to locate Hoy which looked very big, despite being further away than the much nearer Stroma. I reached the outskirts of John O'Groats and became aware of various signs as follows:

John O'Groats

Tourist Information Centre ¾ mile *(and I thought I was nearly there!)*

North & West Highlands Tourist Route - End of Route

Reduce Speed Now.

So I slowed down and made my way to the focal point of 'The End' at 1205 and stood around for a few minutes. There was not much in the way of elation. A party of bikers arrived just after me and after they had had their photos taken, standing by the special indicator post, a lady biker kindly took a photo of me. I looked around one or two of the touristy shops and then retired to the 'Journey's End Café/Bar', where I signed 'The Book'. After some refreshment I continued my journey.

I set off along a coast path, some of which was along a pebbly beach. Then I was walking on grassland above low cliffs, with the sea on my left. Looking out to sea I was aware that this was the Pentland Firth where the Atlantic meets the North Sea. I could see an area of turbulence with white-capped waves and disturbed motion. The caption on the photo I took says 'Hell's Mouth', but I can't find that name on the map. I may have read it somewhere at John O'Groats or I may have invented it. Anyway it seemed to be an appropriate name for what I was seeing. I kept on round the Ness of Duncansby and skirted around the Bay of Sannick with its sandy beach and started to climb up to Duncansby Head.

At 1410 at the car park at the top I was enthusiastically greeted by Peggy, who had come to meet me. I felt I ought to have a little time to be elated but Peggy wanted to whisk me off to look at puffins. We poddled over the grassy top and found a geo and, lo and behold, there were several puffins resting or nesting on ledges on the steep cliffs. Seeing puffins was a first for me so I did feel a little elated. I was then hurried on to view the amazing Duncansby Stacks about half a mile away from our cliff-top viewpoint. These are a couple of large sea stacks, as high as the nearby cliffs, but most unusually coming up to a point at the top rather than roughly parallel sided. This was indeed another great find and Peggy was very proprietorial about them. It was certainly worth the extra distance to view them. So what happened to the elation? The emotional bit had been a few days before, which seemed to suffice. I did, of course, have a great feeling of quiet satisfaction, which is

At John O'Groats - but not quite the end

Duncansby Stacks

still present as I write this now, five years to the day since I travelled south to Penzance.

Having returned to Peggy's car we drove to Dunnet Head, which is the most northerly point of the mainland. Duncansby Head is the furthest point away from Land's End on the British mainland. John O'Groats is neither the furthest point from Land's End, nor the most northerly point, nor the most north-easterly point of the British mainland. But it does have cafés and tourist attractions and a sign post telling you it is 874 miles to Land's End. My calculations led me to believe that I had walked 1077.5 miles on my journey. This involved 97 walking days at an average distance of 11.2 miles a day.

Dunnet Head was well worth visiting with views northwards to Orkney and westwards to distant mountains, which might have included Ben Hope. Peggy then drove me to Thurso where she lives with her husband Mike. They have an interesting large flat with a wonderful view across the town and out to sea. There was lots of news to share and Peggy and Mike were excellent company. I ate well and slept well.

Envoi

I had decided that I needed to start homewards, so on the Monday morning I caught an early train and was able to view the flow country just a little more intimately. I changed onto a bus at Inverness and travelled to Fort William where I booked into the Alexandra Hotel, which was handy for the station in the morning. I was in Room 103, which was the same number of days since I had left home. I caught the 0742 train for Glasgow. It rained for the first time for twelve days. I made this particular train journey because I wanted to have a closer look at the 'proper' Rannoch Moor. My northward journey along General Wade's road had only skirted it along the Black Mount. It will need a further visit some other time as there was too much mist to see very much at all. I changed trains at Glasgow and was eventually home in Buxton by early evening.

And great was the welcome thereof!

….and maybe,

"quiet sleep and a sweet dream…."

"….. the long trick's over".

Post-amble

Well - it looks as though I did it.

This has been a once in a lifetime experience and the enjoyment has been immense. The sense of achievement hides somewhere inside 'enjoyment'. Part of the enjoyment was the open air, the birds, the wind, the flowers, the (early) morning freshness and the views. The just being out in it. Day after day. There was also the freedom from the encumbrance of responsibility. It was sheer escapism. To be allowed to do this was, indeed, a great privilege and I cannot praise too highly the loving and practical support given to me by Ann.

The desire - and plan - not to 'overdo it' was, in the end, a correct decision. There were days when I was having a really lazy afternoon and not minding; but other days, perhaps not many, when I felt I could have been 'getting on'. These days were possibly near the end of the walk, when it seemed to be pretty well established that I hadn't been 'overdoing it' and that a little extra effort would get me to the end of my journey quicker, without undue worry. I toyed briefly with the idea of walking through the night in those late June days when the evenings went on and on, but the practicalities over-ruled it. I would need to sleep through the day. Being unsociable through tiredness when I met Peggy was a no-no. However, it seemed OK to resist such thoughts because I really wanted to continue the 'every-minuteness' of my strolling.

Someone I met along the way said to me that they couldn't do what I was doing because of the monotony of the day after day-ness of it all. For me, as I may have said already, each day was a new adventure and I could step out with my head held high and with a positive outlook.

'In Expectation of a Kingfisher' was the title I have given this book. This name was dreamt up when I was a week or so into Scotland. I never saw one. I don't mind. But there was the expectation of so much else as well. I had hopes and expectations about all sorts of aspects of the walk, like my fitness, the scenery, the weather, the people and the flowers. There was very little that I had hoped for that was not fulfilled. Mostly the fulfilment was over-flowingly so.

I have mentioned flowers a great deal. In all I found about 200 different varieties. I kept a record of flowers seen each day. I wondered whether when I got home I would undertake some sort of analysis of what I had seen, but the task, I felt would be laborious and might not tell me much I hadn't worked out for myself as I went along. Being too analytical would diminish the sense of wonder of actually seeing, and sometimes smelling them. However, I will give a few obvious facts and figures.

The daily count gradually increased as spring and summer came into fullness. Rainy days and stretches of moorland meant fewer flowers to be seen. The highest daily total in March was 31, by the end of April I was seeing 50+, and in May the highest was 73 and in June there was a rainy day with only 52 but the next day there was the highest of the whole walk with 80. So 'Summer' seemed to be more productive then 'Spring'. The whole thing was a kind of indeterminate jumble of factors - a mixture of spring-ness and northerliness. Sometimes altitude and weather and whether I glanced to the ditch on the left or the hedge on the right determined what I actually saw.

Obviously different habitats tend to yield different species. Country lanes were very rich habitats but open moorland was pretty poor. The flower seen every day was the daisy, a wonderful cheerful companion. Dandelion was seen on all but six days. Also seen very often, in descending order of frequency: cow parsley, gorse, germander speedwell, groundsel and stitchwort. The highlights were the marsh cinquefoil - on four separate days, yellow saxifrage - twice and starry saxifrage - twice.

My arthritic knee didn't really get any worse during the walk. I had developed the habit, even long before I started this walk, of favouring my right knee by walking with a straight right leg. This meant that I walked with a limp virtually all the way. There was always some slight pain, which was slightly more than uncomfortable, but not excruciating. Over the next three years since my long trek, the knee gradually became more and more painful and in the summer of 2012 I had a new knee fitted and this has re-opened the possibilities of longer walks which had in the meantime been missing from my agenda.

The weather was absurdly kind to me, which made my journey even more delightful than I had hoped. There were only five days when I commenced the day's walk in the rain. 94% of my walking hours were without inconveniencing rain. The flowers were absolutely delectable. The people I met were almost always unwaveringly kind and helpful. The scenery was, at times, magnificent. Visiting new places was a great joy. I have been blessed and thrice blessed.

To sum up, the achievement was amazingly unbelievable and the enjoyment was unbelievably amazing.

--- ooo ---

I started writing this account of my adventures, not knowing that it might turn into a book. Without being able to remember exactly, I probably started putting finger to keyboard in late 2009. My writing had reached Fort William, when there came a halt to the proceedings as I took on a fairly arduous and responsible Quaker job, which went on all through 2010, 2011 and 2012. I felt unable to give my full concentration to the business of continuing with this tome, as I didn't have a clear space in which to do so. Dangling Quaker tasks occupied the early months of 2013 and then in the late spring I was diagnosed with a cancerous tumour on my bowel and I had an operation at the end of July to have my upper colon removed. I convalesced through August and commenced six months of chemotherapy in September which finished in mid-March 2014. Again there have been interruptions to the preparation of this book, mainly while I concentrated on getting back to full fitness, often in the Lake District.

If my story has inspired you to get out and have a go at something a bit more adventurous than your normal pattern, then go for it. And Happy Walking!

Buxton.
February 2016